# German

## Phrase Book

CONSULTANT
Ulrike Seeberger

> **GEM PHRASE BOOKS**
>
> DUTCH
> FRENCH
> GERMAN
> GREEK
> ITALIAN
> PORTUGUESE
> SPANISH
>
> *Also available Gem Phrase
> Book CD Packs*

First published 1993
This edition published 2003
Copyright © HarperCollins Publishers
Reprint 10 9 8 7 6 5 4 3 2 1
Printed in Italy by Amadeus S.p.A

www.collins.co.uk

ISBN 0-00-714172-6

Your *Collins Gem Phrase Book* is designed to help you locate the exact phrase you need in any situation, whether for holiday or business. If you want to adapt the phrases, we have made sure that you can easily see where to substitute your own words (you can find them in the dictionary section), and the clear, two-colour layout gives you direct access to the different topics.

The *Gem Phrase Book* includes:

■ Over 70 topics arranged thematically. Each phrase is accompanied by a simple pronunciation guide which ensures that there's no problem over pronouncing the foreign words.

■ Practical hints and useful vocabulary highlighted in boxes. Where no article (**der/die/das**) is given, you will generally see the word appearing on signs. We give the pronunciation for all words.

| WORDS APPEARING IN BLACK ARE ENGLISH WORDS | WORDS APPEARING IN BLUE ARE GERMAN WORDS |
|---|---|

■ Possible phrases you may hear in reply to your questions. The foreign phrases appear in blue.

■ A menu-reader for deciphering the menu.

■ A clearly laid-out 5000-word dictionary: English words appear in black and German words appear in blue.

■ A basic grammar section which will enable you to build on your phrases.

It's worth spending time before you embark on your travels just looking through the topics to see what is covered and becoming familiar with what might be said to you.

Whatever the situation, your *Gem Phrase Book* is sure to help!

# CONTENTS

# PRONOUNCING GERMAN

*Spelling and pronouncing German are easy once you know the basic rules. This book has been designed so that as you read the pronunciation of the phrases you can follow the German. This will help you to recognize the different sounds and you will soon be able to pronounce German from the spelling alone (the stressed syllable is marked in **heavy italics**). Here are a few rules you should know:*

| GERMAN | SOUNDS LIKE | EXAMPLE | PRONUNCIATION |
|--------|-------------|---------|---------------|
| ■ AU | **ow** | *Auto* | **ow**to |
| ■ CH | **kh** | *noch* | *nokh* |
| ■ EI | **eye** | *fein* | *fine* |
| ■ IE | **ee** | *sie* | *zee* |
| ■ EU | **oy** | *neun* | *noyn* |
| ■ QU | **kv** | *Quittung* | **kvi**-toong |
| ■ S | **s** | *es* | *es* |
| | **z** | *sie* | *zee* |
| | **sh** | *sprechen* | **shpre**-khen |
| ■ ß | **s** | *Fuß* | *foos* |
| ■ U | **oo** | *gut* | *goot* |
| ■ V | **f** | *von* | *fon* |
| ■ W | **v** | *wir* | *veer* |
| ■ UMLAUTS | | | |
| ■ Ä | **eh** | *hätte* | **het**-te |
| ■ ÄU | **oy** | *läutet* | **loy**-tet |
| ■ Ö | **ur'\*** | *können* | **kur'**-nen |
| ■ Ü | **oo** | *grün* | *groon* |

*A final **e** is always pronounced, but weakly like the **e** in the:*
**Seide** *zy-de*, BITTE *bit-te*

\* **ur'** *as in* **hurt** *without the* **r** *pronounced*

6

*When Germans meet they generally shake hands. The words for Mr and Mrs are **Herr** and **Frau**. Note that **Fräulein** (Miss) is no longer used as it sounds rather patronising.*

**Please**
Bitte
*bi-te*

**Thanks (very much)**
Danke schön
*dang-ke shur'n*

**Don't mention it**
Bitte
*bi-te*

**Yes**
Ja
*ya*

**No**
Nein
*nine*

**OK!**
Ok!
*okay*

**Sir / Mr**
Herr
*hayr*

**Madam / Mrs / Ms**
Frau
*frow*

**Miss** (rarely used nowadays)
Fräulein
*froyline*

**Hello**
Guten Tag
*gooten tahk*

**Hi**
Hallo
*hallo*

**Goodbye**
Auf Widersehen
*owf veeder-zayn*

**Bye**
Tschuss
*tschoos*

**See you later**
Bis später
*bis shpayter*

**See you tomorrow**
Bis morgen
*bis morgen*

**Good morning**
Guten Morgen
*gooten morgen*

**Good evening**
Guten Abend
*gooten ahbent*

**Goodnight**
Gute Nacht
*goo-te nahkt*

**Excuse me / Sorry!**
Entschuldigung
*entshool-digoong*

**Pardon?**
Wie, bitte?
*vee bi-te*

**How are you?**
Wie geht es Ihnen?
*vee gayt es eenen*

**Fine, thanks**
Danke, gut
*dang-ke goot*

**And you?**
Und Ihnen?
*oont eenen*

**I don't speak German**
Ich spreche kein Deutsch
*ikh shpre-khe kine doytch*

**Do you speak English?**
Sprechen Sie Englisch?
*shpre-khen zee eng-lish*

# KEY PHRASES

*You don't need to say complicated things to get what you want.*
*Often simply naming the thing and adding bitte will do the trick.*
*Even when asking for directions.*

| **the** *(masculine)* | *(feminine)* | *(neuter)* | *(plural)* |
|---|---|---|---|
| der/den | die | das | die |
| *der/den* | *dee* | *das* | *dee* |

| **the station** | **the bar** | **the museum** | **the shops** |
|---|---|---|---|
| der Bahnhof | die Bar | das Museum | die Geschäfte |
| *der **bahn**-hof* | *dee bar* | *das moo-**zay**-oom* | *dee ge**shef**-te* |

| **a/one** *(masculine)* | *(feminine)* | *(neuter)* |
|---|---|---|
| ein/einen | eine | ein |
| *ine/**ine**-en* | ***ine**-e* | *ine* |

| **a ticket / one stamp** | **a room / one bottle** |
|---|---|
| eine Fahrkarte / eine Briefmarke | ein Zimmer / eine Flasche |
| ***ine**-e **fahr**kar-te / **ine**-e **bref**mar-ke* | *ine **tsim**mer / **ine**-e **fla**-she* |

**some**
etwas... *(uncountable)* / ein paar... *(countable)*
***et**vas... / ine pahr...*

| **some sugar** | **some jam** | **some cherries** |
|---|---|---|
| etwas Zucker | etwas Marmelade | ein paar Kirschen |
| ***et**vas **tsoo**ker* | ***et**vas mar-me**lah**-de* | *ine pahr **keer**shen* |

| **Do you have...?** | **Do you have leaflets?** |
|---|---|
| Haben Sie...? | Haben Sie Broschüren? |
| ***hah**-ben zee...* | ***hah**-ben zee bro**shoor**-en* |

| **Do you have a room?** | **Do you have some milk?** |
|---|---|
| Haben Sie ein Zimmer? | Haben Sie etwas Milch? |
| ***hah**-ben ze ine **tsim**mer* | ***hah**-ben zee **et**vas milkh* |

| **I'd like...** | **We'd like...** |
|---|---|
| Ich möchte... | Wir möchten... |
| *ikh **mur'kh**-te...* | *veer **mur'kh**-ten...* |

**Some more...**
Etwas mehr...
*etvas meer...*

**Another...**
Noch ein/eine...
*nokh ine/ine-e...*

**Some more bread**
Etwas mehr Brot
*etvas meer broht*

**Some more soup**
Etwas mehr Suppe
*etvas meer soo-pe*

**Some more glasses**
Noch ein paar Gläser
*nokh ine pahr glayzer*

**Another coffee**
Noch einen Kaffee
*nokh ine-en kafay*

**Another beer**
Noch ein Bier
*nokh ine beer*

**How much is it?**
Was kostet das?
*vas kostet das*

**How much is the room?**
Was kostet das Zimmer?
*vas kostet das tsimmer*

**large / small**
gross / klein
*gros / kline*

**with / without**
mit / ohne
*mit / oh-ne*

**Where is/are...?**
Wo ist/sind...?
*vo ist/sint...*

**the nearest...**
der/die nächste...
*der/dee nekh-ste...*

**How do I get...?**
Wie komme ich...?
*vee komme ikh...*

**to the station**
zum Bahnhof
*tsoom bahn-hof*

**to the bar**
zur Bar
*tsoor bar*

**to Berlin**
nach Berlin
*nakh berlin*

**There is/are...**
Es gibt...
*es gipt...*

**There isn't/aren't any...**
Es gibt keine...
*es gipt kine-e...*

**When...?**
Wann...?
*van...*

**At what time...?**
Um wie viel Uhr...?
*oom vee feel oor...*

**today**
heute
*hoy-te*

**tomorrow**
morgen
*morgen*

**Can I...?**
Kann ich...?
*kan ich...*

**smoke here**
hier rauchen
*heer row-khen*

**taste it**
probieren
*proh-beeren*

9

**Eingang** entrance

**Ausgang** exit

**heiß** hot

**kalt** cold

**geöffnet** open

**geschlossen** closed

**Trinkwasser** drinking water

**ZIEHEN** pull

**DRÜCKEN** push

**RECHTS** right

**LINKS** left

*Bitte...* please...

**zum Mitnehmen** take-away

**frei** free, vacant

**besetzt** engaged

**Selbstbedienung** self-service

**HERREN** gents

**DAMEN** ladies

**Außer Betrieb** out of order

**KASSE** cash desk

**zu vermieten** for hire / to rent

**zu verkaufen** for sale

**Baden verboten** no bathing

**Ausverkauf** sale

Untergeschoss ↓
**basement**

Erdgeschoss
**ground floor**

Aufzug →
**lift**

klingeln
**ring**

drücken
**press**

privat
**private**

ZIMMER FREI
**rooms available**

BELEGT
**no vacancies**

NOTAUSGANG
**emergency exit**

Fahrkarten
**tickets**

FAHRPLAN
**timetable**

← ZU DEN ZÜGEN
**to the trains**

(H)
**bus/tram stop**

ABFAHRT
**departure (AB)**

Bitte Wählen Sie
**please select**

Fahrkarte entwerten
**validate your ticket**

ANKUNFT
**arrival (AN)**

zahlbar mit
**pay with**

REISEZENTRUM
**travel centre**

Gepäckaufbewahrung
**left luggage**

GLEIS 2
**platform**

Nicht-raucher
**non-smoking**

Raucher
**smoking**

Rauchen verboten
**no smoking**

# POLITE EXPRESSIONS

*There are two forms of address in German, formal (Sie) and informal (Du). You should always stick to the formal until you are invited to duzen (to use the informal Du).*

**The meal was delicious**
Das Essen war köstlich
*das essen var kur's-tlikh*

**Vou are very kind**
Das ist sehr nett von Ihnen
*das ist zehr net fon ee-nen*

**Delighted to meet you**
Freut mich, Sie kennenzulernen
*froyt mikh zee kenen-tsoolehrnen*

**You have a beautiful house**
Sie haben ein schönes Haus
*zee hah-ben ine shur'nez hows*

**Thanks for everything**
Danke für alles
*dan-ke foor a-lez*

**Enjoy your holiday!**
Schöne Ferien!
*shur'ne fehr-ee-en*

**It was nice seeing you again**
Es war schön, Sie wiederzusehen
*es var shurn zee veedertsoozayen*

**Please come and visit us**
Bitte kommen Sie auf einen Besuch vorbei
*bi-te kom-men zee owf ine-en besookh forbye*

**I have enjoyed myself very much**
Ich habe mich sehr gut amüsiert
*ikh hah-be mikh zehr goot amoo-seeyert*

**Thank you very much**
Vielen Dank
*fee-len dank*

**This is a gift for you**
Hier ist ein Geschenk für Sie
*heer ist ine geshenk foor zee*

**This is my husband / my wife**
Das ist mein Mann / meine Frau
*das ist mine man / mine-e frow*

**You have a beautiful garden**
Sie haben einen schönen Garten
*zee hah-ben ine-en shur'nen garten*

**We'd like to come back**
Wir würden gerne wieder kommen
*veer wur'den gehr-ne veeder kommen*

**We must stay in touch**
Wir müssen in Kontakt bleiben
*veer moos-sen een kontakt blyben*

12

see also **EXCHANGE VISITORS**

**I'd like to wish you...**
Ich wünsche Ihnen...
*ikh **voon**-she ee-nen...*

**I'd like to wish you...** *(familiar)*
Ich wünsche dir...
*ikh **voon**-she deer...*

**Merry Christmas!**
Frohe Weihnachten!
*froh-e vy-nakhten*

**Happy New Year!**
Ein frohes neues Jahr!
*ine froh-es noy-es yahr*

**All the best!**
Alles Gute!
*al-les goo-te*

**Happy** *(Saint's)* **Name Day!**
Alles Gute zum Namenstag!
*al-les goo-te tsoom nah-mens-tahk*

**Happy birthday!**
Herzlichen Glückwunsch zum Geburtstag!
*hayrts-likhen glook-voonsh tsoom ge-boorts-tahk*

**Have a good trip!**
Gute Reise!
*goo-te ry-ze*

**Best wishes!**
Viele Grüße!
*fee-le groo-se*

**Welcome!**
Herzlich willkommen!
*hayrts-likh vil-kommen*

**Enjoy your meal!**
Guten Appetit!
*goo-ten apay-teet*

**Thanks, and the same to you!**
Danke, gleichfalls!
*dang-ke glykh-fals*

**Cheers!**
Prost! or Prosit!
*prohst / proh-zit*

**To your health!**
Zum Wohl!
*tsoom vohl*

**Congratulations!** *(having a baby, getting married, etc.)*
Herzliche Glückwünsche!
*hayrts-likh-e glook-voon-she*

*see also* **MAKING FRIENDS** ☐ **LETTERS**

# MAKING FRIENDS

*We have used the familiar **Du** form for these questions.*

**What's your name?**
Wie heißt du?
*vee hyst doo*

**My name is...**
Ich heiße...
*ikh **hy**-se...*

**How old are you?**
Wie alt bist du?
*vee alt bist doo*

**I'm ... years old**
Ich bin ... Jahre alt
*ikh bin ... **yah**-re alt*

**Where are you from?**
Woher kommst du?
*voh-**her** kommst doo*

**I'm British** *(I come from...)*
Ich komme aus Großbritannien
*ikh **kom**-me ows grohs-bree-**tan**-nee-en*

**Where do you live?**
Wo wohnst du?
*voh vohnst doo*

**Where do you live?** *(plural)*
Wo wohnt ihr?
*voh vohnt eer*

**I live in London**
Ich wohne in London
*ikh **voh**-ne in **lon**don*

**We live in Glasgow**
Wir wohnen in Glasgow
*veer **voh**-nen in **glas**gow*

**I'm still studying**
Ich studiere noch
*ikh shtoo-**dee**-re nokh*

**I work**
Ich arbeite
*ikh **ar**-by-te*

**I'm retired**
Ich bin pensioniert
*ikh bin penzyoh-**neert***

**I'm...**    **(not) married**    **divorced**    **widow(er)**
Ich bin...    (nicht) verheiratet    geschieden    Witwe(r)
*ikh bin...    (nikht) fer-**hy**rah-tet    ge-**shee**den    **vit**-ve(r)*

**I have...**    **a boyfriend**
Ich habe...    einen Freund
*ikh **hah**-be...    **ine**-en froynt*

**a girlfriend**
eine Freundin
***ine**-e **froyn**-din*

**I have ... children**
Ich habe ... Kinder
*ikh **hah**-be ... **kin**der*

**I have no children**
Ich habe keine Kinder
*ikh **hah**-be **kine**-e **kin**der*

**I'm here on holiday**
Ich bin hier auf Urlaub
*ikh bin heer owf **oor**lowp*

**I'm here on business**
Ich bin geschäftlich hier
*ikh bin ge**sheft**-likh heer*

see also **WORK** ☐ **LEISURE/INTERESTS** ☐ **SPORT**

**What work do you do?**
Was machen Sie beruflich?
*vas makhen zee be-rooflikh*

**Do you enjoy it?**
Macht es Ihnen Spaß?
*makht es ee-nen shpahs*

| **I'm...** | **a teacher** | **a manager** | **a postman** |
|---|---|---|---|
| Ich bin... | Lehrer(in) | Manager(in) | Briefträger(in) |
| *ikh bin...* | *lay-rer(in)* | *manager(in)* | *breef-treger(in)* |

| **I work in...** | **a shop** | **a factory** | **a bank** |
|---|---|---|---|
| Ich arbeite in... | einem Geschäft | einer Fabrik | einer Bank |
| *ikh ar-by-te in...* | *ine-em gesheft* | *ine-er fabreek* | *ine-er bank* |

**I work from home**
Ich arbeite zu Hause
*ikh ar-by-te tsoo how-ze*

**I'm self-employed**
Ich bin selbstständig
*ikh bin selbst-shtendikh*

**I am unemployed**
Ich bin arbeitslos
*ikh bin ar-bites-los*

**It's very difficult to get a job at the moment**
Es ist im Augenblick sehr schwer, Arbeit zu finden
*es ist im owgen-blikh zayr shvayr ar-bite tsoo finden*

| **What hours do you work?** | **full-time** | **part-time** |
|---|---|---|
| Wie viele Stunden arbeiten Sie? | ganztags | halbtags |
| *vee fee-le shtoon-den ar-bite-en zee* | *gants-tahks* | *halp-tahks* |

**I work from 9 to 5**
Ich arbeite von neun bis fünf
*ikh ar-by-te fon noyn bis foonf*

**from Monday to Friday**
Montag bis Freitag
*mohntahk bis fry-tahk*

**How much holiday do you get?**
Wie viel Urlaub haben Sie?
*vee feel oorlowp hah-ben zee*

**What do you want to be when you grow up?**
Was möchtest du einmal werden, wenn du groß bist?
*vas mur'kh-test doo ine-mal verden ven doo grohs bist*

see also **MAKING FRIENDS** ▢ **BUSINESS**

| | |
|---|---|
| SONNIG **zon**nikh | SUNNY |
| HEITER **hye**-ter | FAIR |
| BEWÖLKT be**fur'l**kt | CLOUDY |
| SCHAUERHAFT **show**erhaft | SHOWERY |
| GEWITTER ge**vitt**er | THUNDERSTORMS |
| WINDIG **vin**-dikh | WINDY |
| TROCKEN **troh**khen | DRY |

### What is the weather forecast?
Wie ist der Wetterbericht?
*vee ist der **vett**er-berikht*

### It's sunny
Es ist sonnig
*es ist **zonn**ikh*

### It's raining
Es regnet
*es **rayg**net*

### It's snowing
Es schneit
*es shnite*

### It's windy
Es ist windig
*es ist **vin**-dikh*

### What a lovely day!
Was für ein herrlicher Tag!
*vas foor ine **her**-likh-er tahk*

### What awful weather!
Was für ein Mistwetter!
*vas foor ine **mist**-vetter*

### What will the weather be like tomorrow?
Wie wird das Wetter morgen?
*vee virt das **vett**er **mor**gen*

### Do you think it will rain?
Glauben Sie, es wird regnen?
*glowben zee es vird **rayg**nen*

### Do I need an umbrella?
Brauche ich einen Schirm?
***brow**-khe ikh **ine**-en shirm*

### It's very hot
Es ist sehr heiß
*es ist zayr hice*

### What is the temperature?
Wie ist die Temperatur?
*vee ist dee tempe-ra**toor***

### Do you think there will be a storm?
Glauben Sie, es wird einen Sturm geben?
*glowben zee es vird **ine**-en shtoorm **gay**ben*

 see also MAKING FRIENDS

| | |
|---|---|
| GEGENÜBER *gaygen-oober* | **OPPOSITE** |
| NEBEN *nayben* | **NEXT TO** |
| IN DER NÄHE VON *in der nay-e fon* | **NEAR TO** |
| DIE AMPEL *dee ampel* | **TRAFFIC LIGHTS** |
| AN DER ECKE *an der ek-ke* | **AT THE CORNER** |

**Excuse me!**
Entschuldigung!
*entshool-digoong*

**How do I get to...?**
Wie komme ich zum/zur/nach...?
*vee kom-me ikh tsoom/tsoor/nakh...*

**to the station**
zum Bahnhof (m)
*tsoom bahn-hohf*

**to the castle**
zur Burg (f)
*tsoor boork*

**to... (with place name)**
nach...
*nakh...*

**We're looking for...**
Wir suchen...
*veer zookhen...*

**Is it far?**
Ist es weit?
*ist es vite*

**Can I walk there?**
Kann ich dahin laufen?
*kan ikh dahin lowfen*

**We're lost** (on foot)
Wir haben uns verlaufen
*veer hah-ben oons fer-lowfen*

**We're lost** (in car)
Wir haben uns verfahren
*veer hah-ben oons fer-fahren*

**Is this the right way to...?**
Bin ich hier richtig zum/zur/nach...?
*bin ikh heer rikhtikh tsoom/tsoor/nakh...*

**How do I get onto the motorway?**
Wie komme ich zur Autobahn?
*vee kom-me ikh tsoor owto-bahn*

**Can you show me on the map?**
Können Sie mir das auf der Karte zeigen?
*kur'-nen zee meer das owf der kar-te tsy-gen*

■ **YOU MAY HEAR**

**Immer geradeaus**
*immer gay-rah-de-ows*
Straight on

**Biegen Sie links / rechts ab**
*bee-gen zee links / rekhts ap*
Turn left / right

see also **MAPS & GUIDES**

17

*If you are planning to use public transport, you can buy a multiple ticket card – eine **Mehrfahrtenkarte**. You have to stamp it either on board the bus/tram/underground or at the bus stop. Other options are eine **Touristenkarte** or eine **Familienkarte**.*

**Is there a bus to...?**
Gibt es einen Bus nach *(plus place name)* ...?
*gipt es **ine**-en boos nakh...*

**Bonn / Potsdam**
Bonn / Potsdam
*bon / potsdam*

**Where does the bus to ... leave from?**
Wo fährt der Bus zum/zur *(for building, institution)* ... ab?
*voh fayrt der boos tsoom/tsoor ... ap*

| **to the station** | **to the museum** | **to the art gallery** |
|---|---|---|
| zum Bahnhof (m) | zum Museum (nt) | zur Kunsthalle (f) |
| *tsoom **bahn**-hohf* | *zum moo-**zay**-oom* | *tsoor **koonst**-hal-le* |

**What number goes to...?**
Welche Linie fährt zum/zur/nach...?
***vel**-khe **lee**-nee-e fayrt tsoom/tsoor/nakh...*

**Where can I buy tickets?**
Wo kann ich Fahrscheine kaufen?
*voh kann ikh **fahr**-shine-e **kow**-fen*

**On the bus?**
Im Bus?
*im boos*

**How much is it to...?**
Was kostet es bis zum/zur/nach...?
*vas **kost**et es bis tsoom/tsoor/nakh...*

**How often are the buses / trams to...?**
Wie oft fahren die Busse / Straßenbahnen zum/zur/nach...?
*vee oft **fah**-ren dee **boo**-se / **shtrah**-sen-bah-nen tsoom/tsoor/nakh...*

**Please tell me when to get off**
Sagen Sie mir bitte, wann ich aussteigen muss
***zah**-gen zee meer **bit**-te van ikh **ows**-shtygen moos*

**Please let me off**
Kann ich bitte aussteigen
*kan ikh **bit**-te **ows**-shtygen*

**This is my stop**
Das ist meine Haltestelle
*das ist **mine**-e **hal**-te-shte-le*

*Most German cities operate an integrated transport system.
Tickets cover both bus, **U-Bahn** (metro) and **S-Bahn** (suburban
trains).*

### Where is the nearest metro station?
Wo ist die nächste U-Bahn-Haltestelle?
*voh ist dee **nekh**-ste **oo**bahn-hal-te-shte-le*

### How does the ticket machine work?
Wie funktioniert der Automat?
*vee foonk-tsyoh-**neert** der owto-**maht***

### I'm going to...
Ich möchte nach...
*ikh **mur'kh**-te nakh...*

### Do you have a transport map?
Gibt es eine Übersichtskarte für den Nahverkehr?
*gipt es **ine**-e oober-zikhts-**kar**-te foor den **nah**-ferkehr*

### How do I get to...?
Wie komme ich nach...?
*vee **kom**-me ikh nakh...*

### Do I have to change?
Muss ich umsteigen?
*moos ikh **oom**-shtygen*

### Where?
Wo?
*voh*

### Which line is it for...?
Welche Linie fährt nach...?
*vel-khe **lee**-nee-e fayrt nakh...*

### In which direction?
In welche Richtung?
*in **vel**-khe **rikh**toong*

### What is the next stop?
Was ist der nächste Halt?
*vas ist der **nehk**-ste halt*

### May I get past?
Darf ich mal vorbei, bitte?
*darf ikh mal for-**by** bit-te*

### I have to get out here
Ich muss hier aussteigen
*ikh moos heer **ows**-shtygen*

### ■ YOU MAY HEAR

Für welche Zonen?
*foor **vel**-khe **tsoh**-nen*
For which zones?

Für die Innenstadt?
*foor dee **in**en-shtat*
For the city centre?

*see also* **BUS & COACH** ☐ **TAXI** ☐ **LUGGAGE**　　　　　19

*Be sure to check if there is a supplement, **ein Zuschlag**, to pay before you board the train. It costs less if you buy it with your ticket. The ticket and information office are marked **Reisezentrum***

| | |
|---|---|
| DER BAHNHOF der **bahn**-hof | STATION |
| DER HAUPTBAHNHOF (HBF) der **howpt**-bahnhof | MAIN STATION |
| DER FAHRPLAN der **fahr**plan | TIMETABLE |
| DIE ABFAHRT dee **ap**fahrt | DEPARTURE |
| DIE ANKUNFT dee **an**koonft | ARRIVAL |

**When is the next train to....?**
Wann geht der nächste Zug nach...?
*van gayt der **nekh**-ste tzook nakh...*

**Two return tickets to...**
Zwei Rückfahrkarten nach...
*tsvy **rook**far-karten nakh...*

**A single to...**
Einmal einfach nach...
*ine-mal ine-fakh nakh...*

**Ist / 2nd class**
Erster / Zweiter Klasse
*er-ster / tsvy-ter kla-se*

**Smoking / Non smoking**
Raucher / Nichtraucher
*row-kher / nikht-row-kher*

**Is there a supplement to pay?**
Muss ich einen Zuschlag zahlen?
*moos ikh ine-en tsooshlak tsah-len*

**I want to book a seat on the ICE to Hamburg**
Ich möchte einen Platz im ICE nach Hamburg buchen
*ikh mur'kh-te ine-en plats im ee-tsay-ay nakh hamburg boo-khen*

**When does it arrive in...?**
Wann kommt er in ... an?
*van komt er in ... an*

**Do I need to change?**
Muss ich umsteigen?
*moos ikh oom-shty-gen*

**Where?**
Wo?
*voh*

**How long is there to change trains?**
Wie viel Zeit habe ich zum Umsteigen
*vee feel tsite **hab**-be ikh tsoom **oom**-shty-gen*

**Will my connecting train wait?**
Wartet der Anschlusszug?
*var-tet der **an**-shloos-tsook*

**Which platform does it leave from?**
Von welchem Bahnsteig fährt er ab?
*fon **vel**-khem **bahn**-shtike fayrt er ap*

**Does the train to... leave from here?**
Fährt hier der Zug nach ... ab?
*fayrt heer der tsook nakh ... ap*

**Is this the train for...?**
Ist das der Zug nach...?
*ist das der tsook nakh...*

**When will it leave?**
Wann fährt er ab?
*van fayrt er ap*

**Does the train stop at...?**
Hält der Zug in...?
*helt der tsook in...*

**Please let me know when we get to...**
Bitte sagen Sie mir, wann wir in ... ankommen
*bit-te **zah**gen zee meer van veer in ... **an**-kommen*

**Is there a buffet on the train?**
Hat der Zug einen Speisewagen?
*hat der tsook **ine**-en **shpy**-ze-vahgen*

**Is this free?** (seat)
Ist hier noch frei?
*ist heer nokh fry*

**This is my seat**
Das ist mein Platz
*das ist mine plats*

■ **YOU MAY HEAR**

Fahrscheine bitte
***fahr**-shy-ne **bit**-te*
Tickets please?

*see also* **LUGGAGE** ☐ **TAXI**

# TAXI

In Germany it is practically impossible to flag down a taxi in the street. You have to find a taxi rank, **Taxistand**, or phone for one. You can often find adverts for taxi firms in public telephones and you must give your name and the address of the phone box which will be written under the word **Standort**.

**I want a taxi**
Ich hätte gern ein Taxi
*ikh **het**-te gern ine **ta**xi*

**Where can I get a taxi?**
Wo bekomme ich hier ein Taxi?
*voh be-**kom**-me ikh heer ine **ta**xi*

**Please order me a taxi**
Bitte bestellen Sie mir ein Taxi
*bit-te be-**shte**-len zee meer ine **ta**xi*

**straightaway**
sofort
*zo-**fort***

**for** (time)
für ... Uhr
*foor...oor*

**My name is...**
Ich heiße...
*ikh **hy**-se...*

**The address is...**
Die Adresse ist...
*dee a-**dre**-se ist...*

**How much is it...?**
Was kostet die Fahrt ...?
*vas **kos**tet dee fahrt...*

**to the centre**
ins Zentrum
*ins **tsen**troom*

**to the station**
zum Bahnhof
*tsoom **bahn**-hof*

**to the airport**
zum Flughafen
*tsoom **flook**-hafen*

**to this address**
zu dieser Adresse
*tsoo **dee**zer a-**dre**-se*

**How much is it?**
Was kostet das?
*vas **kos**tet das*

**Why is it so much?**
Warum ist das so teuer?
*vah**room** ist das zoh **toy**-er*

**I'm afraid I've nothing smaller**
Ich habe es leider nicht kleiner
*ikh **hah**-be es **ly**-der nikht **kline**-er*

**I need a receipt**
Ich brauche eine Quittung
*ikh **brow**-khe **ine**-e **kvi**-toong*

**I'm in a hurry**
Ich habe es sehr eilig
*ikh **hah**-be es zayr **eye**-likh*

**Is it far?**
Ist es weit?
*ist es vite*

**I have to catch the ... o'clock flight to...**
Ich muss zum Flug um ... Uhr nach...
*ikh moos tsoom flook oom ... oor nakh...*

see also **LUGGAGE** ☐ **BUS** ☐ **METRO**

**When is the next boat / the next ferry to...?**
Wann fährt das nächste Schiff / die nächste Fähre nach ... ab?
*van fayrt das **nekh**-ste shif / dee **nekh**-ste **fay**-re nakh ... ap*

**Is there a timetable?**
Gibt es einen Fahrplan?
*gipt es **ine**-en **fahr**-plahn*

**Is there a car ferry to...?**
Gibt es eine Autofähre nach...?
*gipt es **ine**-e **owto**-fay-re nakh...*

**How much is...?**       **a single**          **a return**
Was kostet...?            die einfache Fahrt    eine Rückfahrkarte
*vas **kost**et...*       *dee **ine**-fakh-e fahrt*   ***ine**-e **rook**-fahr-kar-te*

**a tourist ticket**                **a family card**
eine Touristenkarte                 eine Familienkarte
***ine**-e too-**ris**-ten-kar-te*  ***ine**-e fa-**mee**-lee-en-kar-te*

**How much is it for a car and ... people?**
Was kostet es für ein Auto mit ... Personen?
*vas **kost**et es foor ine **owto** mit ... per-**zoh**nen*

**How long does the trip take?**    **When do we get to...?**
Wie lange dauert die Fahrt?         Wann kommen wir in ... an?
*vee **lang**-e **dow**-ert dee fahrt*   *van **kom**men veer in ... an*

**Where does the boat leave from?**
Wo fährt das Schiff ab?
*voh fayrt das shif ap*

**When is the first / last boat?**
Wann geht das erste / letzte Schiff?
*van gayt das **er**-ste / **lets**-te shif*

**Is there somewhere to eat on the boat?**
Kann man auf dem Schiff etwas zu essen bekommen?
*kan man owf daym shif **et**vas tsoo **es**sen be-**kom**men*

■ **YOU MAY HEAR**

Wollen Sie heute noch zurück?
***vol**-len zee **hoy**-te nokh tsoo**rook***
Do you want to come back today?

*see also* **LUGGAGE**

**To the airport, please**
Zum Flughafen, bitte
tsoom *flook*-hafen *bit*-te

**How do I get to** (name town) **...?**
Wie komme ich nach...?
vee *kom*-me ikh nakh...

| **How much is a taxi...?** | **into town** | **to the hotel** |
| Wie viel kostet ein Taxi...? | in die Stadt | zum Hotel |
| vee feel *kos*tet ine *ta*xi... | in dee shtat... | tsoom ho*tel* |

**Is there an airport bus to the city centre?**
Gibt es einen Airport-Bus zum Stadtzentrum?
gipt es *ine*-en *air*port-boos tsoom *shtat*-tsentroom

**Where do I check in for...** (airline) **?**
Wo ist der Check-in für...?
voh ist der *check*-in foor...

**Which is the departure gate for the flight to...?**
Welches Gate hat der Flug nach...?
*vel*-khes gate hat der flook nakh...

**Where is the luggage for the flight from...?**
Wo ist das Gepäck vom Flug aus...?
voh ist das ge*pek* fom flook ows...

## ■ YOU MAY HEAR

Sie steigen von Gate Nummer ... ein
zee *shty*-gen fon gate *noo*mer ... ine
**Boarding will take place at gate number...**

Gehen Sie sofort zu Gate Nummer...
*gay*en zee zo-*fort* tsoo gate *noo*mer...
**Go immediately to gate number...**

Ihr Flug hat Verspätung
eer flook hat fer-*shpay*-toong
**Your flight is delayed**

see also LUGGAGE ☐ BUS ☐ METRO ☐ TAXI

*With the single European Market, European Union (EU) citizens
are subject only to highly selective spot checks and they can go
through the blue customs channel when arriving from another
EU country. There is no restriction, either by quantity or value,
on goods purchased by travellers in another EU country provided
they are **for their own personal use** (guidelines have been
published). If you are unsure of certain items, check with the
customs officials as to whether payment of duty is required.*

| | |
|---|---|
| DIE PASSKONTROLLE dee **pas**-kontroh-le | PASSPORT CONTROL |
| DER ZOLL der tsoll | CUSTOMS |

**Do I have to pay duty on this?**
Muss ich das verzollen?
*moos ikh das fer-**tsoll**en*

**I bought this in ... as a gift**
Ich habe das in ... als Geschenk gekauft
*ikh **hah**-be das in ... als ge-**shenk** ge**kowft***

**It is for my own personal use**
Es ist für meinen persönlichen Gebrauch
*es ist foor **mine**-en per-**zur'n**-likhen ge-**browkh***

**We are on our way to...** (if in transit to another country)
Wir sind auf der Durchreise nach...
*veer zint owf der **doorkh**-ry-ze nakh...*

**The children are on this passport**
Die Kinder stehen in diesem Pass
*dee **kin**der **shtay**-en in **dee**-zem pass*

**This is the baby's passport**
Hier ist der Pass für das Baby
*heer ist der pass foor das **ba**by*

**I have a visa**
Ich habe ein Visum
*ikh **hah**-be ine **vee**zoom*

25

switch on
headlights

diversion

**LANGSAM**

slow down

one way street

**VORFAHRT**

you have priority
at next junction

*yellow centre*

priority road

**VORFAHRT
GEWÄHREN**

give way

customs
control

**GEFAHRSTELLE**

danger zone

**AUTOBAHN**

motorway

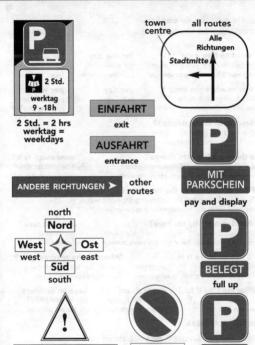

**P**

**P** 2 Std.
werktag
9 - 18h

2 Std. = 2 hrs
werktag
= weekdays

town centre
*Stadtmitte*

all routes
Alle
Richtungen

**EINFAHRT**

exit

**AUSFAHRT**

entrance

ANDERE RICHTUNGEN ➤   other routes

**P**

**MIT PARKSCHEIN**

pay and display

north
**Nord**

**West**   **Ost**

west   east

**Süd**

south

**P**

**BELEGT**

full up

**!**

**SCHRITTGESCHWINDIGKEIT**

dead slow

**PARKVERBOT**

no parking

**P**

**FREI**

spaces

27

DER FÜHRERSCHEIN *der **foo**rershine*
DIE ZULASSUNG *dee tsoo**las**-soong*

**DRIVING LICENCE**
**LOG BOOK**

**I want to hire a car**
Ich möchte ein Auto mieten
*ickh **mur'kh**-te ine **ow**to **mee**ten*

**for one day**
für einen Tag
*foor **ine**-en tahk*

**for ... days**
für ... Tage
*foor ... **ta**-ge*

**How much is the car...?**
Was kostet das Auto...?
*vas kostet das **ow**to...*

**per day**
pro Tag
*proh tahk*

**per week**
pro Woche
*proh **vo**-khe*

**How much is the deposit?**
Wie hoch ist die Kaution?
*vee hokh ist dee kow-**tsyon***

**Is there a kilometre charge?**
Verlangen Sie eine Kilometergebühr?
*fer-**lang**en zee **ine**-e keelo-**may**ter-geboor*

**How much is it?**
Wie viel ist das?
*vee feel ist das*

**What is included in the insurance?**
Was ist alles in der Versicherung inbegriffen?
*vas ist **al**-les in der fer-**zikh**eroong **in**-be-griffen*

**Must I return the car here?**
Muss ich das Auto hierher zurückbringen?
*moos ikh das **ow**to **heer**-her tsoo**rook**-bringen*

**By what time?**
Bis wann?
*bis van*

**I'd like to leave it in...**
Ich würde es gern in ... abgeben
*ikh **voor**-de es gern in ... **ap**-gayben*

**Where is the reverse gear?**
Wo ist der Rückwärtsgang?
*voh ist der **rook**-verts-gang*

**What do I do if I...?**
Was mache ich...?
*vas **ma**-khe ikh...*

**break down**
bei einer Panne
*by **ine**-er **pan**-ne*

**have an accident**
bei einem Unfall
*by **ine**-em **oon**-fall*

■ **YOU MAY HEAR**

Bitte bringen Sie das Auto voll betankt zurück
***bit**-te **bring**en zee das **ow**to fol be-**tankt** tsoo**rook***
Please return the car with a full tank

*The speed limits in Germany are 50 km/h in built up areas, 100 km/h on ordinary roads. There is no speed restriction on motorways though 130 km/h is recommended. But be careful, some sections will have restrictions and these will be signposted. Most cities have controlled parking areas – watch out for **Zone** signs. You cannot park inside these zones.*

**We're going to....**
Wir fahren nach...
*veer **fah**-ren nakh...*

**What's the best route?**
Was ist der beste Weg?
*vas ist der **bes**-te vayk*

**Is this the road to...?**
Ist das die Straße nach...?
*is das dee **shtra**-se nakh...*

**How do I get to the motorway?**
Wie komme ich zur Autobahn?
*vee **kom**-me ich tsoor **owto**-bahn*

**Which junction is it for...?**
Welche Anschlussstelle führt nach...?
*vel-khe anshlus-**ste**-le foort nakh...*

**Where is there a car park?**
Wo ist hier ein Parkplatz?
*voh ist heer ine **park**plats*

**Do I need a parking disk?**
Braucht man eine Parkscheibe?
*browkht man **ine**-e **park**-shy-be*

**Can I park here?**
Kann ich hier parken?
*kan ikh heer **park**en*

**How long for?**
Für wie lange?
*foor vee **lang**-e*

**Where is the best place to park?**
Wo sollte ich am besten parken?
*voh **zoll**-te ikh am **bes**-ten **park**en*

**Is the pass open?**
Ist der Pass offen?
*ist der pas **off**en*

**Do I/we need snow chains?**
Braucht man Schneeketten?
*browkht man **shnay**-ketten*

see also **ROAD SIGNS** □ **PETROL** □ **BREAKDOWN**

# PETROL

*Petrol is more expensive at motorway service stations. An **Autohof** (a trucker stop) is a cheaper alternative.*

| | | | |
|---|---|---|---|
| SUPER **tsoo**per | 4 STAR | DAS BENZIN das bent**seen** | PETROL |
| BLEIFREI **bly**-fry | UNLEADED | DAS ÖL das ur'l | OIL |

**Is there a petrol station near here?**
Ist hier in der Nähe eine Tankstelle?
ist heer in der **nay**-e **ine**-e **tank**-shte-le

**Fill it up, please**
Voll tanken, bitte
fol **tang**-ken **bit**-te

**Please check the oil / the water**
Bitte überprüfen Sie den Öl / das Wasser
**bit**-te oober-**proo**fen zee das ur'l / das **vas**ser

**...euro worth of unleaded petrol**
Für ... Euro bleifrei bitte
foor ... **oyro bly**-fry **bit**-te

**Please check the tyre pressure**
Bitte überprüfen Sie den Reifendruck
**bit**-te oober-**proo**fen zee den **ry**fen-drook

**Can you fill this can with petrol, please?**
Könnten Sie diesen Kanister mit Benzin füllen?
**kur'n**-ten zee **dee**zen ka-**ni**ster mit bent**seen fool**len

**Do you take this credit card?**
Nehmen Sie diese Kreditkarte?
**nay**men zee **dee**-ze kre**deet**-kar-te

**Where do I pay?**
Wo kann ich zahlen?
voh kan ikh **tsah**-len

**Pump number...**
Säule Nummer...
**soy**-le **noo**mer...

■ **YOU MAY HEAR**

**Welche Säule?**
**vel**-khe **soy**-le
Which pump?

see also **BREAKDOWN** ☐ **CAR**

*If you break down on the German motorway, by law you should place a warning triangle 100 metres behind your vehicle.*

**Can you help me?**
Können Sie mir helfen?
*kur'-nen zee meer hel-fen*

**My car has broken down**
Ich habe eine Autopanne
*ikh hah-be ine-e owto-pan-ne*

**The car won't start**
Das Auto springt nicht an
*das owto shpringt nikht an*

**Can you give me a push?**
Können Sie mich anschieben?
*kur'-nen zee mikh an-sheeben*

**I've run out of petrol**
Ich habe kein Benzin mehr
*ikh hah-be kine bentseen mayr*

**Is there a garage near here?**
Ist eine Werkstatt in der Nähe?
*ist ine-e verk-shtat in der nay-e*

**The engine is overheating**
Der Motor wird zu heiß
*der mohtor virt tsoo hice*

**The battery is flat**
Meine Batterie ist leer
*mine-e ba-teree ist layr*

**I have a flat tyre**
Ich habe einen Platten
*ikh hah-be ine-en pla-ten*

**I can't get the wheel off**
Ich bekomme das Rad nicht ab
*ikh be-kom-me das rat nikht ap*

**I need water**
Ich brauche Wasser
*ikh brow-khe vas-ser*

**The petrol tank / radiator is leaking**
Der Tank / Kühler leckt
*der tank / kooler lekht*

**Can you tow me to the nearest garage?**
Könnten Sie mich bis zur nächsten Werkstatt abschleppen?
*kur'n-ten zee mikh bis tsoor nekh-sten verk-shtat ap-shleppen*

**Do you have parts for a** (make of car )**...?**
Haben Sie Ersatzteile für einen...?
*hah-ben zee erzats-tile-e foor ine-en...*

**Something is wrong with...**
Es stimmt etwas nicht mit...
*es shtimt etvas nikht mit...*

**Can you put in a new windscreen?**
Können Sie eine neue Windschutzscheibe einsetzen?
*kur'-nen zee ine-e noy-e vintshoots-shy-be ine-zetsen*

*see also* **CAR PARTS**

# CAR PARTS

**The ... doesn't work**
Der/Die/Das ... funktioniert nicht
*der/dee/das...foonk-tsyoh-neert nikht*

**The ... don't work**
Die ... funktionieren nicht
*dee...foonk-tsyoh-neeren nikht*

| | | |
|---|---|---|
| accelerator | das Gaspedal | *gas-paydal* |
| battery | die Batterie | *ba-teree* |
| brakes | die Bremsen | *brem-zen* |
| central locking | die Zentralverriegelung | *tsentral-fer-ree-geloong* |
| choke | der Choke | *choke* |
| clutch | die Kupplung | *kooploong* |
| distributor | der Verteiler | *fayr-tyler* |
| engine | der Motor | *mohtor* |
| exhaust pipe | das Auspuffrohr | *owspoof-rohr* |
| fanbelt | der Keilriemen | *kile-reemen* |
| fuse | die Sicherung | *zikh-eroong* |
| gears | das Getriebe | *getree-be* |
| handbrake | die Handbremse | *hantbrem-ze* |
| headlights | die Scheinwerfer | *shine-verfer* |
| heating | die Heizung | *hyt-soong* |
| ignition | die Zündung | *tsoon-doong* |
| indicator | der Blinker | *blinker* |
| points | der Unterbrecher | *oonter-brekh-er* |
| radiator | der Kühler | *kooler* |
| rear lights | das Rücklicht | *rook-likht* |
| seat belt | der Sicherheitsgurt | *zikher-hites-goort* |
| spare wheel | das Ersatzrad | *erzats-rat* |
| spark plugs | die Zündkerzen | *tsoont-kayrtsen* |
| steering | die Lenkung | *lenkoong* |
| tyre | der Reifen | *ry-fen* |
| wheel | das Rad | *raht* |
| windscreen | die Windschutzscheibe | *vintshoots-shy-be* |
| windscreen wiper | der Scheibenwischer | *shyben-visher* |

see also **BREAKDOWN** □ **PETROL**

You can book accommodation over the internet using the German tourist office website **www.deutschland-tourismus.de**.

| | | |
|---|---|---|
| **Anreise am** <br> *start of stay* | | **(TT/MM/JJ)** <br> *(dd/mm/yy)* |
| **Abreise am** <br> *date of departure* | | **(TT/MM/JJ)** <br> *(dd/mm/yy)* |
| **Anreiseart** <br> *arriving by* | ☐ **Auto** *car*  ☐ **Bahn** *train* | ☐ **Flugzeug** *aeroplane* |
| **Gästeanzahl** <br> *no. of guests* | ☐ **Erwachsene** *adults* | ☐ **Kinder** *children* |
| **Zimmerart** <br> *type of room* | ☐ **Einzelzimmer** *single room* | ☐ **Doppelzimmer** *double room* |
| | ☐ **Mehrbettzimmer** *family room* | ☐ **Appartement** *appartment* |

**I'd like (to book) a room**
Ich möchte ein Zimmer (buchen)
*ikh mur'kh-te ine tsimmer (boo-khen)*

**a double room**
ein Doppelzimmer
*ine doppel-tsimmer*

**a single room**
ein Einzelzimmer
*ine ine-tsel-tsimmer*

**with bath**
mit Bad
*mit baht*

**with shower**
mit Dusche
*mit doo-she*

**a twin-bedded room**
ein Zweibettzimmer
*ine tsvy-bet-tsimmer*

**with an extra bed for a child**
mit einem zusätzlichen Kinderbett
*mit ine-em tsoo-sets-likhen kin-derbet*

**How much is it...?**
Was kostet es...?
*vas kostet es...*

**per night**
pro Nacht
*pro nakht*

**per week**
pro Woche
*pro vo-khe*

**We'd like to stay ... nights**
Wir möchten ... Nächte bleiben
*veer mur'kh-ten ... nekh-te bly-ben*

**from ... till ...**
vom ... bis zum ...
*fom ... bis tsoom ...*

*cont...*

# HOTEL (BOOKING)

| **How much is...?** | **half board** | **full board** |
|---|---|---|
| Was kostet...? | Halbpension | Vollpension |
| *vas **kost**et...* | ***halp**-pen-zyohn* | ***fol**-pen-zyohn* |

**Is breakfast included?**
Ist das Frühstück inbegriffen?
*ist das **froo**-shtook **in**-be-griffen*

**I'll confirm by e-mail**
Ich schicke eine E-Mail zur Bestätigung
*ikh **shi**-ke ine-e **e**-mail tsoor be-**shtay**-ti-goong*

**I'll arrive at ... o'clock**
Ich komme an um ... Uhr
*ikh **kom**-me an oom ... oor*

**Can you recommend another hotel?**
Können Sie ein anderes Hotel empfehlen?
***kur'**-nen zee ine **an**-de-res ho**tel** emp-**fay**len*

## ■ YOU MAY HEAR

| **Wir sind ausgebucht** | **Für wie viele Nächte?** |
|---|---|
| *veer zint **ows**-gebookht* | *foor vee **fee**-le **nekh**-te* |
| We're full up | For how many nights? |

**Wie heißen Sie, bitte?**
*vee **hy**-sen zee **bit**-te*
What is your name, please?

| **Bitte bestätigen Sie...** | **per E-Mail** | **per Fax** |
|---|---|---|
| ***bit**-te be-**shtay**-tigen zee...* | *per e-mail* | *per fax* |
| Please confirm... | by e-mail | by fax |

**Wann kommen Sie an?**
*van **kom**-men zee an*
What time will you arrive?

**Wie brauchen Ihre Kreditkartennummer**
*vee **brow**khen **ee**-re kredit**kar**tenoo-mer*
We need your credit card number

*A **Hotel Garni** is a bed and breakfast. A **Gasthof** is usually a pub or wine bar with a few guestrooms. They are generally good value.*

**Have you any vacancies?**     **for tonight / for 2 nights**
Haben Sie Zimmer frei?     für heute Nacht / für zwei Nächte
*hah-ben zee **tsim**mer fry*     *foor **hoy**-te nakht / foor tsvy **nekh**-te*

**I booked a room in the name of...**
Ich habe ein Zimmer auf den Namen ... reserviert
*ikh **hah**-be ine **tsim**mer owf den **nah**-men ... ray-zer-**veert***

**Where can I park the car?**
Wo kann ich mein Auto parken?
*voh kan ich mine **ow**to **par**ken*

**What time is...?**     **dinner** *(evening)*     **breakfast**
Wann gibt es...?     Abendessen     Frühstück
*van gipt es...*     ***ah**bent-essen*     ***froo**-shtook*

**We'll be back late tonight**
Wir kommen heute abend spät zurück
*veer **kom**men **hoy**-te **ah**bent shpayt tsoo**rook***

**Can you put this in the safe, please?**
Können Sie das bitte in den Safe legen?
***kur'**-nen zee das **bit**-te in den safe **lay**-gen*

**The key, please**     **Room number...**
Den Schlüssel, bitte     Zimmer *(number)*...
*den **shloo**-sel **bit**-te*     ***tsim**mer...*

**Are there any messages for me?**
Sind Nachrichten für mich da?
*zint **nahkh**-rikhten foor mikh dah*

**I'm leaving tomorrow**     **Please prepare the bill**
Ich reise morgen ab     Machen Sie bitte die Rechnung fertig
*ikh **ry**-ze **mor**gen ap*     ***ma**khen zee **bit**-te dee **rekh**-noong **fer**tikh*

*see also* **PAYING**

*Local tourist offices should have details of campsites and prices.*

**Do you have a list of campsites with prices?**
Haben Sie eine Liste von Campingplätzen mit Preisen?
*hah-ben zee ine-e lis-te fon kam-ping-pletsen mit pri-zen*

**Is the campsite sheltered?**
Liegt der Campingplatz geschützt?
*leekt der kam-ping-platz ge-shootst*

**How far is the lake?**
Wie weit ist es bis zum See?
*vee vite ist es bis tsoom zay*

**Is there a restaurant?**
Gibt es ein Restaurant?
*gipt es ine restoh-rong*

**Is there a shop?**
Gibt es einen Laden?
*gipt es ine-en lah-den*

**Do you have any vacancies?**
Haben Sie noch Plätze frei?
*hah-ben zee nokh plet-se fry*

**Are showers...**
Ist Duschen...
*ist doo-shen...*

**Is hot water...**
Ist Heißwasser...
*ist hice-vasser...*

**Is electricity...**
Ist Strom...
*ist shtrohm...*

**...included in the price?**
...im Preis inbegriffen?
*...im price in-be-griffen?*

**We'd like to stay for ... nights**
Wir möchten ... Nächte bleiben
*veer mur'kh-ten ... nekh-te bly-ben*

**How much is it per night...?**
Was kostet die Nacht...?
*vas kos-tet dee nakht...*

**for a tent**
pro Zelt
*pro tselt*

**per person**
pro Person
*pro per-zohn*

**Can we camp here overnight?** *(for tent)*
Können wir über Nacht hier zelten?
*kur'-nen veer oober nakht heer tsel-ten*

*Recycling in Germany is taken very seriously. Bins are colour-coded according to what can be put into them: brown is for biodegradable material, blue is for paper, black is for general waste and yellow is for any packaging carrying the recycling symbol.*

**Can we have an extra set of keys?**
Können wir ein Extraset Schlüssel bekommen?
*kur'-nen veer ine extraset **shloo**-sel be**kom**men*

**When does the cleaner come?**
Wann kommt die Putzfrau?
*van komt dee **poots**frow*

**Who do we contact if there are problems?**
An wen können wir uns wenden, wenn wir ein Problem haben?
*an ven **kur'**-nen veer oonts **ven**den ven veer ine proh**blem** hah-ben*

**How does the heating work?**
Wie funktioniert die Heizung?
*vee foonksyon**eert** dee **hyt**soong*

**Is there always hot water?**
Gibt es immer Heißwasser?
*gipt es **im**-mer **hys**was-ser*

**Where is the nearest supermarket?**
Wo ist der nächste Supermarkt?
*voh ist der **nehkh**-ste **soo**permarkt*

**Where do we leave the rubbish?**
Wo sollen wir den Müll entsorgen?
*voh **sol**-len veer den mool ent**sor**gen*

**When is the rubbish collected?**
Wann kommt die Müllabfuhr?
*van komt dee **mool**abfoor*

**What are the neighbours called?**
Wie heißen die Nachbarn?
*vie **hy**-sen dee **nakh**barn*

see also **SIGHTSEEING & TOURIST OFFICE**

# SHOPPING PHRASES

**DER AUSVERKAUF** der **ow**sverkowf                                          **SALE**
**DAS STÜCK** das **shtook**                                                          **SINGLE ITEM**

**Do you have...?**                         **Where is the nearest...?**
Haben Sie...?                               Wo ist der/die/das nächste...?
*hah-ben zee...*                            *voh ist der/dee/das **nekh**-ste...*

**How do I get to the main shopping area?**
Wie komme ich zum Hauptgeschäftszentrum?
*vee **kom**-me ikh tsoom howpt-ge**shefts**-tsentroom?*

**I'm looking for a present for...**      **my mother**          **a child**
Ich suche ein Geschenk für...              meine Mutter          ein Kind
*ikh **zoo**-khe ine ge**shenk** foor...*  ***mine**-e **moo**ter*  *ine kint*

**Can you recommend any good shops?**
Können Sie ein paar gute Geschäfte empfehlen?
***kur'**-nen zee ine pahr **goo**-te ge**shef**-te emp-**fay**len*

**Which floor are shoes on?**
Auf welchem Stockwerk sind die Schuhe?
*owf **vel**-khem **shtok**-verk zint dee **shoo**-e*

**It's too expensive for me**
Das ist mir zu teuer
*das ist meer tsoo **toy**-er*

**Have you anything else?**
Haben Sie noch etwas anderes?
*hah-ben zee nokh **et**vas **an**-de-res*

**Is there a market?**                      **When?**
Gibt es hier einen Markt?                   Wann?
*gipt es heer **ine**-en markt*             *van*

## ■ YOU MAY HEAR

**Kann ich Ihnen helfen?**                  **Darf es sonst noch etwas sein?**
*kan ikh **ee**-nen **helf**en*             *darf es zonst nokh **et**vas zine*
Can I help you?                             Would you like anything else?

*Most large shops in Germany are open all day approx. 9am to 6pm Mon. to Fri. On Saturdays they are open until 4pm. There is late night shopping on Thursdays until 8pm. Shops are shut on Sundays.*

| | | |
|---|---|---|
| baker's | BÄCKEREI | be-ke-**ry** |
| bookshop | BUCHHANDLUNG | **bookh**-hantloong |
| butcher's | FLEISCHEREI | fly-sher-**ry** |
| cake shop | KONDITOREI | kondi-toh-**ry** |
| clothes | KLEIDUNG | **kly**-doong |
| department store | WARENHAUS | **vah**ren-hows |
| dry-cleaner's | REINIGUNG | **ry**-nigoong |
| electrical goods | ELEKTROGESCHÄFT | elek-tro-gesheft |
| fishmonger's | FISCHGESCHÄFT | **fish**-gesheft |
| gifts | GESCHENKARTIKEL | ge-**shenk**-arteekel |
| greengrocer's | GEMÜSELADEN | ge**moo**-ze-lahden |
| grocer's | LEBENSMITTELLADEN | **lay**bens-mittel-**lah**den |
| hairdresser's | FRISEUR | free-**zu'r** |
| health food shop | REFORMHAUS | ray**form**-hows |
| household (goods) | HAUSHALTSWAREN | **hows**-halts-vahren |
| hardware | EISENWARENHANDLUNG | **ize**-en-vahren-**hant**loong |
| jeweller's | JUWELIER | yoovay-**leer** |
| market | MARKT | markt |
| pharmacy | APOTHEKE | apoh-**tay**-ke |
| self-service | SELBSTBEDIENUNG | **zelpst**-bedee-noong |
| shoe shop | SCHUHGESCHÄFT | **shoo**-gesheft |
| shop | LADEN | **lah**-den |
| sports shop | SPORTGESCHÄFT | **sport**-gesheft |
| stationer's | SCHREIBWARENHANDLUNG | **shripe**-vahren**hant**loong |
| supermarket | SUPERMARKT | **zoo**per-markt |
| tobacconist's | TABAKLADEN | **tab**ak-lahden |
| toy shop | SPIELWARENLADEN | **shpeel**-vahren-lahden |

| | | |
|---|---|---|
| biscuits | die Kekse | **kek**-se |
| bread | das Brot | broht |
| bread (brown) | das Vollkornbrot | **fol**korn-broht |
| bread roll | das Brötchen | **brur't**-khen |
| butter | die Butter | **boo**ter |
| cheese | der Käse | **kay**-ze |
| coffee (instant) | der Instantkaffee | instant-ka**fay** |
| cream | die Sahne | **zah**-ne |
| crisps | die Chips | chips |
| eggs | die Eier | **eye**-er |
| flour | das Mehl | mayl |
| ham | der Schinken | **shin**ken |
| herbal tea | der Kräutertee | **kroy**ter-tay |
| honey | der Honig | **hoh**nikh |
| jam | die Marmelade | mar-me**lah**-de |
| margarine | die Margarine | marga-**ree**-ne |
| marmalade | die Orangenmarmelade | o**ron**jen-mar-me**lah**-de |
| milk | die Milch | milkh |
| mustard | der Senf | zenf |
| oil | das Öl | ur'l |
| orange juice | der Orangensaft | o**ron**-jen-zaft |
| pasta | die Nudeln | **noo**-deln |
| pepper | der Pfeffer | **pfef**fer |
| rice | der Reis | rice |
| saccharin | der Süßstoff | **zoos**-shtof |
| salt | das Salz | zalts |
| sausage | die Wurst | voorst |
| stock cube | der Suppenwürfel | **zoo**-pen-vur'-fel |
| sugar | der Zucker | **tsoo**ker |
| tea | der Tee | tay |
| tin of tomatoes | die Dose Tomaten | **doh**-ze to**mah**-ten |
| vinegar | der Essig | **es**sikh |
| yoghurt | der Jogurt | **yoh**-goort |

*see also* **MEASUREMENTS & QUANTITIES**

| **FRUIT** | OBST *opst* |
|---|---|
| apples | die Äpfel *epfel* |
| apricots | die Aprikosen *apri-koh-zen* |
| bananas | die Bananen *bana-nen* |
| cherries | die Kirschen *keershen* |
| grapefruit | die Grapefruit *grapefruit* |
| grapes | die Trauben *trowben* |
| lemon | die Zitrone *tsitroh-ne* |
| melon | die Melone *meloh-ne* |
| nectarines | die Nektarinen *nek-ta-reenen* |
| oranges | die Orangen *oron-jen* |
| peaches | die Pfirsiche *pfir-zi-khe* |
| pears | die Birnen *bir-nen* |
| pineapple | die Ananas *ananas* |
| plums | die Pflaumen *pflow-men* |
| raspberries | die Himbeeren *him-bayren* |
| strawberries | die Erdbeeren *ert-bayren* |

| **VEGETABLES** | GEMÜSE *gemooz-e* |
|---|---|
| asparagus | der Spargel *shpargel* |
| broccoli | der Brokkoli *brokoli* |
| carrots | die Karotten *ka-rot-ten* |
| cauliflower | der Blumenkohl *bloomen-kohl* |
| courgettes | die Zucchini *tsoo-keenee* |
| French beans | die grünen Bohnen *groonen bohnen* |
| garlic | der Knoblauch *knohp-lowkh* |
| leeks | der Lauch *lowkh* |
| lettuce | der Kopfsalat *kopf-zalaht* |
| mushrooms | die Pilze *pilt-se* |
| onions | die Zwiebeln *tsveebeln* |
| peas | die Erbsen *erpsen* |
| peppers | die Paprika *papreeka* |
| potatoes | die Kartoffeln *kar-tofeln* |
| spinach | der Spinat *shpinaht* |
| tomatoes | die Tomaten *tomah-ten* |

*see also* **SHOPPING PHRASES**

# CLOTHES

| women | | men – suits | | shoes | | | |
|---|---|---|---|---|---|---|---|
| **sizes** | | **sizes** | | **sizes** | | | |
| UK | EC | UK | EC | UK | EC | UK | EC |
| 8 | 36 | 36 | 46 | 2 | 35 | 7 | 41 |
| 10 | 38 | 38 | 48 | 3 | 36 | 8 | 42 |
| 12 | 40 | 40 | 50 | 4 | 37 | 9 | 43 |
| 14 | 42 | 42 | 52 | 5 | 38 | 10 | 44 |
| 16 | 44 | 44 | 54 | 6 | 39 | 11 | 45 |
| 18 | 46 | 46 | 56 | | | | |

**May I try this on?**
Kann ich das anprobieren?
*kan ikh das anproh-beeren*

**Do you have this in size...?**
Haben Sie das in Größe...?
*hah-ben zee das in grur'-se...*

**Do you have this in other colours?**
Haben Sie das noch in anderen Farben?
*hah-ben zee das nokh in an-de-ren farben*

**Where are the changing rooms?**
Wo sind die Umkleidekabinen?
*voh zint dee oom-kly-de-ka-beenen*

**bigger**
größer
*grur'-ser*

**smaller**
kleiner
*kline-er*

| **It's too big** | **It's too small** | **It's too expensive** |
|---|---|---|
| Es ist zu groß | Es ist zu klein | Es ist zu teuer |
| *es ist tsoo grohs* | *es ist tsoo kline* | *es ist tsoo toy-er* |

**I'm just looking**
Ich schaue mich nur um
*ikh show-e mikh noor oom*

**I'll take it**
Ich nehme es
*ikh nay-me es*

## ■ YOU MAY HEAR

**Welche Größe haben Sie?**
*vel-khe grur'-se hah-ben zee*
What size are you?

**Passt es?**
*past es*
Does it fit you?

see also **NUMBERS**

| belt | der Gürtel *goor*-tel |
|---|---|
| blouse | die Bluse *bloo*-se |
| bra | der BH bay-*hah* |
| coat | der Mantel *man*tel |
| dress | das Kleid *klite* |
| fleece | das Fleece *flees* |
| gloves | die Handschuhe *hant*-shoo-e |
| hat | der Hut *hoot* |
| jacket | das Jackett ya*ket* |
| knickers | der Slip *slip* |
| nightdress | das Nachthemd *nakht*-hemt |
| pyjamas | der Pyjama pee-*jah*-ma |
| raincoat | der Regenmantel *ray*gen-mantel |
| sandals | die Sandalen zan-*dah*-len |
| scarf (silk) | das Tuch *tookh* |
| scarf (wool) | der Schal *shal* |
| shirt | das Hemd *hemt* |
| shorts | die Shorts *shorts* |
| skirt | der Rock *rock* |
| slippers | die Pantoffeln pan*tof*-feln |
| socks | die Socken *zok*-ken |
| suit (man's) | der Anzug *an*-tsook |
| suit (woman's) | das Kostüm kos-*toom* |
| swimsuit | der Badeanzug *bah*-de-antsook |
| tie | die Krawatte kra*vat*-te |
| tights | die Strumpfhose *shtroompf*-hoh-ze |
| tracksuit | der Trainingsanzug *train*ings-antsook |
| trousers | die Hose *hoh*-ze |
| underpants | die Unterhose *oon*-terhoh-ze |
| zip | der Reißverschluss *rice*-fer-shloos |

see also **SHOPPING** ❏ **SHOPPING PHRASES** ❏ **PAYING**    43

# MAPS & GUIDES

*Large railway stations and airport bookshops usually stock English newspapers and books, but they can be very expensive.*

**Have you...?**    **a map of the town / a map of the region**
Haben Sie...?    einen Stadtplan / eine Karte der Umgebung
*hah-ben zee...    ine-en shtat-plan / ine-e kar-te der oom-gayboong*

**Can you show me where ... is on the map?**
Können Sie mir auf der Karte zeigen, wo ... ist?
*kur'-nen zee meer owf der kar-te tsy-gen, voh ... ist*

**Do you have a more detailed map of the area?**
Haben Sie eine genauere Karte der Gegend?
*hah-ben zee ine-e ge-nower-e kar-te der gaygent*

**Can you draw me a map?**
Können Sie mir einen Plan zeichnen?
*kur'-nen zee meer ine-en plan tsykh-nen*

**Do you have a guide book / a leaflet in English?**
Gibt es einen Reiseführer / eine Broschüre auf Englisch?
*gipt es ine-en ry-ze-foorer / ine-e bro-shoo-re owf eng-lish*

**Could I have this in English?**
Könnte ich das auf Englisch haben?
*kur'n-te ikh das owf eng-lish hah-ben*

**Where can I/we buy an English newspaper?**
Wo kann man englische Zeitungen kaufen?
*voh kan man english-e tsy-toongen kowfen*

**Do you have any English newspapers / books?**
Haben Sie englische Zeitungen / Bücher?
*hah-ben zee english-e tsy-toongen / boo-kher*

**When do the English newspapers arrive?**
Wann kommen die englischen Zeitungen an?
*van kommen dee english-en tsy-toongen an*

**Please put** *(name newspaper)* **aside for me**
Bitte legen Sie für mich ... zurück
*bit-te laygen zee foor mikh ... tsoorook*

*Main Post Offices are open all day 9am to 6pm Mon. to Fri. and on Saturday mornings. A red dot on German postboxes indicates that there is a late/weekend collection.*

| | |
|---|---|
| DAS POSTAMT / DIE POST *das **post**amt/dee post* | **POST OFFICE** |
| DER BRIEFKASTEN *der **bref**kasten* | **POSTBOX** |
| DIE BRIEFMARKEN *dee **bref**marken* | **STAMPS** |

### Where is the nearest post office?
Wo ist das nächste Postamt?
*voh ist das **nekh**-ste **post**amt*

### When is it open?
Wann hat es auf?
*van hat es owf*

### Is there a postbox near here?
Ist hier ein Briefkasten in der Nähe?
*ist heer ine **bref**-kasten in der **nay**-e*

### Where can I buy stamps?
Wo bekomme ich Briefmarken?
*voh be-**kom**-me ikh **bref**-marken*

### Stamps for ... postcards to Great Britain, please
Briefmarken für ... Postkarten nach England, bitte
***bref**-marken foor ... **post**-karten nakh **eng**-lant **bit**-te*

### I want to send this parcel to...
Ich möchte dieses Paket nach ... schicken
*ikh **mur'kh**-te **dee**zes pa-**kayt** nakh ... **shi**-ken*

### How much is it for this small packet?
Was kostet dieses Päckchen?
*vas **kost**et **dee**zes **pek**-khen*

### by airmail
per Luftpost
*per **looft**post*

### It's a gift
Es ist ein Geschenk
*es ist ine ge-**shenk***

### The value is...
Der Wert ist...
*der vayrt ist...*

### ■ YOU MAY HEAR

Füllen Sie das bitte aus
*fool**len zee das **bit**-te ows*
Fill in this form, please

see also **MONEY** □ **PAYING**

**Where can I buy tapes for a camcorder?**
Wo kann man Bänder für einen Camcorder kaufen?
*voh kan man **ben**der foor **ine**-en **cam**corder **kow**fen*

| **A colour film** | **with 24 / 36 exposures** |
|---|---|
| Einen Farbfilm | mit 24 / 36 Bildern |
| ***ine**-en **farp**-film* | *mit **feer**-oont-tsvan-tsikh / **zekh**s-oont-drysikh **bil**dern* |

**A tape for this camcorder**
Ein Band für diesen Camcorder
*ine bant foor **dee**-zen **cam**corder*

| **Have you batteries...?** | **for this camera / camcorder** |
|---|---|
| Haben Sie Batterien...? | für diese Kamera / diesen Camcorder |
| ***hah**-ben zee ba-te**ree**-en...* | *foor dee-ze **ka**mera / **dee**-zen **cam**corder* |

| **Can you develop this film?** | **How much will it be?** |
|---|---|
| Können Sie diesen Film entwickeln? | Was kostet das? |
| ***kur'**-nen zee **dee**zen film ent**vi**-keln* | *vas **kos**tet das* |

**When will the photos be ready?**
Wann sind die Fotos fertig?
*van zint dee **fo**tos **fer**tikh*

| **The film is stuck** | **Can you take it out, please?** |
|---|---|
| Der Film klemmt | Können Sie ihn bitte herausnehmen? |
| *der film klemt* | ***kur'**-nen zee een **bit**-te her**ows**-naymen* |

**Is it OK to take pictures here?**
Darf man hier fotografieren?
*darf man heer foto-gra-**fee**ren*

**Would you take a picture of us, please?**
Könnten Sie bitte ein Foto von uns machen?
***kur'n**-ten zee **bit**-te ine **fo**to fon oons **ma**khen*

■ **YOU MAY HEAR**

| **Matt oder Hochglanz?** | **Die Fotos sind am ... fertig** |
|---|---|
| *matt oder **hokh**-glans* | *dee **fo**tos zint am ... **fer**tikh* |
| **Matt or Glossy?** | **The photos will be ready at...** |

see also **SHOPPING**

*Monday is not a good day for sightseeing in Germany as most museums and art galleries close on Mondays.*

**Where is the tourist office?**
Wo ist das Touristeninformation?
*voh ist das toorist-en-informa-**tsyon***

**What can we visit in the area?**
Was gibt es in der Gegend zu besichtigen?
*vas gipt es in der **gay**-gent tsoo be**zich**-tigen*

**Have you any leaflets about it?**
Haben Sie Broschüren davon?
*hah-ben zee bro-**shoo**ren da-**fon***

**When can we visit...?**
Wann können wir ... besichtigen?
*van **kur'**-nen veer ... be**zich**-tigen*

**What day does it close?**
An welchem Tag ist es zu?
*an **vel**-khem tahk ist es tsoo*

**We'd like to go to...**
Wir möchten nach...
*veer **mur'kh**-ten nakh...*

**Are there any excursions?**
Gibt es Ausflugsfahrten?
*gipt es **ows**-flooks-fahrten*

**When does it leave?**
Wann ist die Abfahrt?
*van ist dee **ap**-fahrt*

**Where does it leave from?**
Wo ist die Abfahrt?
*voh ist dee **ap**-fahrt*

**How much does it cost to get in?**
Was kostet der Eintritt?
*vas **kos**tet der **ine**-trit*

**Are there any reductions for...?**
Gibt es eine Ermäßigung für...?
*gipt es **ine**-e er-**may**-sigoong foor...*

| children | students | unemployed | senior citizens |
|---|---|---|---|
| Kinder | Studenten | Arbeitslose | Rentner |
| **kin**der | shtoo-**den**ten | **ar**-bites-loh-ze | **rent**ner |

see also **MAPS & GUIDES** ☐ **LEISURE/INTERESTS**

# ENTERTAINMENT

*Larger towns usually have magazines listing cultural and political events and TV programmes.*

### What is there to do in the evenings?
Was kann man hier abends unternehmen?
*vas kan man heer **ah**-bents oonter-**nay**men*

### Do you have a list of events for this month?
Haben Sie einen Veranstaltungskalender für diesen Monat?
***hah**-ben zee **ine**-en fer-**an**shtal-toongs-ka**len**der foor **dee**zen **moh**nat*

### Is there anything for children?
Gibt es Veranstaltungen für Kinder?
*gipt es fer-**an**shtal-toongen foor **kin**der*

### Where is there a play park?
Wo gibt es hier einen Spielplatz?
*voh gipt es heer **ine**-en **shpeel**-plats*

### Where can I get tickets?
Wo kann ich Karten kaufen?
*vo kan ikh **kar**-ten **kow**fen*

### for tonight
für heute Abend
*foor **hoy**-te **ah**bent*

### for the show
für die Show
*foor dee shoh*

### for the football match
für das Fußballspiel
*foor das **foos**-ball-shpeel*

### I'd like ... tickets
Ich möchte ... Karten
*ikh **mur'kh**-te ... **kar**-ten*

### ...adults
...Erwachsene
*...er**vak**-se-ne*

### ...children
...Kinder
*...**kin**der*

### Where can we go dancing?
Wo kann man hier tanzen gehen?
*voh kan man heer **tan**tsen **gay**en*

### What time does it open?
Wann macht das auf?
*van makht das owf*

### How much is it to get in?
Was kostet der Eintritt?
*vas **kos**tet der **ine**-trit*

### What is there to do here at weekends?
Was kann man hier am Wochenende machen?
*vas kan man heer am **vo**khen-**en**-de **ma**khen*

see also **MUSIC** ☐ **CINEMA** ☐ **THEATRE/OPERA**

**Where can I/we go...?**
Wo kann man hier ... gehen?
*voh kan man heer ... gay*en

fishing
angeln
**angel**n

riding
reiten
**ry**-ten

**Are there any good beaches near here?**
Gibt es hier in der Nähe gute Strände?
*gipt es heer in der nay-e goo-te shtren-de*

**Is there a swimming pool near here?**
Gibt es hier in der Nähe ein Schwimmbad?
*gipt es heer in der nay-e ine shvim-baht*

**Where can I/we hire bikes?**
Wo kann man hier Fahrräder leihen?
*voh kan man heer fah-rehder lye-en*

**Do you have cycling helmets?**
Haben Sie Fahrradhelme?
*hah-ben zee fah-radhelm-e*

**How much is it...?**
Was kostet das...?
*vas kostet das...*

per hour
pro Stunde
pro **shtoon**-de

per day
pro Tag
pro tahk

**What do you do in your spare time?** *(familiar)*
Was machst du in deiner Freizeit?
*vas makhst doo in dine-er fry-tsite*

**I like gardening**
Ich arbeite gern im Garten
*ikh ar-by-te gern im garten*

**I like photography**
Ich fotografiere gern
*ikh fotogra-fee-re gern*

**I like playing...**
Ich spiele gern...
*ikh shpee-le gern...*

tennis
Tennis
**ten**nis

football
Fußball
**foos**-ball

**Do you like playing...?**
Spielen Sie gern...?
**shpee**len zee gern...

**Do you like playing...?** *(familiar)*
Spielst du gern...?
*shpeelst doo gern...*

see also **SPORT** ☐ **SKIING** ☐ **WALKING**

# MUSIC

**Are there any good concerts on?**
Gibt es zur Zeit gute Konzerte?
*gipt es tsoor tsayt **goo**-te kon-**tser**-te*

**Where can I/we get tickets for the concert?**
Wo gibt es Karten für das Konzert?
*voh gipt es **kar**-ten foor das kon-**tsert***

**Where can I/we hear some classical music / jazz?**
Wo kann man hier klassische Musik / Jazz hören?
*voh kan man heer **klas**-sish-e moo**zeek** / jazz **hur**-en*

**What sort of music do you like?**
Welche Musik mögen Sie?
*vel-khe moo**zeek** mur'gen zee*

**I like...**
Ich mag...
*ikh mahk...*

**Which is your favourite band?** *(familiar)*
Was ist deine Lieblingsband?
*vas ist **dine**-e **leep**lings-bant*

**Who is your favourite singer?** *(familiar)*
Wer ist dein Lieblingssänger?
*ver ist dine **leep**lings-zenger*

**Can you play any musical instruments?** *(familiar)*
Spielst du ein Instrument?
*shpeelst doo ine in-stroo-**ment***

| **I play...** | **the guitar** | **the piano** | **the violin** |
|---|---|---|---|
| Ich spiele... | Gitarre | Klavier | Geige |
| *ikh **shpee**-le...* | *gee-**ta**-re* | *kla-**veer*** | ***gy**-ge* |

**Have you been to any good concerts recently?** *(familiar)*
Warst du in letzter Zeit in einem guten Konzert?
*vahrst doo in **lets**-ter tsite in **ine**-em **goo**ten kon-**tsert***

**Do you like opera?**
Mögen Sie Oper?
***mur**'gen zee **oh**-per*

**Do you like rap music?** *(familiar)*
Magst du Rap?
*mahkst doo rap*

see also **MAKING FRIENDS** ☐ **ENTERTAINMENT**

*Films are generally dubbed in Germany. New films are usually
released on Thursdays and many cinemas offer a discount of up to
50% (mostly on Tuesdays), the so-called **Kinotag** (cinema day).*

**What's on at the cinema?**
Was gibt es im Kino?
*vas gipt es im **kee**no*

**When does the film start?**
Wann fängt der Film an?
*van fengt der film an*

**When does the film finish?**
Wann ist der Film zu Ende?
*van ist der film tsoo **en**-de*

**Is the film dubbed?**
Ist der Film synchronisiert?
*ist der film zoon-kroh-ni**zeert***

**How much is it to get in?**
Was kostet der Eintritt?
*vas **kos**tet der **ine**-trit*

**Two for** (name film) ...
Zwei für...
*tsvy foor...*

**What films have you seen recently?**
Welche Filme haben Sie in letzter Zeit gesehen?
***vel**-khe **fil**-me **hah**-ben zee in **lets**-ter tsite ge**zay**-en*

**What is ... called in German?**
Wie heißt ... auf Deutsch?
*vee hyst ... owf doytch*

**Who is your favourite actress?**
Wer ist Ihre Lieblingsschauspielerin?
*vayr ist **ee**-re **leep**lings-show-shpeelerin*

**Who is your favourite actor?**
Wer ist Ihr Lieblingsschauspieler?
*vayr ist eer **leep**lings-show-shpeeler*

■ **YOU MAY HEAR**

**Für Kino 1/2...**
*foor **kee**no ines/tsvy...*
**For screen 1/2...**

**ist ausverkauft**
*ist **ows**-ferkowft*
**it's sold out**

*see also* **ENTERTAINMENT** ☐ **LEISURE/INTERESTS**

| | |
|---|---|
| DIE GARDEROBE *dee garde**roh**-be* | **CLOAKROOM** |
| DAS THEATERSTÜCK *das tay-**ah**tershtook* | **PLAY** |
| DER PLATZ *der plats* | **SEAT** |

**What's on at the theatre?**
Was gibt es im Theater?
*vas gipt es im tay-**ah**ter*

**How do I/we get there?**
Wie kommt man hin?
*vee komt man hin*

**How much are the tickets?**
Was kosten die Karten?
*vas **kos**ten dee **kar**-ten*

**I'd like two tickets...**
Ich hätte gern zwei Karten...
*ikh **het**-te gern tsvy **kar**-ten...*

**for tonight**
für heute Abend
*foor **hoy**-te **ah**bent*

**for tomorrow night**
für morgen Abend
*foor **mor**gen **ah**bent*

**for 5th August**
für den fünften August
*foor den **foonf**-ten ow**goost***

**in the stalls**
im Parkett
*im par-**kett***

**in the circle**
im ersten Rang
*im **er**-sten rang*

**in the upper circle**
im zweiten Rang
*im **tsvy**-ten rang*

**How long is the interval?**
Wie lang ist die Pause?
*vee lang ist dee **pow**-ze*

**Is there a bar?**
Gibt es eine Bar?
*gipt es **ine**-e bar*

**When does the performance end?**
Wann ist die Vorstellung zu Ende?
*van ist dee **for**-shtelloong tsoo **en**-de*

**I didn't enjoy that**
Das hat mir nicht gefallen
*das hat meer nikht ge**fal**-en*

**It was very good**
Es war sehr gut
*es vahr zayr goot*

see also **ENTERTAINMENT** ❑ **LEISURE/INTERESTS**

| | |
|---|---|
| DIE FERNBEDIENUNG dee fernbaydeenoong | **REMOTE CONTROL** |
| DIE SEIFENOPER dee **zye**-fenoper | **SOAP** |
| DER VIDEORECORDER der **vee**dayorekorder | **VIDEO RECORDER** |
| DIE NACHRICHTEN dee **nakh**rikhten | **NEWS** |
| EINSCHALTEN **ine**shalten | **TO SWITCH ON** |
| AUSSCHALTEN **ows**-shalten | **TO SWITCH OFF** |
| DER CARTOON der **kar**toon | **CARTOONS** |

### Is there a TV?
Gibt es hier einen Fernseher?
gipt es heer ine-en **fern**-zayer

### What's on television?
Was gibt es im Fernsehen?
vas gipt es im **fern**-zayen

### When is the news?
Wann kommen die Nachrichten?
van **kom**men **nakh**-rikhten

### Please could you lower the volume?
Könnten Sie bitte leiser stellen?
**kur'n**-ten zee **bit**-te **ly**-zer **shte**-len

### May I turn the volume up?
Darf ich lauter stellen?
darf ikh **low**-ter **shte**-len

### Are there any English-speaking channels?
Haben Sie englischsprachige Fernsehkanäle?
**hah**-ben zee **eng**-lish-shpra-khi-ge **fern**-zay-kanay-le

### Do you have satellite TV?
Haben Sie Satellitenfernsehen?
**hah**-ben zee zatel-**lit**en-**fern**-zay-en

### When are the children's programmes?
Wann sind die Kinderprogramme?
van zint dee **kin**der-pro**gram**-me

### Is there a cartoon channel?
Gibt es einen Kanal mit Cartoons?
gipt es **ine**-en ka**nahl** mit **car**toons

# SPORT

| | |
|---|---|
| DER WETTKAMPF / DAS SPIEL *der **vet**kampf/das shpeel* | MATCH / GAME |
| DER TENNISPLATZ *der **ten**nisplats* | TENNIS COURT |
| DER GOLFPLATZ *der **golf**plats* | GOLF COURSE |
| GEWINNEN *gay**vin**-nen* | TO WIN |

**Where can we...?**
Wo können wir...?
*voh **kur'**-nen veer...*

**play tennis**
Tennis spielen
***ten**nis **shpee**len*

**play golf**
Golf spielen
*golf **shpee**len*

**go swimming**
schwimmen
***shvim**men*

**go jogging**
joggen
***jog**gen*

**How much is it per hour?**
Was kostet es pro Stunde?
*vas **kos**tet es proh **shtoon**-de*

**Can we hire rackets/clubs?**
Kann man Schläger leihen?
*kan man **shlay**-ger **ly**-en*

**We'd like to go to see** (name team) **play**
Wir möchten ein Spiel von ... sehen
*veer **mur'kh**-ten ine shpeel fon ... **zay**-en*

**Where can I/we get tickets?**
Wo gibt es Karten?
*voh gipt es **kar**ten*

**How do I/we get to the stadium?**
Wie kommt man zum Stadion?
*vee komt man tsoom **shta**-dyohn*

**Which is your favourite team?** (familiar)
Was ist deine Lieblingsmannschaft?
*vas ist **dine**-e **leep**lings-**man**shaft*

**Would you like to play...?**
Möchten Sie ... spielen?
***mur'kh**-ten zee ... **shpee**len*

see also **LEISURE/INTERESTS** ☐ **SKIING** ☐ **WALKING**

DER SKIPASS der **ski**pass — SKI PASS

DER LANGLAUF der **lang**lowf — CROSS-COUNTRY SKIING

**I want to hire skis**
Ich möchte Skier leihen
*ikh **mur'kh**-te **shee**-er **ly**-en*

**Are the boots / the poles included in the price?**
Sind die Schuhe / die Stöcke im Preis inbegriffen?
*zint dee **shoo**-e / dee **shtur'**-khe im price **in**-be-griffen*

**Can you adjust my bindings, please?**
Könnten Sie bitte meine Bindungen einstellen?
*kur'n-ten zee **bit**-te **mine**-e **bin**-doongen **ine**-shte-len*

**How much is a pass for...?** — **a day** — **a week**
Was kostet ein Pass für...? — einen Tag — eine Woche
*vas **kos**tet ine pas foor...* — ***ine**-en tahk* — ***ine**-e **vo**-khe*

**Do you have a map of the ski runs?**
Haben Sie eine Pistenkarte?
*hah-ben zee **ine**-e **pis**ten-kar-te*

**When is the last chair-lift?**
Wann ist der letzte Skilift?
*van ist der **let**-ste **ski**lift*

■ **YOU MAY HEAR**

**Welche Länge brauchen Sie?**
*vel-khe **leng**-e **brow**-khen zee*
**What length skis do you want?**

**Welche Schuhgröße haben Sie?**
*vel-khe **shoo**-grur'-se **hah**-ben zee*
**What is your shoe size?**

**Es besteht Lawinengefahr**
*es be**shtayt** la**vee**-nen-gefahr*
**There is danger of avalanches**

**Diese Piste ist gesperrt**
*dee-ze **pis**-te ist ge**shpert***
**This run is closed off**

*see also* **LEISURE/INTERESTS** ❒ **SPORT** ❒ **WALKING**    55

**Are there any guided walks?**
Gibt es geführte Wanderungen?
*gipt es ge-**foor**-te **van**-de-roongen*

**Do you have details?**
Haben Sie Informationen dazu?
*hah-ben zee infor-matsyoh-nen datsoo*

**Is there a guide to local walks?**
Gibt es einen Wanderführer von dieser Gegend?
*gipt es **ine**-en **van**der-**foor**er fon **dee**zer **gay**gent*

**How many kilometres is the walk?**
Wie lang ist die Wanderung?
*vee lang ist dee **van**-deroong*

**Is the path very steep?**
Ist der Weg sehr steil?
*ist der Veg zayr shtyl*

**How long will the walk take?**
Wie lange werden wir für die Wanderung brauchen?
*vee **lang**-e **ver**den veer foor dee **van**-deroong **brow**-khen*

**We'd like to go climbing**
Wir möchten klettern gehen
*veer **mur'kh**-ten **klet**tern **gay**en*

**Do I/we need walking boots?**
Braucht man Wanderstiefel?
*browkht man **van**der-shteefel*

| **Should we take...?** | water | food | waterproofs |
|---|---|---|---|
| Müssen wir ... mitnehmen? | Essen | Wasser | Regenzeug |
| *moo**sen veer ... **mit**-naymen* | *essen* | *vasser* | *raygen-tsoyk* |

**What time does it get dark?**
Wann wird es dunkel?
*van virt es **doon**kel*

*To phone Germany from the UK, the international code is 00 49,
then the German area code less the first 0, e.g., Bonn (0)228,
Leipzig (0)341, followed by the number you require. (Other international codes: Austria 00 43, Switzerland 00 41). To phone the
UK from abroad dial 00 44, plus the UK area code less the first 0,
e.g., Glasgow (0)141. Most phone boxes operate with phonecards.*

| | |
|---|---|
| DAS HANDY *das handy* | MOBILE |
| DIE TELEFONKARTE *dee taylayfon-kar-te* | PHONECARD |
| DIE GELBEN SEITEN *dee gelben zye-ten* | YELLOW PAGES |
| DAS R-GESPRÄCH *das ayr-geshpraykh* | COLLECT / REVERSE CHARGE CALL |

### Where can I buy a phonecard?
Wo kann ich eine Telefonkarte kaufen?
*voh kan ikh ine-e taylayfon-kar-te kowfen*

### A phonecard, please
Eine Telefonkarte, bitte
*ine-e taylayfon-kar-te bit-te*

### I want to make a phone call
Ich möchte telefonieren
*ikh mur'kh-te taylay-fo-neeren*

### Do you have a mobile?
Haben Sie ein Handy?
*hah-ben zee ine handy*

### What is your mobile number?
Wie lautet Ihre Handynummer?
*vee lau-tet ee-re handy-noomer*

### My mobile number is...
Meine Handynummer ist...
*mine-e handy-noomer ist...*

### Herr Braun, please
Herr Braun, bitte
*hayr brown bit-te*

### Extension ..., please
Apparat ..., bitte
*apa-raht ... bit-te*

### Can I speak to Mr.../Mrs...?
Kann ich mit Herrn.../Frau... sprechen?
*kan ikh mit hayrn.../frow... shpre-khen*

### This is Jim Brown
Hier ist Jim Brown
*heer ist jim brown*

cont...

**I'll call back later**
Ich rufe später wieder an
ikh **roo**-fe **shpay**ter **vee**der an

**I'll call back tomorrow**
Ich rufe morgen wieder an
ikh **roo**-fe **mor**gen **vee**der an

**An outside line, please**
Eine Amtsleitung, bitte
**ine**-e **amts**-ly-toong **bit**-te

**I can't get through**
Ich komme nicht durch
ikh **kom**-me nikht doorkh

**We were cut off**
Wir sind unterbrochen worden
veer zint oonter-**bro**-khen **vor**den

**It's constantly engaged**
Da ist immer besetzt
da ist **im**mer be**zetst**

### ■ YOU MAY HEAR

Hallo
**hal**lo
Hello

Wer spricht, bitte?
ver shprikht **bit**-te
Who is calling?

Augenblick, ich verbinde
**owg**en-blik ikh fer**bin**-de
Just a moment, I'm trying to connect you

Es ist besetzt
es ist be**zetst**
It's engaged

Bitte rufen Sie später wieder an
**bit**-te **roo**fen zee **shpay**ter **vee**der an
Please try again later

Soll ich etwas ausrichten?
zoll ikh **et**vas **ows**-rikhten
Can I take a message?

Sie haben sich verwählt
zee **hah**-ben zikh fer**vaylt**
You've got a wrong number

Bitte sprechen Sie nach dem Signalton
**bit**-te **shpre**-khen zee nakh dem zig-**nahl**-ton
Please leave a message after the tone

Sie müssen Ihre Handys abschalten
zee **moos**-sen **ee**-re **han**dys **ap**-shalten
You must turn off your mobile phones

58　　see also **E-MAIL** □ **INTERNET** □ **FAX** □ **BUSINESS**

*As the case with many computer-related expressions and indeed with everyday speech, the Germans tend to use a lot of English when writing SMS. Most of the short forms used in mobile phone mesages are English abbreviations such as '4U'. When German is used at all, general abbreviations (also used in letters etc.) such as **'bzgl.'** (short for **'bezüglich'**, meaning 'with regard to') are employed or German abbreviations (often forming a funny new word) invented. There are, however, some German abbreviations which seem to be more common than others, although they may not all be universally understood (you are probably safer with the English ones there).*

**Can I text you?** *(informal)*
Kann ich Dir eine SMS schicken?
*kan ikh deer **ine**-e sms **shick**en*

**Can you text me?** *(informal)*
Kannst Du mir eine SMS schicken?
*kanst do meer **ine**-e sms **shick**en*

**Good Night!**
N8 (Gute *Nacht!*)

**Have a nice day!**
STN (Schönen*Tag* noch!)

**(That was) cheeky!**
3st (*Das war dreist*)

**To be continued**
FF (Fortsetzung *folgt*)

**Attention! (Important!)**
8ung (Attention)

**Phone me**
RUMIN (Ruf mich an)

**Shall we meet?**
TWU (Treffen wir uns?)

**I'll soon be there**
BIGBED (Bin *gleich bei Dir*)

**I immediately need money**
BSG (Brauche sofort Geld)

**Miss you**
HASE (Habe Sehnsucht)

**Thinking of you**
DAD (Denk an Dich)

**I feel so lonely**
BSE (Bin so einsam)

**I like you**
MAD (Mag Dich)

**I love you**
ILD (Ich liebe Dich)

**I'm happy**
*freud* (Ich freue mich)

**I'm sad**
*heul* (ich bin traurig)

*see also* **E-MAIL**

# E-MAIL

| | |
|---|---|
| SCANNEN **skan**nen | TO SCAN |
| DRUCKEN **droo**khen | TO PRINT |
| CD-BRENNEN see-dee **bren**nan | TO BURN CDS |
| DOWNLOADEN **down**loaden | TO DOWNLOAD |
| LÖSCHEN **lűr'**-shen | TO DELETE |

**Do you have e-mail?**
Haben Sie E-Mail?
**hah**-ben zee ee-mail?

**What's the your e-mail address?**
Wie ist Ihre E-Mail-Adresse?
vee ist **ee**-re ee-mail-a**dres**-se

**caroline.smith@anycompany.co.uk**
caroline.smith@anycompany.co.uk
caroline poonkt smith at anycompany poonkt tsay oh poonkt oo kah

**How do you spell it?**
Wie buchstabiert man das?
vee **bookh**-shtabyert man das

| **All lower case** | **All upper case** |
|---|---|
| Alles kleingeschrieben | Alles großgeschrieben |
| **al**-les **kline**-ges-shreeben | **al**-les **gros**-ge-shreeben |

**Can I send an e-mail?**
Kann ich eine E-Mail schicken?
kan ikh **ine**-e ee-mail **shi**-ken

**Did you get my email**
Haben Sie meine E-Mail bekommen?
**hah**-ben zee min-e ee-mail be-**kom**men

**Can I send and receive e-mail here?**
Kann ich hier E-Mails schicken und erhalten?
kan ikh heer ee-mails **shi**-ken oont **er**-halten

60          see also **TEXT** ☐ **INTERNET** ☐ **FAX** ☐ **BUSINESS**

*German e-mail addresses end in **.de** for **Deutschland** (Germany).*

| | |
|---|---|
| DIE STARTSEITE *dee **shtart**-zye-te* | **HOME** |
| DIE AUSWAHL *dee **ows**vahl* | **MENU** |
| DER BENUTZERNAME *der be**noots**ernah-me* | **USERNAME** |
| DIE SUCHMASCHINE *dee **sookh**mashee-ne* | **SEARCH ENGINE** |
| DAS PASSWORT *das **pass**vort* | **PASSWORD** |

**Are there any internet cafés here?**
Gibt es hier Internet-Cafés?
*gipt es heer **int**ernet ka**fays***

**How much is it to log on for an hour?**
Was kostet das Einloggen für eine Stunde?
*vas **kost**et das **ine**-logen foor **ine**-e **shtoon**de*

**Do you have a website?**
Haben Sie eine Homepage?
***hab**en zee **ine**-e homepage*

**The website address is...**
Die Homepage-Adresse lautet...
*dee homepage-a**dres**-se **low**tet...*

**www.collins.co.uk**
www.collins.co.uk
*vay vay vay poonkt collins poonkt tsay oh poonkt oo kah*

**Do you know any good sites for...?**
Kennen Sie gute Homepages für...?
***ken**nen zee **goo**-te homepage foor...*

**Which is the best search engine to use?**
Welche Suchmaschine sollte ich am besten benutzen?
***vel**khe **zookh**-mashin-e **zol**-te ikh am **best**en be**noot**zen*

**I can't log on**
Ich kann nicht einloggen.
*ikh kan nikht **ine**-logen*

*see also* **TEXT** ☐ **E-MAIL** ☐ **FAX** ☐ **BUSINESS**

# FAX

*The code to send faxes to Germany from the UK is **00 49** followed by the German area code (less the first 0), e.g. Munich (0)**89**. You should then add the fax number you require. The code from Germany to the UK is **00 44**. For e-mail see p. 60.*

| ADDRESSING A FAX | |
|---|---|
| AN *an* | TO |
| VON *fon* | FROM |
| DATUM *dahtoom* | DATE |
| BETREFF: *bet-ref* | RE: |
| IN DER ANLAGE *in der anlah-ge* | PLEASE FIND ATTACHED |
| EINE KOPIE VON... *ine-e kopee fon...* | A COPY OF... |
| ...SEITEN INSGESAMT ...*sy-ten insgesamt* | ...PAGES IN TOTAL |

**I want to send a fax**
Ich möchte ein Fax schicken
*ikh **mur'kh**-te ine fax **shi**-ken*

**Do you have a fax?**
Haben Sie ein Fax?
***hah**-ben zee ine fax*

**Can I send a fax from here?**
Kann ich von hier ein Fax schicken?
*kan ikh fon heer ine fax **shi**-ken*

**What is your fax number?**
Wie ist Ihre Faxnummer?
*vee ist **ee**-re fax-noomer*

**My fax number is...**
Meine Faxnummer ist...
***mine**-e fax-noomer ist...*

**Did you get my fax?**
Haben Sie mein Fax bekommen?
***hah**-ben zee mine fax be**kom**men*

**Please resend your fax**
Bitte schicken Sie Ihr Fax noch einmal
***bit**-te **shi**-ken zee eer fax nokh **ine**-mal*

**I can't read it**
Ich kann es nicht lesen
*ikh kan es nikht **lay**-zen*

**Your fax is constantly engaged**
Ihr Fax ist immer besetzt
*eer fax ist **im**mer be**zetst***

*see also* **INTERNET** ☐ **E-MAIL** ☐ **BUSINESS**

| | |
|---|---|
| **17 May 2003** | 17. Mai 2003 |
| **Dear Sir / Madam** | Sehr geehrte Damen und Herren *(Sie)* |
| **Yours faithfully** | Mit freundlichen Grüßen |
| **Dear Mr...** | Sehr geehrter Herr.... *(Sie)* |
| **Dear Mrs...** | Sehr geehrte Frau.... *(Sie)* |
| **Yours sincerely** | Mit freundlichen Grüßen |
| **Dear Christian** | Lieber Christian |
| **Dear Petra** | Liebe Petra |
| **Best regards** | Mit besten Grüßen |
| **Dear ...** | Lieber / Liebe... *(du)* |
| **Love** | Viele liebe Grüße |

**Further to our telephone conversation...**
Bezugnehmend auf unser Telefongespräch...

**Please find enclosed...**
In der Anlage finden Sie...

**Thank you for the information / for your price list**
Vielen Dank für die Information / für Ihre Preisliste

**I look forward to hearing from you soon**
Ich freue mich auf Ihre baldige Antwort

Familie Grün
Berliner Str. 23
65205 Wiesbaden
Deutschland

*Addressing an envelope*

*road and number of house*
**(Str.** *is the abbreviation for*
**Straße,** *street)*
*postcode and town*
*country*

*see also* **INTERNET** ☐ **E-MAIL** ☐ **FAX** ☐ **BUSINESS**        63

*The euro is the currency of Germany. You can change money and traveller's cheques where you see the sign **Geldwechsel**. Cash dispensers usually let you choose which language to carry out the transaction in. Banks are generally open longer on Tuesdays and Thursdays.*

**Where can I change some money?**
Wo kann ich hier Geld wechseln?
*voh kan ikh heer gelt **vek**-selln*

**Where is the nearest cash dispenser?**
Wo ist der nächste Geldautomat?
*voh ist der **nekh**-ste **gelt**-owto-**maht***

**When does the bank open?**
Wann macht die Bank auf?
*van makht dee bank owf*

**When does the bank close?**
Wann macht die Bank zu?
*van makht dee bank tsoo*

**I want to change these traveller's cheques**
Ich würde gern diese Reiseschecks einlösen
*ikh **voor**-de gern **dee**-ze ry-ze-sheks **ine**-lur'-zen*

**My credit card number is...**
Meine Kreditkartennummer ist...
*mine-e kre**deet**-kar-ten-noommer ist...*

| | |
|---|---|
| **expiry date...** | **valid until...** |
| Auslaufdatum... | Gueltig bis... |
| *ows*lowfdatoom... | *gur'l-tikh bis...* |

**Can I use my credit card to get euros?**
Kann ich hier mit meiner Kreditkarte Euro bekommen?
*kan ikh heer mit mine-er kre**deet**-kar-te oyro be-**kom**men*

**The cash dispenser has swallowed my credit card**
Der Geldautomat hat meine Kreditkarte geschluckt
*der **gelt**-owto-maht hat mine-e kre**deet**-kar-te ge-**shlookt***

see also **PAYING**

| | |
|---|---|
| DER BETRAG der be**trag** | AMOUNT TO BE PAID |
| DIE RECHNUNG dee **rekh**-noong | BILL |
| DIE KASSE dee **kas**-se | CASH DESK |
| DIE QUITTUNG dee **kvi**-toong | RECEIPT |

**How much is it?**
Was kostet das?
vas **kost**et das

**Can I pay...?**
Kann ich ... bezahlen?
kan ikh ... be**tsah**-len

**by credit card**
mit Kreditkarte
mit kre**deet**-kar-te

**by cheque**
mit Scheck
mit shek

**Do you take credit cards?**
Nehmen Sie Kreditkarten?
**nay**men zee kre**deet**-karten

**My credit card number is...**
Meine Kreditkartennummer ist...
**mine**-e kre**deet**-kar-ten-noommer ist...

**expiry date...**
Auslaufdatum...
**ows**lowfdatoom...

**valid until...**
Güeltig bis...
**gur'l**-tikh bis...

**Is service / VAT included?**
Ist die Bedienung / die Mehrwertsteuer inbegriffen?
ist dee be-**dee**noong / dee **mayr**-vayrt-shtoy-er **in**-be-griffen

**Put it on my bill**
Setzen Sie es auf meine Rechnung
**set**-sen zee es owf **mine**-e **rekh**-noong

**Could I have a receipt, please?**
Könnte ich eine Quittung haben, bitte?
**kur'n**-te ikh **ine**-e **kvi**-toong **hah**-ben **bit**-te

**Do I have to pay in advance?**
Muss ich im Voraus zahlen?
moos ikh im **for**-ows **tsah**-len

**Do you require a deposit?**
Verlangen Sie eine Kaution?
fer**langen** zee **ine**-e kow-**tsyohn**

**I'm sorry**
Tut mir Leid
toot meer lite

**I've nothing smaller**
Ich habe es nicht kleiner
ikh **hah**-be es nikht **kline**-er

**Keep the change**
Stimmt so
shtimt zoh

see also **SHOPPING □ MONEY**

*You often need a coin to unlock the trolley, so make sure you have some small change on arrival.*

| | | |
|---|---|---|
| DIE GEPÄCKAUSGABE *dee gepek**ows**gah-be* | | **BAGGAGE RECLAIM** |
| DIE GEPÄCKAUFBEWAHRUNG *dee gepek**owf**bevaroong* | | **LEFT-LUGGAGE OFFICE** |
| DAS SCHLIESSFACH *das sch**lees**-fakh* | | **LEFT-LUGGAGE LOCKER** |

**My luggage isn't there**
Mein Gepäck ist nicht da
*mine ge**pek** ist nikht dah*

**My suitcase has been damaged on the flight**
Mein Koffer wurde beim Flug beschädigt
*mine **kof**fer **voor**-de bime flook be-**shay**-dikht*

**What's happened to the luggage on the flight from...?**
Was ist mit dem Gepäck vom Flug aus ... passiert?
*vas ist mit dem ge**pek** fom flook ows ... pas-**see**-ert*

**Can you help me with my luggage, please?**
Könnten Sie mir bitte mit meinem Gepäck helfen?
***kur'n**-ten zee meer **bit**-te mit **mine**-em ge**pek** **helf**en*

**When does the left luggage office open / close?**
Wann macht die Gepäckaufbewahrung auf / zu?
*van makht dee ge**pek**-owf-be**vah**-roong owf / tsoo*

**We'd like to leave this overnight**
Wir möchten das über Nacht aufgeben
*veer **mur'kh**-ten das **oo**ber nakht **owf**-geben*

**Can I leave my luggage here?**
Kann ich mein Gepäck hier lassen?
*kan ikh mine ge**pek** heer **las**sen*

**I'll collect it at...**
Ich hole es um ... Uhr ab
*ikh **hoh**-le es oom ... oor ap*

■ **YOU MAY HEAR**

Sie können es bis sechs Uhr da lassen
*zee **kur'**-nen es bis zekhs oor dah **las**sen*
**You may leave it here until 6 o'clock**

see also **TRAIN** ▢ **AIR TRAVEL**

**DER SCHUHMACHER** *der shoo*makher    **SHOE REPAIR SHOP**

**DIE SCHNELLREPARATUR** *dee shnelraypa-ra-toor*    **REPAIRS WHILE YOU WAIT**

**This is broken**
Das ist kaputt
*das ist kapoot*

**Where can I get this repaired?**
Wo kann ich das reparieren lassen?
*voh kan ikh das raypa-reeren lassen*

**Is it worth repairing?**
Lohnt sich die Reparatur?
*lohnt zikh dee raypa-ra-toor*

**How much will it be?**
Was kostet das?
*vas kostet das*

**Can you repair...?**
Können Sie ... reparieren?
*kur'-nen zee ... raypa-reeren*

**these shoes**
diese Schuhe
*dee-ze shoo-e*

**my watch**
meine Uhr
*mine-e oor*

**Can you do it straightaway?**
Können Sie das gleich machen?
*kur'-nen zee das glykh makhen*

**Can I wait?**
Kann ich warten?
*kan ikh var-ten*

**How long will it take?**
Wie lange dauert das?
*vee lang-e dow-ert das*

**When will it be ready?**
Wann ist es fertig?
*van ist es fertikh*

**Where can I have my shoes reheeled?**
Wo kann ich neue Absätze an meine Schuhe machen lassen?
*voh kan ikh noy-e ap-zet-se an mine-e shoo-e makhen lassen*

**I need some glue**
Ich brauche Klebstoff
*ikh brow-khe clayp-shtoff*

**I need some Sellotape®**
Ich brauche Tesafilm®
*ikh brow-khe tayza-film*

**Do you have a needle and thread?**
Haben Sie Nadel und Faden?
*hah-ben zee nahdel oont fahden*

**The fuse has blown**
Die Sicherung ist raus
*dee zikh-eroong ist rows*

*see also* **BREAKDOWN**

# LAUNDRY

| | |
|---|---|
| DIE REINIGUNG *dee ry-nee-goong* | DRY-CLEANER'S |
| DER WASCHSALON *der **vash**-salong* | LAUNDERETTE |
| DAS WASCHPULVER *das **vash**-poolver* | WASHING POWDER |
| DER WEICHSPÜLER *der **vykh**-shpooler* | FABRIC SOFTENER |

**Where can I do some washing?**
Wo kann ich hier Wäsche waschen?
*voh kan ikh heer **ve**-she **va**shen*

**Can I have my laundry washed here?**
Kann ich hier Wäsche waschen lassen?
*kan ikh heer **ve**-she **va**shen **las**sen*

**When will my things be ready?**
Wann sind meine Sachen fertig?
*van zint **mine**-e **zakh**-en **fer**tikh*

**Where is the nearest launderette?**
Wo ist der nächste Waschsalon?
*voh ist der **nekh**-ste **vash**-salong*

**Where is the nearest dry-cleaner's?**
Wo ist die nächste Reinigung?
*voh ist dee **nekh**-ste **ry**-nee-goong*

**What coins do I need?**
Was für Münzen brauche ich?
*vas foor **moon**-tsen **brow**-khe ikh*

**Is there somewhere I can hang my clothes to dry?**
Kann ich hier irgendwo Sachen zum Trocknen aufhängen?
*kan ikh heer ir-gent-**voh zakh**-en tsoom **trok**nen **owf**-hengen*

**Can you iron this for me?**
Könnten Sie das für mich bügeln?
*kur'n-ten zee das foor mikh **boo**geln*

**Can I borrow an iron?**
Kann ich hier ein Bügeleisen leihen?
*kan ikh heer ine **boo**gel-ize-en **lye**-en*

see also **HOTEL DESK**

**The ... doesn't work**
Der/Die/Das ... funktioniert nicht
*der/dee/das...foonk-tsyoh-neert nikht*

**The ... don't work**
Die ... funktionieren nicht
*die...foonk-tsyoh-neeren nikht*

| | | | |
|---|---|---|---|
| **light** | **lock** | **toilet** | **heating** |
| das Licht | das Schloss | die Toilette | die Heizung |
| *das likht* | *das shlos* | *dee twa-le-te* | *dee hyt-soong* |

**There's a problem with the room**
Ich habe ein Problem mit dem Zimmer
*ikh hah-be ine proh-blaym mit dem tsimmer*

**It's too noisy**
Es ist zu laut
*es ist tsoo lowt*

**It's too hot / too cold**
Es ist zu warm / zu kalt
*es ist tsoo varm / tsoo kalt*

**It's too small**
Es ist zu klein
*es ist tsoo kline*

**It's too hot / too cold** (food)
Das ist zu heiß / zu kalt
*das ist tsoo hice / tsoo kalt*

**This isn't what I ordered**
Das habe ich nicht bestellt
*das hah-be ikh nikht beshtelt*

**To whom can I complain?**
Bei wem kann ich mich beschweren?
*by vaym kan ikh mikh be-shvayren*

**I want my money back**
Ich möchte mein Geld zurück
*ikh mur'kh-te mine gelt tsoorook*

**This is dirty**
Das ist schmutzig
*das ist shmoo-tsig*

**We have been waiting for a very long time**
Wir warten schon sehr lange
*veer var-ten shohn sayr lang-e*

**The bill is not correct**
Die Rechnung stimmt nicht
*dee rekh-noong shtimt nikht*

see also **HOTEL DESK** ☐ **REPAIRS** ☐ **PROBLEMS**    69

## PROBLEMS

**Can you help me?**
Können Sie mir helfen?
*kur'-nen zee meer **helf**en*

**I don't speak German**
Ich spreche kein Deutsch
*ikh **shpre**-khe kayn doytch*

**Does anyone here speak English?**
Spricht hier jemand Englisch?
*shprikht heer **yay**mant **eng**-lish*

**What's the matter?**
Was ist los?
*vas ist lohs*

**I have a problem**
Ich habe ein Problem
*ikh **hah**-be ine pro**blem***

**I'm lost**
Ich habe mich verlaufen *(on foot)*
*ikh **hah**-be mikh fer-**low**fen*

**How do I get to...?**
Wie komme ich nach...?
*vee **kom**-me ikh nakh...*

**I've missed...**
Ich habe ... verpasst
*ikh **hah**-be ... fer-**past***

**my plane**
mein Flugzeug
*mine **flook**-tsoyk*

**my connection**
meinen Anschluss
*mine-en **an**-shloos*

**My coach has left without me**
Mein Bus ist ohne mich abgefahren
*mine boos ist **oh**-ne mikh **ap**-gefahren*

**Can you show me how this works?**
Können Sie mir zeigen, wie das geht?
*kur'-nen zee meer **tsy**-gen vee das gayt*

**I've lost my money**
Ich habe mein Geld verloren
*ikh **hah**-be mine gelt fer-**loh**ren*

**I need to get to...**
Ich muss nach...
*ikh moos nakh...*

**Is there a lost property office?**
Gibt es hier ein Fundbüro?
*gipt es heer ine **foont**-booroh*

**Where is it?**
Wo ist es?
*voh ist es*

**I need to phone the British consulate**
Ich muss das britische Konsulat anrufen
*ikh moos das **brit**ish-e konsoo-**laht** an-roofen*

**Leave me alone!**
Lassen Sie mich in Ruhe!
*lassen zee mikh in **roo**-e*

**Go away!**
Hau ab!
*how ap*

see also **COMPLAINTS**

| | |
|---|---|
| DIE POLIZEI dee poli-**tsy** | **POLICE** |
| DER KRANKENWAGEN der **kran**ken-vahgen | **AMBULANCE** |
| DIE FEUERWEHR dee **foy**-er-vehr | **FIRE BRIGADE** |
| DIE NOTAUFNAHME dee notowf**nah**-me | **CASUALTY DEPARTMENT** |

**Help!**
Hilfe!
*hil*-fe

**Fire!**
Feuer!
*foy*-er

**Can you help me?**
Können Sie mir helfen?
*kur'n*-en zee meer **hel**-fen

**There's been an accident**
Ein Unfall ist passiert
*ine oon*fal ist pa**seert**

**Someone is injured**
Es ist jemand verletzt worden
es ist **yay**mant fer**letst vor**den

**Someone has been run over**
Es ist jemand überfahren worden
es ist **yay**mant oober-**fah**ren **vor**den

**Please call...**
Bitte rufen Sie...
*bit*-te **roo**fen zee...

**the police**
die Polizei
*dee* poli-**tsy**

**an ambulance**
einen Krankenwagen
*ine*-en **kran**ken-vahgen

**Where is the police station / the hospital?**
Wo ist die Polizeiwache / das Krankenhaus?
*voh ist dee* poli-**tsy**-va-khe / *das* **kran**ken-hows

**I want to report a theft**
Ich möchte einen Diebstahl melden
*ikh* **mur'kh**-te **ine**-en **deep**-shtahl **mel**den

**I've been robbed**
Ich bin beraubt worden
*ikh bin* be-**rowpt vor**den

**I've been attacked**
Ich bin überfallen worden
*ikh bin* oober-**fal**len **vor**den

**Someone has stolen...**
Jemand hat ... gestohlen
**yay**mant hat ... ge**shtoh**-len

**my money**
mein Geld
*mine* gelt

**my passport**
meinen Pass
**mine**-en pass

**My car has been broken into**
Mein Auto ist aufgebrochen worden
*mine* **ow**to ist **owf**-gebro-khen **vor**den

cont...

**My car has been stolen**
Mein Auto ist gestohlen worden
*mine owto ist geshtoh-len vorden*

**I've been raped**
Ich bin vergewaltigt worden
*ikh bin fer-geval-tikht vorden*

**I want to speak to a policewoman**
Ich möchte mit einer Polizistin sprechen
*ikh mur'kh-te mit ine-er poli-tsis-tin shpre-khen*

**I need to make an urgent telephone call**
Ich muss dringend telefonieren
*ikh moos dringent taylay-fo-neeren*

**I need a report for my insurance**
Ich brauche einen Bericht für meine Versicherung
*ikh brow-khe ine-en berikht foor mine-e ferzhikh-eroong*

**How much is the fine?**
Wie viel Strafe muss ich zahlen?
*vee feel shtrah-fe mooss ikh tsah-len*

**Where do I pay it?**
Wo kann ich das bezahlen?
*voh kan ikh das be-tsah-len*

**Do I have to pay it straightaway?**
Muss ich sofort bezahlen?
*mooss ikh zo-fort be-tsahlen*

**I'm very sorry**
Es tut mir sehr Leid
*es toot meer zayr lite*

**I would like to phone my embassy**
Ich möchte mit meiner Botschaft telefonieren
*ikh mur'kh-te mit mine-er bohtshaft taylay-fo-neeren*

### ■ YOU MAY HEAR

Sie sind bei Rot über die Ampel gefahren
*zee zint by roht oober dee ampel ge-fahren*
**You went through a red light**

Sie sind zu schnell gefahren
*zee zint tsoo shnell ge-fahren*
**You were driving too fast**

| | |
|---|---|
| DIE APOTHEKE *dee apo**teh**-ke* | **PHARMACY** |
| DIE NOTAPOTHEKE *dee notapo**teh**-ke* | **DUTY CHEMIST** |
| DAS REZEPT *das ret**sept*** | **PRESCRIPTION** |

**I don't feel well**
Ich fühle mich nicht wohl
*ikh **foo**-le mikh nikht vohl*

**Have you something for…?**
Haben Sie etwas gegen…?
*hah-ben zee et**vas **gay**-gen…*

**a headache**
Kopfschmerzen
*kopf-shmertsen*

**car sickness**
Reisekrankheit
*ry-ze-krank-hite*

**diarrhoea**
Durchfall
*doorkh-fal*

**I have a rash**
Ich habe einen Ausschlag
*ikh **hah**-be ine-en **ows**-shlahk*

**Is it safe to give children?**
Kann man es bedenkenlos auch Kindern geben?
*kan man es be-**deng**-ken-lohs owkh **kin**dern **gay**ben*

■ **YOU MAY HEAR**

Dreimal täglich vor dem / beim / nach dem Essen
*dry-mal **tayk**-likh for dem / bime / nakh dem **es**sen*
Three times a day before / with / after meals

■ **WORDS YOU MAY NEED**

| antiseptic | das Antiseptikum | anti-**zepti**-koom |
|---|---|---|
| aspirin | das Aspirin | aspi-**reen** |
| cold | die Erkältung | er-**kel**toong |
| condoms | die Kondome | kon**dom**-e |
| cotton wool | die Watte | **vat**-te |
| dental floss | die Zahnseide | **tsahn**-zy-de |
| plaster | das Pflaster | **pfla**ster |
| sanitary pads | die Binden | **bin**den |
| sore throat | die Halsschmerzen | **halts**-shmertsen |
| tampons | die Tampons | **tam**pons |
| toothpaste | die Zahnpasta | **tsahn**-pasta |

see also **BODY** ☐ **DOCTOR**

# BODY

| My ... hurts | Mein (with **der** and **das**) ... tut weh |
| | Meine (with **die**) ... tut weh |
| My ... hurt | Meine (with all plurals) ... tun weh |

| | | |
|---|---|---|
| ankle | der Knöchel | **knur'**-khel |
| arm | der Arm | arm |
| back | der Rücken | **roo**-ken |
| bone | der Knochen | **knokh**-en |
| chin | das Kinn | kin |
| ear | das Ohr | ohr |
| elbow | der Ellbogen | **ell**-boh-gen |
| eye | das Auge | **ow**-ge |
| finger | der Finger | **fing**-er |
| foot | der Fuß | foos |
| hand | die Hand | hant |
| head | der Kopf | kopf |
| heart | das Herz | hayrts |
| hip | die Hüfte | **hoof**-te |
| joint | das Gelenk | ge-**lenk** |
| kidney | die Niere | **nee**-re |
| knee | das Knie | k-nee |
| leg | das Bein | bine |
| liver | die Leber | **lay**-ber |
| mouth | der Mund | moont |
| nail | der Nagel | **nah**-gel |
| neck | der Nacken | **na**-ken |
| nose | die Nase | **nah**-ze |
| stomach | der Magen | **mah**-gen |
| throat | der Hals | halts |
| thumb | der Daumen | **dow**-men |
| toe | die Zehe | **tsay**-e |
| wrist | das Handgelenk | **hant**-ge-lenk |

see also **DOCTOR** ☐ **PHARMACY**

| | |
|---|---|
| DAS KRANKENHAUS das **kran**ken-hows | **HOSPITAL** |
| DIE AMBULANZ dee amboolants | **OUT-PATIENTS** |
| DIE SPRECHSTUNDEN dee **shprekh**stoonden | **SURGERY HOURS** |

**I need a doctor**
Ich brauche einen Arzt
ikh **brow**-khe **ine**-en artst

**My son / My daughter is ill**
Mein Sohn / Meine Tochter ist krank
mine zohn / **mine**-e **tokh**ter ist krank

**I have a pain here** (point)
Ich habe Schmerzen hier
ikh **hah**-be **shmer**tsen heer

**He/She has a high temperature**
Er/Sie hat hohes Fieber
er/zee hat **hoh**-es **fee**ber

**I'm diabetic**
Ich habe Zucker
ikh **hah**-be **tsoo**ker

**I'm pregnant**
Ich bin schwanger
ikh bin **shvan**ger

**I'm on the pill**
Ich nehme die Pille
ikh **nay**-me dee **pil**-le

**I'm allergic to penicillin**
Ich bin allergisch gegen Penizillin
ikh bin a-**ler**-gish **gay**-gen peni-tsi**leen**

**My blood group is...**
Meine Blutgruppe ist...
**mine**-e **bloot**groo-pe ist...

**Will he / she have to go to hospital?**
Muss er / sie ins Krankenhaus?
moos er / zee ins **kran**ken-hows

**Will I have to pay now?**
Muss ich gleich bezahlen?
moos ikh glykh be**tsah**-len

**How much will it cost?**
Was wird es kosten?
vas virt es **kos**ten

**I need a receipt for the insurance**
Ich brauche eine Quittung für meine Versicherung
ikh **brow**-khe **ine**-e **kvi**-toong foor **min**-e fer**zikh**-eroong

■ **YOU MAY HEAR**

**Sie müssen ins Krankenhaus**
zee **moos**sen ins **kran**ken-hows
**You will have to go to hospital**

**Ich muss Sie röntgen**
ikh moos zee **rur'nt**-gen
**I'll have to give you an X-ray**

see also **EMERGENCIES** □ **PHARMACY**

| | |
|---|---|
| DIE FÜLLUNG *dee **fool**-lung* | **FILLING** |
| DIE KRONE *dee **kroh**-ne* | **CROWN** |
| DIE PROTHESE *dee proh-**tay**-ze* | **DENTURES** |

**I need a dentist**
Ich brauche einen Zahnarzt
*ikh **brow**-khe ine-en **tsahn**artst*

**He/She has toothache**
Er/Sie hat Zahnschmerzen
*er/zee hat **tsahn**-shmer-tsen*

**Can you do a temporary filling?**
Können Sie mir eine provisorische Füllung machen?
*kur'-nen zee meer ine-e provi-**zor**ish-e **fool**-lung **ma**khen*

**I think I have an abscess**
Ich glaube, ich habe einen Abszess
*ikh **glow**-be ikh **hah**-be ine-en ap**stsess***

**It hurts**
Das tut weh
*das toot vay*

**Can you give me something for the pain?**
Können Sie mir etwas gegen die Schmerzen geben?
*kur'-nen zee meer **et**vas **gay**-gen dee **shmer**-tsen **gay**ben*

**Can you repair my dentures?**
Können Sie meine Prothese reparieren?
*kur'-nen zee **mine**-e proh-**te**-ze raypa-**ree**ren*

**Do I have to pay now?**
Muss ich das gleich bezahlen?
*moos ikh das **glykh** be**tsah**-len*

**How much will it be?**
Wie teuer wird es?
*vee **toy**-er virt es*

**I need a receipt for my insurance**
Ich brauche eine Quittung für meine Krankenkasse
*ikh **brow**-khe ine-e **kvi**-toong foor **mine**-e **krang**-ken-ka-se*

■ **YOU MAY HEAR**

**Bitte weit aufmachen**
*bit-te vite **owf**-makhen*
Please open wide

**Möchten Sie eine Spritze?**
*mur'kh-ten zee ine-e **shprit**-se*
Do you want an injection?

*see also* **PHARMACY**

**What facilities do you have for disabled people?**
Welche Einrichtungen haben Sie für Behinderte?
*vel-khe ine-rikht-toongen hah-ben zee foor be-hin-der-te*

**Do you have toilets for the disabled?**
Haben Sie Toiletten für Behinderte?
*hah-ben zee twa-le-ten foor be-hin-der-te*

**Do you have any bedrooms on the ground floor?**
Haben Sie Zimmer im Erdgeschoss?
*hah-ben zee tsimmer im ert-geshoss*

**How many steps are there?**
Wie viele Stufen sind es?
*vee fee-le shtoo-fen zint es*

**Do you have a lift?**
Haben Sie einen Aufzug?
*hah-ben zee ine-en owftsook*

**Where is the lift?**
Wo ist der Aufzug?
*voh ist der owftsook*

**Do you have wheelchairs?**
Haben Sie Rollstühle?
*hah-ben zee rol-shtoo-le*

**Can you visit ... in a wheelchair?**
Kann man ... im Rollstuhl besuchen?
*kann man ... im rol-shtool bezookhen*

**Where is the wheelchair-accessible entrance?**
Wo ist der Eingang für Rollstuhlfahrer?
*voh ist der ine-gang foor rol-shtool-fahrer*

**Is there an induction loop for the hard of hearing?**
Haben Sie eine Induktionsschleife für Schwerhörige?
*hah-ben zee ine-e in-dook-tsyohns-shly-fe foor shvayr-hur'-ri-ge*

**Is there a reduction for the disabled?**
Gibt es eine Ermäßigung für Behinderte?
*gipt es ine-e er-may-sigoong foor be-hin-der-te*

*see also* **HOTEL**

# EXCHANGE VISITORS

*We have used the familiar **Du** form for these phrases.*

**What would you like for breakfast?**
Was möchtest du frühstücken?
*vas **mur'kh**-test doo **froo**-shtooken*

**What would you like to eat?**
Was möchtest du essen?
*vas **mur'kh**-test doo es-sen*

**What would you like to drink?**
Was möchtest du trinken?
*vas **mur'kh**-test doo **trin**ken*

**Did you sleep well?**
Hast du gut geschlafen?
*hast doo goot ge**shlah**fen*

**what would you like to do today?**
Was möchtest du heute gerne machen?
*vas **mur'kh**-test doo **hoy**-te **ger**-ne **makh**en*

**I will pick you up at...**
Ich hole dich um ... ab
*ikh **hoh**-le dikh oom ... ap*

**may I phone home?**
Kann ich daheim anrufen?
*kan ikh da-**hime** an**roof**en*

**I like...**
Ich mag...
*ikh makh...*

**I don't like...**
Ich mag kein(e) / nicht...
*ikh makh kine(-e) / nikht...*

**Take care**
Mach's gut
*makhs goot*

**Thanks for everything**
Danke für alles
***dang**-ke foor **al**-les*

**Thank you very much**
Vielen Dank
***fee**-len dank*

**I've had a great time**
Ich hatte eine super Zeit
*ikh **hat**-te **ine**-e **zoop**er tsite*

see also **POLITE EXPRESSIONS**

Public transport is free for children under 4. Children between 4 and 12 pay half price.

**A child's ticket**
Eine Kinderfahrkarte
*ine-e kinderfarkar-te*

**He/She is ... years old**
Er/Sie ist ... Jahre alt
*er/zee ist ... yah-re alt*

**Is there a reduction for children?**
Gibt es eine Ermäßigung für Kinder?
*gipt es ine-e er-may-sigoong foor kinder*

**Do you have a children's menu?**
Haben Sie eine Speisekarte für Kinder?
*hah-ben zee ine-e shpy-ze-kar-te foor kinder*

**Is it OK to take children?**
Kann man Kinder mitnehmen?
*kan man kinder mitnaymen*

**what is there for children to do?**
Was können Kinder dort unternehmen?
*vas kur'-nen kinder dort oonter-naymen*

**Is there a play park near here?**
Gibt es einen Spielplatz in der Nähe?
*gipt es ine-en shpeelplats in der nay-e*

**Is it safe for children?**
Ist das ungefährlich für Kinder?
*ist das oon-gefayrlikh foor kinder*

**Do you have...?**
Haben Sie...?
*hah-ben zee...*

**a high chair**
einen Hochstuhl
*ine-en hokh-shtool*

**a cot**
ein Kinderbett
*ine kinderbet*

**I have two children**
Ich habe zwei Kinder
*ikh hah-be tsvy kinder*

**He/She is 10 years old**
Er/Sie ist 10 Jahre alt
*er/zee ist tsayn yah-re alt*

**Do you have any children?**
Haben Sie Kinder?
*hah-ben zee kinder*

| DIE AUFSICHTSRATSITZUNG *dee owfzeekhsratzeetsoong* | BOARD MEETING |
| DAS KONFERENZZIMMER *das konferents-tsimmer* | CONFERENCE ROOM |
| DIE BESPRECHUNG *dee be-shpre-khoong* | MEETING |
| DAS PROTOKOLL *das proh-tokol* | MINUTES |
| DAS MUSTER *das mooster* | SAMPLE |
| DIE MESSE *dee mes-se* | TRADE FAIR |

**I'd like to arrange a meeting with...**
Ich möchte einen Termin mit ... ausmachen
*ikh mur'kh-te ine-en ter-min mit ... ows-makhen*

**Are you free to meet...?**
Haben Sie Zeit für eine Besprechung...?
*hah-ben zee tsite foor ine-e be-shpre-khoong...*

**on April 4th at 11 o'clock**
am vierten April um elf Uhr
*am feer-ten april oom elf oor*

**for lunch**
zum Mittagessen
*tsoom mitak-essen*

**I will send an e-mail / a fax to confirm**
Ich schicke eine E-Mail / ein Fax zur Bestätigung
*ikh shi-ke ine-e e-mail / ine fax tsoor be-shtay-ti-goong*

**I'm staying at Hotel...**
Ich wohne im Hotel...
*ikh voh-ne im hotel...*

**How do I get to your office?**
Wie komme ich zu Ihrem Büro?
*vee kom-me ikh tsoo ee-rem booroh*

**Please let ... know that I will be ... minutes late**
Bitte sagen Sie ..., dass ich ... Minuten später komme
*bit-te zah-gen zee ... das ikh ... minoo-ten shpayter kom-me*

**I have an appointment with Herr/Frau...**
Ich habe einen Termin mit Herrn/Frau...
*ikh hah-be ine-en ter-meen mit hayrn/frow...*

**at ... o'clock**
um ... Uhr
*oom ... oor*

**I'm ...**
Ich bin...
*ikh bin...*

**Here is my card**
Hier ist meine Karte
*heer ist mine-e kar-te*

**I'm delighted to meet you at last**
Schön, dass wir uns endlich persönlich kennen lernen
*shur'n das veer oons ent-likh per-sur'n-likh kennen layr-nen*

**My German isn't very good**
Mein Deutsch ist nicht sehr gut
*mine doytch ist nikht sayr goot*

**Please speak slowly**
Bitte sprechen Sie langsam
*bit-te shpre-khen zee lang-zahm*

**I'm sorry I'm late**
Entschuldigen Sie, dass ich zu spät komme
*entshool-digen zee das ikh tsoo shpayt kom-me*

**My flight was delayed**
Mein Flug hatte Verspätung
*mine flook hat-te fer-shpay-toong*

**May I introduce you to...**
Darf ich Ihnen ... vorstellen
*darf ikh ee-nen ... for-shte-len*

**Can I offer you dinner?**
Darf ich Sie zum Essen einladen?
*darf ikh zee tsoom essen ine-lahden*

### ■ YOU MAY HEAR

**Haben Sie einen Termin?**
*hah-ben zee ine-en ter-meen*
Do you have an appointment?

**...ist im Augenblick nicht im Büro**
*...ist im ow-genblik nikht im booroh*
... isn't in the office at the moment

**Er/Sie kommt in ein paar Minuten wieder**
*er/zee komt in ine pahr minoo-ten veeder*
He/She will be back in a few minutes

see also **TELEPHONE** □ **E-MAIL** □ **INTERNET** □ **FAX**     81

# ALPHABET

*Except for ä, ö, ü and ß (which corresponds to double s), the German alphabet is the same as the English. Below are the words used for clarification when spelling something out.*

**How do you spell it?**
Wie schreybt man das?
*vee shrybt man das*

**A as in Anton, b as in Berta**
A wie Anton, B wie Berta
*ah vee anton bay vee berta*

| | | | |
|---|---|---|---|
| A (ä) | *ah (ah oom-lowt)* | Anton | *an-ton* |
| B | *bay* | Berta | *ber-ta* |
| C | *tsay* | Caesar | *tsay-zar* |
| D | *day* | Dora | *do-rah* |
| E | *ay* | Emil | *ay-meel* |
| F | *ef* | Friedrich | *freed-rikh* |
| G | *gay* | Gustav | *goos-tahf* |
| H | *hah* | Heinrich | *hine-rikh* |
| I | *ee* | Ida | *ee-dah* |
| J | *yot* | Julius | *yoo-lee-oos* |
| K | *kah* | Konrad | *kon-rat* |
| L | *el* | Ludwig | *lood-vikh* |
| M | *em* | Martin | *mar-tin* |
| N | *en* | Nordpol | *nort-pol* |
| O (ö) | *oh (oh oom-lowt)* | Otto | *ot-toh* |
| P | *pay* | Paula | *pow-la* |
| Q | *koo* | Quelle | *kvel-le* |
| R | *ayr* | Richard | *ri-khart* |
| S | *es* | Siegfried | *zeek-freet* |
| ß | *es-tset* | Eszett | *ess-tset* |
| T | *tay* | Theodor | *tay-o-dor* |
| U (ü) | *oo (oo oom-lowt)* | Ulrich | *ool-rikh* |
| V | *fow* | Victor | *vik-tor* |
| W | *vay* | Wilhelm | *vil-helm* |
| X | *iks* | Xanten | *ksan-ten* |
| Y | *oop-si-lon* | Ypsilon | *oop-si-lon* |
| Z | *tset* | Zeppelin | *tse-pe-leen* |

## ■ LIQUIDS

| | | |
|---|---|---|
| **1/2 litre** (c.1 pint) | einen halben Liter | *ine*-en **hal**ben **lee**ter |
| **a litre of...** | einen Liter... | *ine*-en **lee**ter... |
| **a bottle of...** | eine Flasche... | *ine*-e **fla**-she... |
| **a glass of...** | ein Glas... | *ine* glahs... |
| **a small glass** | ein kleines Glas | *ine* **kline**-es glahs |
| **a large glass** | ein großes Glas | *ine* **groh**-ses glahs |

## ■ WEIGHTS

| | | |
|---|---|---|
| **100 grams of...** | hundert Gramm... | **hoon**dert gram... |
| **a pound** (=500 g) | ein Pfund | *ine* pfoont |
| **a kilo of...** | ein Kilo... | *ine* **kee**lo... |

## ■ FOOD

| | | |
|---|---|---|
| **a slice of...** | eine Scheibe... | *ine*-e **shy**-be... |
| **a portion of...** | eine Portion... | *ine*-e por-**tsyohn**... |
| **a dozen...** | ein Dutzend... | *ine* **doo**-tsent... |
| **a packet of...** | ein Paket... | *ine* pa**kayt**... |
| **a tin of...** | eine Dose... | *ine*-e **doh**-ze... |
| **a jar of...** | ein Glas... | *ine* glahs... |

## ■ MISCELLANEOUS

| | | |
|---|---|---|
| **10 euro worth of...** | für zehn Euro... | foor tsayn **oy**ro... |
| **a third** | ein Drittel | *ine* **drit**tel |
| **a quarter** | ein Viertel | *ine* **feer**tel |
| **ten per cent** | zehn Prozent | tsayn pro-**tsent** |
| **more...** | noch etwas... | nokh **et**vas... |
| **less...** | weniger... | **vay**ni-ger... |
| **enough** | genug | ge-**nook** |
| **double** | doppelt | **dop**-pelt |
| **twice** | zweimal | **tsvy**-mal |
| **three times** | dreimal | **dry**-mal |

# NUMBERS

| | | | | | | |
|---|---|---|---|---|---|---|
| 0 | null | *nool* | | | | |
| 1 | eins | *ines* | | 1st | erste | *er-ste* |
| 2 | zwe | *tsvy* | | | | |
| 3 | drei | *dry* | | 2nd | zweite | *tsvy-te* |
| 4 | vier | *feer* | | | | |
| 5 | fünf | *foonf* | | 3rd | dritte | *drit-te* |
| 6 | sechs | *zekhs* | | | | |
| 7 | sieben | *zee*ben | | 4th | vierte | *feer-te* |
| 8 | acht | *akht* | | | | |
| 9 | neun | *noyn* | | 5th | fünfte | *foonf-te* |
| 10 | zehn | *tsayn* | | | | |
| 11 | elf | *elf* | | 6th | sechste | *zekhs-te* |
| 12 | zwölf | *tsvur'lf* | | | | |
| 13 | dreizehn | *dry-tsayn* | | 7th | siebte | *zeep-te* |
| 14 | vierzehn | *feer-tsayn* | | | | |
| 15 | fünfzehn | *foonf-tsayn* | | 8th | achte | *akh-te* |
| 16 | sechzehn | *zekh-tsayn* | | | | |
| 17 | siebzehn | *zeep-tsayn* | | 9th | neunte | *noyn-te* |
| 18 | achtzehn | *akh-tsayn* | | | | |
| 19 | neunzehn | *noyn-tsayn* | | 10th | zehnte | *tsayn-te* |
| 20 | zwanzig | *tsvan-tsikh* | | | | |

| | | |
|---|---|---|
| 21 | einundzwanzig | *ine-oont-tsvan-tsikh* |
| 22 | zweiundzwanzig | *tsvy-oont-tsvan-tsikh* |
| 23 | dreiundzwanzig | *dry-oont-tsvan-tsikh* |
| 24 | vierundzwanzig | *feer-oont-tsvan-tsikh* |
| 25 | fünfundzwanzig | *foonf-oont-tsvan-tsikh* |
| 30 | dreißig | *dry-sikh* |
| 40 | vierzig | *feer-tsikh* |
| 50 | fünfzig | *foonf-tsikh* |
| 60 | sechzig | *zekh-tsikh* |
| 70 | siebzig | *zeep-tsikh* |
| 80 | achtzig | *akh-tsikh* |
| 90 | neunzig | *noyn-tsikh* |
| 100 | hundert | *hoon*dert |
| 101 | hunderteins | *hoon*dert-ines |
| 200 | zweihundert | *tsvy*-hoondert |
| 1,000 | tausend | *tow*zent |
| 2,000 | zweitausend | *tsvy*-towzent |
| 1 million | eine Million | *ine*-e milyohn |

**days** *(all der words)*

| | | |
|---|---|---|
| MONTAG *mon*tahk | | MONDAY |
| DIENSTAG *deens*tahk | | TUESDAY |
| MITTWOCH *mit*vohk | | WEDNESDAY |
| DONNERSTAG *donn*erstahk | | THURSDAY |
| FREITAG *fry*tahk | | FRIDAY |
| SAMSTAG *zams*tahk | | SATURDAY |
| SONNTAG *zon*-tahk | | SUNDAY |

**seasons** *(all der words)*

| | |
|---|---|
| FRÜHLING *froo*ling | SPRING |
| SOMMER *zom*mer | SUMMER |
| HERBST *herpst* | AUTUMN |
| WINTER *vin*ter | WINTER |

**months** *(all der words)*

| | |
|---|---|
| JANUAR *yan*ooar | JANUARY |
| FEBRUAR *feb*rooar | FEBRUARY |
| MÄRZ *mehrts* | MARCH |
| APRIL ap*reel* | APRIL |
| MAI *mye* | MAY |
| JUNI *yoo*nee | JUNE |
| JULI *yoo*lee | JULY |
| AUGUST ow*goost* | AUGUST |
| SEPTEMBER sep*tem*ber | SEPTEMBER |
| OKTOBER ok*to*ber | OCTOBER |
| NOVEMBER no*vem*ber | NOVEMBER |
| DEZEMBER dayts*em*ber | DECEMBER |

## What is today's date?
Was für ein Datum haben wir heute?
*was foor ine **dah**toom **hah**-ben veer **hoy**-te*

## It's the 5th of March 2003
Heute ist der fünfte März zweitausenddrei
***hoy**-te ist der **foonf**-te merts **tsvy**towzent-dry*

| **on Saturday** | **on Saturdays** | **every Saturday** |
|---|---|---|
| am Samstag | samstags | jeden Samstag |
| *am **zams**tahk* | ***zams**tahks* | ***yay**-den **zams**tahk* |

| **this Saturday** | **next Saturday** | **last Saturday** |
|---|---|---|
| diesen Samstag | nächsten Samstag | letzten Samstag |
| ***dee**zen **zams**tahk* | ***nekh**-sten **zams**tahk* | ***lets**-ten **zams**tahk* |

| **in June** | **at the beginning of June** | **at the end of June** |
|---|---|---|
| im Juni | Anfang Juni | Ende Juni |
| *im **yoo**nee* | *anfang **yoo**nee* | *en-de **yoo**nee* |

| **before summer** | **during the summer** | **after summer** |
|---|---|---|
| vor dem Sommer | im Sommer | nach dem Sommer |
| *for dem **zom**mer* | *im **zom**mer* | *nakh dem **zom**mer* |

*see also* **NUMBERS**

*The 24-hour clock is used a lot more in continental Europe than in Britain. After 1200 midday, it continues: **1300**–dreizehn Uhr, **1400**–vierzehn Uhr, **1500**–fünfzehn Uhr, etc. until **2400**–vierundzwanzig Uhr. With the 24-hour clock, the words Viertel (quarter) and Halb (half) aren't used:*

| | |
|---|---|
| **13.15** (1.15pm) | dreizehn Uhr fünfzehn |
| **19.30** (7.30pm) | neunzehn Uhr dreißig |
| **22.45** (10.45pm) | zweiundzwanzig Uhr fünfundvierzig |

| **What time is it, please?** | **am** | **pm** |
|---|---|---|
| Wie spät ist es, bitte? | morgens | abends |
| *vee shpayt ist es bit-te* | **mor**gens | **ah**-bents |

| **It's ...** | **2 o'clock** | **3 o'clock** | **6 o'clock** (etc.) |
|---|---|---|---|
| Es ist... | zwei Uhr | drei Uhr | sechs Uhr |
| *es ist...* | *tsvy oor* | *dry oor* | *zekhs oor* |

| **It's half past 8** | **at midnight** |
|---|---|
| Es ist halb neun (in German you say half to 9) | um Mitternacht |
| *es ist halp noyn* | *oom **mit**ter-nakht* |

| | |
|---|---|
| **9** | neun Uhr <br> *noyn oor* |
| **9.10** | neun Uhr zehn <br> *noyn oor tsayn* |
| **quarter past 9** | Viertel nach neun (Austria: viertel zehn) <br> ***feer**tel nakh noyn* |
| **9.20** | neun Uhr zwanzig <br> *noyn oor **tsvan**-tsikh* |
| **half past 9/9.30** | halb zehn / neun Uhr dreißig <br> *halp tsayn / noyn oor **dry**-sikh* |
| **9.35** | neun Uhr fünfunddreißig <br> *noyn oor foonf-oont-**dry**-sich* |
| **quarter to 10** | Viertel vor zehn (Austria: drei viertel zehn) <br> ***feer**tel for tsayn* |
| **10 to 10** | zehn vor zehn <br> *tsayn for tsayn* |

**When do you open?**
Wann öffnen Sie?
van **ur'f**-nen zee

**When do you close?**
Wann schließen Sie?
van **shlee**-sen zee

**at 3 o'clock**
um drei Uhr
oom dry oor

**before 3 o'clock**
vor drei Uhr
for dry oor

**after 3 o'clock**
nach drei Uhr
nakh dry oor

**today**
heute
**hoy**-te

**tonight**
heute Abend
**hoy**-te **ah**bent

**tomorrow**
morgen
**mor**gen

**yesterday**
gestern
**ges**tern

**the day before yesterday**
vorgestern
**for**-gestern

**the day after tomorrow**
übermorgen
**oo**ber-morgen

**in the morning**
morgens
**mor**gens

**this morning**
heute Morgen
hoy-te **mor**gen

**in the afternoon**
am Nachmittag
am **nakh**-mi-tahk

**in the evening**
am Abend
am **ah**bent

**at half past 7**
um halb acht
oom halp akht

**at about 10 o'clock**
gegen zehn Uhr
**ge**gen tsayn oor

**in an hour's time**
in einer Stunde
in **ine**-er **shtoon**-de

**in a while**
bald
balt

**two hours ago**
vor zwei Stunden
for tsvy **shtoon**den

**soon**
bald
balt

**early**
früh
froo

**late**
spät
shpayt

**later**
später
**shpay**ter

**I'll do it...**
Ich mache es...
ikh **ma**-khe es...

**as soon as possible**
so bald wie möglich
zo balt vee **mur'k**-likh

**...at the latest**
...spätestens
...**shpay**-testens

see also **NUMBERS**

## Café

*Generally attached to a cake shop, Konditorei, where you can sit down and sample some of the cakes. Can be quite expensive.*

## Biergarten

*An open-air pub offering a selection of meals, usually hearty food (like pretzels, or sausages).*

## Selbstbedienung

*Self-service*

## BISTRO

*A good place for breakfast, snacks, coffees and cakes.*

## Eisdiele

*Ice-cream parlour*

## Kneipe

*Similar to a pub*

## Restaurant

*Generally open 11.30pm to 2.30pm and 7.30pm to 10.30pm. The menu is posted outside.*

## Ratskeller

*German town halls often have restaurants open to the public.*

## Weinstube

*A winebar where light, usually cold meals are served.*

## Imbiss

*These stalls serve cheap snacks like hamburgers, sausages, chips and soup.*

| **a black coffee** | **a white coffee** | **...please** |
|---|---|---|
| einen schwarzen Kaffee | einen Milchkaffee | ...bitte |
| *ine-en shvar-tsen kafay* | *ine-en milkh-kafay* | ...*bit-te* |

| **a tea...** | **with milk** | **with lemon** | **no sugar** |
|---|---|---|---|
| einen Tee... | mit Milch | mit Zitrone | ohne Zucker |
| *ine-en tay...* | *mit milkh* | *mit tsitroh-ne* | *oh-ne tsooker* |

| **for two** | **for me** | **for him / her** | **for us** | **with ice** |
|---|---|---|---|---|
| für zwei | für mich | für ihn / sie | für uns | mit Eis |
| *foor tsvy* | *foor mikh* | *foor een / zee* | *foor oons* | *mit ice* |

| **a lager** | **a bitter** | **a half pint** | **a pint** (approx.) |
|---|---|---|---|
| ein helles Bier | ein Altbier | ein Kleines | ein Großes |
| *ine hel-les beer* | *ine altbeer* | *ine kline-es* | *ine groh-ses* |

| **A bottle of mineral water** | **sparkling** | **still** |
|---|---|---|
| Eine Flasche Mineralwasser | mit Kohlensäure | still |
| *ine-e fla-she mi-nerahl-vasser* | *mit kohlen-zoy-re* | *shtill* |

| **Would you like a drink?** | **What will you have?** |
|---|---|
| Möchten Sie etwas trinken? | Was möchten Sie? |
| *mur'kh-ten zee etvas trinken* | *vas mur'kh-ten zee* |

| **I'm very thirsty** | **I'd like something cool to drink** |
|---|---|
| Ich habe großen Durst | Ich möchte etwas Kühles trinken |
| *ikh hah-be groh-sen doorst* | *ikh mur'kh-te etvas koo-les trinken* |

**Do you have anything non-alcoholic?**
Haben Sie auch Getränke ohne Alkohol?
*hah-ben zee owkh ge-treng-ke oh-ne al-kohol*

## ■ OTHER DRINKS TO TRY

ein Kölsch *a strong lager from Cologne*
ein dunkles Bier *a dark beer similar to brown ale*
ein Fruchtsaft *a fruit juice*
eine heiße Schokolade *a rich-tasting hot chocolate*
ein Pils *a strong, slightly bitter lager*
ein Radler *a type of shandy*

*see also* **IN A RESTAURANT**

# IN A BAR/CAFÉ

*Typical German snacky food (**Imbiss**) includes **Bratwurst** (fried sausage), **Bockwurst** (boiled sausage, i.e. frankfurter) and **Buletten** (thick hamburgers).*

| Getränke nicht inklusive | drink not included |
|---|---|

| Tagesgericht für 7 € 50<br>Fisch<br>oder Fleisch<br>oder Geflügel | dish of the day 7 € 50<br>fish<br>or meat<br>or poultry |
|---|---|

| **Mittagsmenü**<br>**Vorspeise + Hauptgericht +**<br>**Kaffee** | lunchtime menu<br>starter + main course +<br>coffee |
|---|---|

| *Speisekarte* | *Menu* |
|---|---|
| *Vorspeisen* | *Starters* |
| *Suppen* | *soups* |
| *Salate* | *salads* |
| *Knoblauchbrot* | *garlic bread* |
| *Fleisch* | *Meat* |
| *Wild und Geflügel* | *Game & Poultry* |
| *Fisch* | *Fish* |
| *Meeresfrüchte* | *seafood* |
| *Gemüse* | *Vegetables* |
| *Käse* | *Cheese* |
| *Dessert* | *Dessert* |
| *Getränke* | *Drinks* |

In Germany the main meal of the day is lunch – **Mittagessen**.
Breakfast – **Frühstück** – is also often a substantial meal. Look out
for breakfast buffets – **Frühstücksbüfett**. Those preferring
vegetarian dishes, turn to p. 92 for further phrases.

**Where can we have a snack?**
Wo kann man hier eine Kleinigkeit essen?
*voh kan man heer **ine**-e **kline**-ikh-kite **ess**en*

**Can you recommend a good restaurant?**
Können Sie ein gutes Restaurant empfehlen?
***kur**'-nen zee ine **goo**-tes restoh-**rong** emp-**fay**len*

**I'd like to book a table for ... people**
Ich möchte einen Tisch für ... Personen reservieren
*ikh **mur'kh**-te **ine**-en tish foor ... per-**zoh**nen ray-zer-**vee**ren*

| for tonight... | for tomorrow night... | for 8 pm |
|---|---|---|
| für heute Abend... | für morgen Abend... | für acht Uhr |
| *foor **hoy**-te **ah**bent...* | *foor **mor**gen **ah**bent...* | *foor akht oor* |

**The menu, please**
Die Speisekarte, bitte
*dee **shpy**-ze-kar-te **bit**-te*

**What is the dish of the day?**
Was ist das Tagesgericht?
*vas ist das **tah**ges-gerikht*

**Have you a set-price menu?**
Haben Sie eine Tageskarte?
***hah**-ben zee **ine**-e **tah**ges-kar-te?*

**I'll have this**
Ich nehme das
*ikh **nay**-me das*

**What is in this?**
Was ist das?
*vas ist das*

**Can you recommend a local dish?**
Können Sie eine Spezialität aus der Gegend empfehlen?
***kur**'-nen zee **ine**-e shpe-tsee-ali-**tayt** ows der **gay**gent emp-**fay**len*

| Excuse me! | more bread... | more water... | please |
|---|---|---|---|
| Entschuldigung | noch Brot... | noch Wasser... | bitte |
| *ent**shool**-digoong* | *nokh broht...* | *nokh **vass**er...* | ***bit**-te* |

**The bill, please**
Zahlen, bitte
***tsah**-len **bit**-te*

**Is service included?**
Ist die Bedienung inbegriffen?
*ist dee be-**dee**noong **in**-be-griffen*

see also **EATING PLACES** □ **WINES & SPIRITS**

# VEGETARIAN

*Although vegetarianism is gradually becoming more popular, few restaurants offer vegetarian options.*

### Are there any vegetarian restaurants here?
Gibt es hier vegetarische Restaurants?
*gipt es heer vaygay-**ta**rish-e restoh-**rongs***

### Do you have any vegetarian dishes?
Haben Sie vegetarische Gerichte?
*hah-ben zee vaygay-**ta**rish-e ge-**rikh**-te*

### Which dishes have no meat / fish?
Welche Gerichte sind ohne Fleisch / Fisch?
*vel-khe ge-**rikh**-te zint **oh**-ne flysh / fish*

### What fish dishes do you have?
Was für Fischgerichte haben Sie?
*vas foor **fish**-gerikh-te **hah**-ben zee*

### I'd like pasta as a main course
Ich möchte als Hauptgericht Nudeln
*ikh **mur'kh**-te als **howpt**-gerikht **noo**deln*

### I don't eat meat
Ich esse kein Fleisch
*ikh **es**-se kine flysh*

### What do you recommend?
Was können Sie empfehlen?
*vas **kur'**-nen zee emp-**fay**len*

### Is it made with vegetable stock?
Ist das mit Gemüsebrühe gemacht?
*ist das mit ge**moo**-ze-broo-he ge-**makht***

### ■ POSSIBLE DISHES

**Gemüsestrudel** *vegetable-filled strudel*

**Kartoffelpuffer** *potato pancakes*

**Käseplatte** *selection of cheeses*

**Omelette mit Champignons** *mushroom omelette*

**Pfifferling mit Semmelklops** *chanterelle mushrooms with dumpling and sauce*

**Topfenstrudel** *strudel filled with soft cheese*

see also EATING PLACES

**The wine list, please**
Die Weinkarte, bitte
dee **vine**kar-te **bit**-te

**Can you recommend a good wine?**
Können Sie mir einen guten Wein empfehlen?
**kur'**-nen zee meer **ine**-en **goo**-ten vine emp-**fay**len

**A bottle of house wine**
Eine Flasche Hauswein
**ine**-e **fla**-she **hows**vine

**A glass of white wine / red wine**
Ein Glas Weißwein / Rotwein
ine glahs **vice**vine / **roht**vine

**A bottle of red wine**
Eine Flasche Rotwein
**ine**-e **fla**-she **roht**vine

**A bottle of white wine**
Eine Flasche Weißwein
**ine**-e **fla**-she **vice**vine

---

*Wines are usually categorized according to three criteria: the overall growing area, the village or even vineyard where they are produced, and the type of grape they are made from. Major grape varieties include* **Riesling, Silvaner, Gewürztraminer,** *and* **Müller-Thurgau**

---

*Important wine-growing areas in Germany and Austria include:*

**Ahr** *small valley north of the Moselle, producing mainly pleasant, light red wines*

**Baden** *the region around Freiburg in the Upper Rhine valley, producing pleasant, light, mainly white and rosé wines*

**Burgenland** *region in Austria producing mainly sweet wines*

**Franken** *important wine-growing area in Northern Bavaria, producing dry, full-bodied wines*

**Mosel-Saar-Ruwer** *region along the rivers Moselle, Saar and Ruwer, producing white wines, many of them dry*

**Rheinpfalz** *Palatinate region, producing mainly white wines*

**Rheinhessen** *quality wine region along the banks of the Rhine*

**Wachau** *major wine-growing area in Austria, just west of Vienna
The names of the villages and vineyards producing wines are innumerable. The name of the wine is often the name of the village (e.g. Nierstein) plus the name of the particular vineyard (e.g. Gutes Domtal) which combined become* **Niersteiner Gutes Domtal**

*cont...*

*Amongst the most well-known names are:*

**Bereich Bernkastel** *on the river Moselle, producing crisp whites*

**Erbach** *area near Eltville in the Rheingau/Palatinate region, producing scented white wines mainly from the Riesling grape*

**Gumpoldskirchen** *spicy white wine from Austria*

**Hochheim** *strong white wines the from the Rheingau region*

**Kaiserstuhl** *region near Freiburg, producing light white and rosé wines which are best drunk young*

**Nierstein** *village in the Rheingau region, producing medium to sweet white Rheinwein (e.g.* **Niersteiner Gutes Domtal***)*

**Oppenheim** *village on the Rhine, producing fine white wines*

**Volkach** *town in Franken, producing fine, rather dry white wines*

*Other words to look out for are:*

**Eiswein** *a rich, naturally sweet, white wine made from grapes which are harvested only after a period of frost*

**halbtrocken** *medium-dry*

**Landwein** *similar to French 'vin de pays'*

**Prädikatswein** *highest category of quality wines*

**QbA** *quality wine from a specified region*

**Tafelwein** *lowest quality wine, similar to French 'vin de table'*

**trocken** *dry*

## ■ OTHER DRINKS

### What liqueurs do you have?
Was für Liköre haben Sie?
*vas foor lee-__kur__'-re __hah__-ben zee*

**Apfelkorn** *apple brandy*

**Danziger Goldwasser** *brandy with tiny bits of gold leaf*

**Himbeergeist** *raspberry brandy which is very strong and clear*

**Kirschwasser** *cherry brandy*

**Schnaps** *strong spirit*

**Sliwowitz** *plum brandy (Austria)*

**Erdäpfelkren** relish with potato and horseradish
**Erdäpfelnudeln** fried, boiled potato balls tossed in fried breadcrumbs
**Erdbeeren** strawberries
**erster Gang** first course
**Essig** vinegar
**Export Bier** premium beer

## F

**Falscher Hase** baked mince meatloaf
**Fasan** pheasant
**Feigen** figs
**Fenchel** fennel
**fettarm** low in fat
**Fisch** fish
**Fischfilet** fish fillet
**Fischgerichte** fish and seafood
**Fischklöße** fish dumplings
**Fischsuppe** fish soup
**flambiert** flambé
**Fledermaus** boiled beef in horseradish cream browned in the oven
**Fleisch** meat
**Fleischgerichte** meat dishes
**Fleischklößchen** meatballs
**Fleischlaberln** highly seasoned meat cake
**Fleischpflanzerl** thick hamburgers

**Fleischsalat** sausage salad with onions
**Fleischsuppe** meat soup served with dumplings
**Flunder** flounder
**Fondue** melted cheese with wine and bread for dipping
**Forelle** trout
**Forelle blau** steamed trout with potatoes and vegetables
**Forelle Müllerin** trout fried in batter with almonds
**Forelle Steiermark** trout fillet with bacon in white sauce
**Frikadelle** thick hamburger
**frisch** fresh
**Fritattensuppe** beef broth with strips of pancake
**Froschschenkel** frogs' legs
**Frucht** fresh fruit
**Früchtetee** fruit tea
**Fruchtsaft** fruit juice
**Fünfkernbrot** wholemeal bread made with five different cereals

## G

**Gang** course
**Gans** goose
**Gänseleber** foie gras
**Gänseleberpastete** goose liver pâté
**Gebäck** pastries
**gebacken** baked
**gebackene Leber** liver fried in breadcrumbs

## A

**Aal** eel
**Aalsuppe** eel soup
**Allgäuer Emmentaler** whole-milk hard cheese from the Allgäu
**Allgäuer Käsespätzle** cheese noodles from the Allgäu
**Alpzirler** cow's milk cheese from Austria
**Alsterwasser** lager shandy
**Altbier** top-fermented beer from the lower Rhine
**Ananas** pineapple
**Apfel** apple
**Apfelkorn** apple brandy
**Apfelkuchen** apple cake
**Apfelsaft** apple juice
**Apfelsalami** salami with apple
**Apfelstrudel** flaky pastry filled with apples and spices
**Apfelwein** cider (apple wine)
**Aprikose** apricot
**Art** style or fashion of
**Artischocken** artichokes
**Aubergine** aubergine
**Auflauf** baked dish, can be sweet or savoury
**Aufschnitt** sliced cold meats
**Austern** oysters

## B

**Bäckerofen** 'baker's oven', pork and lamb bake from Saarland
**Backpflaumen** prunes
**Banane** banana
**Bandnudeln** ribbon pasta
**Barack** apricot brandy
**Barsch** perch
**Bauernfrühstück** scrambled eggs, bacon, cooked diced potatoes, onions, tomatoes
**Baunzerl** little bread roll with distinctive cut on top
**Bayrisch Kraut** shredded cabbage cooked with sliced apples, wine and sugar
**Beilage** side dish
**Bereich Bernkastel** area along the Moselle producing crisp white wines
**Bergkäse** cheese from the Alps
**Berliner** doughnut filled with jam
**Berliner Weiße** fizzy beer with fruit syrup added
**Berner Erbsensuppe** soup made of dried peas with pig's trotters
**Bienenstich** type of cake, baked on a tray with a coating

95

of almonds and sugar
and a cream filling
**Bierschinken** beer
sausage with ham
**Bierwurst** beer
sausage
**Birchermüsli** muesli
**Birne** pear
**Birnenmost** pear wine
**Birnensekt** sparkling pear wine
**Blattsalat** green salad
**blau** rare (meat); poached (fish)
**Blauschimmelkäse** blue cheese
**Blumenkohl** cauliflower
**Blunz'n** black pudding
**Blutwurst** black pudding
**Bockbier** strong beer (light
or dark), drunk especially in
Bavaria
**Bockwurst** boiled sausage.
A popular snack served with
a bread roll
**Böhmische Knödel** sliced
dumpling
**Bohnen** beans
**Bohnensalat** bean salad
**Bohnensuppe** thick bean
and bacon soup
**Bosniakerl** wholemeal roll with
caraway seeds
**Brathähnchen** roast chicken
**Brathering** fried herring
(eaten cold)
**Bratkartoffeln** fried potatoes
**Bratwurst** fried sausage.

A popular snack served with
a bread roll
**Brauner** strong black coffee
with a little milk
**Bremer Kükenragout** Bremen
chicken fricassée
**Broiler** spit-roasted chicken
**Brombeeren** blackberries
**Bröselknödel** soup with little
dumplings prepared with bone
marrow and breadcrumbs
**Brot** bread
**Brötchen** bread roll
**Brühwurst** thick frankfurter
**B'soffene** pudding soaked in
mulled wine
**Buletten** thick hamburgers
**Buletten mit Kartoffelsalat**
thick hamburgers with potato
salad
**Bündnerfleisch** raw beef
smoked and dried, served
thinly sliced
**Burgenländische Krautsuppe**
thick cabbage and vegetable
soup
**Butter** butter
**Butterbrot** open sandwich
**Butterkäse** high-fat cheese

## C

**Cervelat** fine beef and pork
salami
**Chindbettering** ring of bread
**Cremeschnitten** cream slices

**Champignons** button
mushrooms
**Currywurst** sausage served
with a spicy sauce. A popular
snack originally from Berlin

## D

**Damenkäse** mild buttery cheese
**Dampfnudeln** hot yeast
dumplings with vanilla sauce
**Danziger Goldwasser**
schnapps containing tiny bits
of gold leaf
**Datteln** dates
**Deutsches Beefsteak** thick
hamburger
**dicke Bohnen** broad beans
**Doppelbockbier** like
Bockbier, but still stronger
**Dorsch** cod
**Dresdner Suppentopf**
Dresden vegetable soup with
dumplings
**Dunkles** dark beer

## E

**Ei** egg
**Eier im Glas** soft boiled eggs
served in a glass
**Eierkuchen** pancakes
**Eierschwammerln** chanterelles
**Eierspeispfandl** special
Viennese omelette
**eingelegt** pickled

**Einmachsuppe**
chicken or veal
broth with cream
and egg
**Einspänner** coffee
with whipped
cream served in a
glass

**Eintopf** stew
**Eis** ice cream
**Eisbecher** knickerbocker glory
**Eisbein** boiled pork knuckle
often served with sauerkraut
**Eiskaffee** iced coffee served
with vanilla ice cream
**Eiswein** a rich, naturally sweet,
white wine made from
grapes which are harvested
only after a period of frost
**Emmentaler** Swiss Emmental,
whole-milk hard cheese
**Ennstaler** blue cheese from
mixed milk
**Ente** duck
**Erbach** area producing scent-
ed white wines mainly from
Riesling grape
**Erbsen** peas
**Erbsenpüree** green pea purée
**Erbsensuppe** pea soup
**Erdäpfel** potatoes
**Erdäpfelgulasch** spicy
sausage and potato ste
**Erdäpfelknödel** potat
semolina dumplings

98

**gebraten** roasted/fried
**gedämpft** steamed
**Geflügel** poultry
**gefüllt** stuffed/filled
  **gefüllte Kalbsbrust** stuffed
  breast of veal
  **gefüllte Paprika** peppers
  filled with mince
**gegrillt** grilled
  **gegrillter Lachs** grilled salmon
**Gehacktes** mince
**gekocht** boiled
  **gekochtes Rindfleisch mit**
  **grüner Soße** boiled beef
  with green sauce
**gemischter Salat** mixed salad
**Gemüse** vegetables
  **Gemüse und Klöße**
  vegetables and dumplings
  **Gemüselasagne** vegetable
  lasagne
  **Gemüseplatte** mixed
  vegetables
  **Gemüsesuppe** vegetable
  soup
**geräuchert** smoked
**Gericht** dish
**geschmort** braised
**Geschnetzeltes** thinly sliced
  meat in sauce served with
  potatoes or rice
**Geselchtes** smoked meats
**Gespritzter** spritzer, white
  wine and soda water
**Gewürzgurken** gherkins

**Gitziprägel** baked
  rabbit in batter (a
  Swiss dish)
**Glühwein** mulled
  wine
**Goldbarsch** redfish
**Graf Görz** Austrian soft
  cheese
**Grammeln** croissant stuffed
  with bacon
**Grießklößchensuppe** soup
  with semolina dumplings
**Grießtaler** gnocchi
**Grog** hot rum
**grüne Bohnen** green beans
**grüne Veltlinersuppe** green
  wine soup
**grüner Salat** green salad
**Gruyère** gruyère cheese
**Güggeli** roast chicken with
  onions and mushrooms in
  white wine sauce
**Gulasch** stewed diced beef and
  pork with paprika served with
  dumplings and red cabbage
**Gulaschsuppe** spicy meat
  soup with paprika
**Gulyas** beef stew with paprika
**Gumpoldskirchner** spicy white
  wine from Austria
**Gurke** cucumber
**Gurkensalat** cucumber salad
**gutbürgerliche Küche**
  traditional German cooking
**Gyros** kebab

99

## H

**Hackbraten** mince-meat roast
**Hackepeter auf Schrippen mit Zwiebeln** spiced minced pork on rolls, with onions
**Hackfleisch** mince
**Hähnchen** chicken
  **Hähnchenbrust** chicken breast
**halbtrocken** medium-dry
**Hamburger Rundstück** Hamburg meat roll
**Hammel** mutton
**Hartkäse** hard cheese
**Hase** hare
**Hasenbraten** roast hare
**Hauptgericht** main course
**Hausbrauerei** house beer
**hausgemacht** home-made
**Hausmannskost** good traditional home cooking
**Hecht** pike
**Hefeweizen** wheat beer
**Heidschnuckenragout** lamb stew
**heiß** hot
**Helles** light beer
**Hering** herring
  **Heringsschmaus** herring in creamy sauce
**Herz** heart
**Heuriger** new wine

**Himbeeren** raspberries
  **Himbeergeist** raspberry brandy
**Hirn** brain
**Hirsch** venison
**Hockheim** strong white wines from the Rheingau
**Honig** honey
**Hühnchen** chicken
**Hühnerfrikasse** chicken fricassée
**Hühnerschenkel** chicken drumsticks
**Hühnerleber** chicken liver
**Hummer** lobster

## I

**Ingwer** ginger

## J

**Jägerschnitzel** cutlet served with mushrooms and wine sauce
**Jogurt** yoghurt
**Johannisbeeren** redcurrants
**Jura Omelette** bacon, potato and onion omelette

## K

**Kabeljau** cod
**Kaffee** coffee
  **Kaffee komplett** coffee with milk and sugar

**Kaffee mit Milch** coffee with milk

**Kaisermelange** black coffee with an egg yolk

**Kaiserschmarren** strips of pancake served with raisins, sugar and cinnamon

**Kakao** cocoa

**Kalb** veal

  **Kalbsbraten** roast veal

  **Kalbshaxe** knuckle of veal

  **Kalbskoteletts** veal cutlets

  **Kalbsleber** calf's liver

  **Kalbsschnitzel** veal escalope

**kalt** cold

  **kalte Platte** cold meat platter

**Kaninchen** rabbit

**Kapuziner** Austrian equivalent to a cappuccino which is black coffee with a drop of milk

**Karotten** carrots

**Karpfen** carp

  **Karpfen blau** poached carp

  **Karpfen in Bier** carp poached in beer with herbs

**Kartoffeln** potatoes

  **Kartoffelklöße** potato dumplings

  **Kartoffelpuffer** potato pancakes. A popular snack

  **Kartoffelpüree** mashed potatoes

  **Kartoffelsalat** potato salad

**Kartoffelsuppe** potato soup

**Käse** cheese

  **Käsebrötchen** roll with small bacon pieces in the dough and melted cheese on top

  **Käsefondue** dish made from melted cheese and flavoured with wine and kirsch into which you dip bread

  **Käsekuchen** cheesecake

  **Käsenudeln** noodles served with cheese

  **Käseplatte** cheese platter with various cheeses

  **Käsesuppe** cheese soup

**Kasseler** smoked pork

  **Kasseler Rippe mit Sauerkraut** smoked pork rib with sauerkraut

**Kastanienroulade** roulade with chestnut filling

**Katenspeck** streaky bacon

**Kaviar** caviar

**Kekse** biscuits

**Kirschen** cherries

**Kirschwasser** cherry schnapps

**Kirtagssuppe** soup with caraway seed thickened with potato

**Klops** rissole

**Klöße** dumplings

**Knackwurst** hot spicy sausage. A popular snack served with bread
**Knoblauch** garlic
**Knödel** dumpling
**Knödelbeignets** fruit dumplings
**Knöderl** dumplings
**Kohl** cabbage
**Kohlsprossen** Brussels sprouts
**Kölsch** top-fermented beer from Cologne
**Kompott** stewed fruit
**Königsberger Klopse** meatballs served in thick white sauce with capers
**Kopfsalat** lettuce salad
**Korn** rye spirit
**Kotelett** pork chop/cutlet dipped in breadcrumbs and deep fried
**Krabben** prawns
**Krabbencocktail** prawn cocktail
**Kraftbrot** wheatgerm bread
**Kraftfleisch** corned beef
**Kraftsuppe** consommé
**Krapfen** doughnut
**Kräutertee** herbal tea
**Krautwickerl** stuffed cabbage
**Kren** horseradish
**Kristallweizen** a kind of sparkling beer
**Kroketten** croquettes
**Kürbis** pumpkin

## L

**Labskaus** cured pork, herring and potato stew
**Lachs** salmon
**Lachsbrot** smoked salmon with bread
**Lamm** lamb
**Lammkeule** leg of lamb
**Lasagne** lasagne
**Lauch** leeks
**Leber** liver
**Leberkäse** pork liver meatloaf
**Leberknödelsuppe** light soup with chicken liver dumplings
**Leberpastete** liver paté
**Leberwurst** liver sausage
**Leinsamenbrot** wholemeal bread with linseed
**Leipziger Allerlei** vegetable dish made from peas, carrots, cauliflower and cabbage
**Likör** liqueur
**Limburger** strong cheese flavoured with herbs
**Limonade** lemonade
**Linsen** lentils
**Linsenspecksalat** lentil salad with bacon
**Linsensuppe** lentil and sausage soup
**Linzer Torte** latticed tart with jam topping
**Liptauer Quark** cream cheese with paprika and herbs
**Lunge** lungs

# M

**Mais** sweetcorn
**Maiskolben** corn on the cob
**Makrele** mackerel
**Malzbier** dark malt beer
**Mandarine** tangerine
**Marillenknödel** apricot
 dumplings
**Marmelade** jam
**Maronitorte** chestnut tart
**Märzenbier** stronger beer
 brewed for special occasions
**Mastochsenhaxe** knuckle of
 beef (with sauce) from
 Sachsen-Anhalt
**Matjes** herring
**Maultaschen** ravioli-like pasta
 filled with pork, veal and
 spinach mixture
**Meeresfrüchte** seafood
**Mehrkornbrötchen** rolls made
 with several kinds of whole-
 meal flour
**Melange** milky coffee
**Melone** melon
**Mettenden** sausage with a
 filling similar to mince
**Milch** milk
  **Milchrahmstrudel** strudel
  filled with egg custard and
  soft cheese
  **Milchshake** milk shake
**Mineralwasser** mineral water

**Mirabellen** small
 yellow plums
**Mischbrot** grey
 bread made with
 rye and wheat
 flour
**Mohn** poppy seed
  **Mohnnudeln** noodles with
  poppy seeds, cinnamon,
  sugar and butter
  **Mohntorte** gâteau with
  poppy seeds
**Möhren** carrots
  **Möhrensalat** carrot salad
**Mohr im Hemd** chocolate
 pudding
**Most** fruit juice; (in the south)
 fruit wine
**Münchener** a kind of dark
 lager from Munich
**Muscheln** mussels

# N

**Nachspeisen** desserts
**Nieren** kidneys
**Nierstein** village on the Rhine
 producing medium to sweet
 white Rheinwein
**Nockerln** small dumplings
**Nudeln** noodles
  **Nudelsuppe** noodle soup
**Nüsse** nuts
  **Nusskuchen** nut cake
  **Nusstorte** nut gâteau

### O

Obst fruit
Obstkuchen fruit cake
Obstsalat fruit salad
Ochsenschwanz oxtail
Ochsenschwanzsuppe oxtail soup
Öl oil
Oppenheim village on the Rhine producing fine white wines
Orange orange
Orangensaft orange juce

### P

Palatschinken pancakes filled with curd mixture or jam or ice cream
Pampelmuse grapefruit
paniert coated with breadcrumbs
Paprika peppers
Pellkartoffeln small jacket potatoes served with their skins, often accompanied by Quark
Pfannkuchen pancakes
Pfeffer pepper
Pfefferkäse mit Schinken ham and pepper cheese log
Pfifferlinge chanterelles
Pfirsich peach
Pflaumen plums
Pflaumenkuchen plum tart
Pils, Pilsner a strong, slightly bitter lager
Pilze mushrooms
Pilzsuppe mushroom soup
Pommes frites chips
Powidltascherl ravioli-like pasta filled with plum jam
Pumpernickel very dark bread made with wholemeal coarse rye flour
Punschpudding pudding containing alcohol
Pute turkey
Putenschnitzel turkey breast in breadcrumbs

### Q

Quark curd cheese

### R

Raclette melted cheese and potatoes
Ragout stew
Rahm sour cream
Rahmschnitzel cutlet with a creamy sauce
Rahmsuppe creamy soup
Räucherkäse mit Schinken smoked cheese with bacon pieces in it
Räucherkäse mit Walnüssen smoked cheese with pieces of walnut in it

Räucherlachs smoked salmon
Räucherspeck smoked bacon
Reh venison
  Rehrücken roast saddle of
  venison
Reibekuchen potato cakes
Reis rice
Riesling Riesling wine
  Rieslingsuppe wine soup
  made with Riesling
Rind(fleisch) beef
  Rinderbraten roast beef
  Rinderrouladen rolled beef
  (beef olives)
Rippenbraten roast spare ribs
Risi lisi, Risibisi rice with peas
Rollmops marinated herring
  fillets rolled up with small
  pieces of onion, gherkins and
  white peppercorns
Rosenkohl Brussels sprouts
Roséwein rosé wine
Rosinen raisins
Rösti fried diced potatoes,
  onions and bacon
Rotbarsch rosefish
rote Bete beetroot
rote Grütze raspberry, red
  currant and wine jelly served
  with fresh cream
rote Rübe beetroot
Rotkohl red cabbage
Rotwein red wine
Roulade beef olive
Rübe turnip

Rührei scrambled
  eggs

## S

Sachertorte rich
  chocolate gâteau
Saft juice
Sahne cream
Salat salad
Salz salt
Salzkartoffeln boiled potatoes
Sardellen anchovies
Sardinen sardines
Sauerbraten braised pickled
  beef served with dumplings
  and vegetables
Sauerkraut shredded pickled
  white cabbage
Scampi scampi
Schafskäse ewe's milk cheese
Schaschlik shish kebab
Schellfisch haddock
Schnaps strong spirit
Schinken ham
  Schinkenkipferl ham-filled
  croissant
  Schinkenwurst ham
  sausage
Schlachtplatte mixture of cold
  sausages and meat
Schmelzkäse cheese spread
Schmorgurken hotpot with
  cucumber and meat
Schnecke snail
Schnittlauch chives

**Schnittlauchbrot** chives on bread

**Schnitzel** escalope served with potatoes and vegetables

**Schokolade** chocolate

**Schokoladentorte** chocolate gateaux

**Scholle** plaice

**Schwäbischer Apfelkuchen** apple cake from Swabia

**Schwammerlgulasch** mushroom stew

**Schwarzbrot** rye bread

**schwarze Johannisbeeren** blackcurrants

**schwarzer Tee** black tea

**Schwarzwälder Kirschtorte** Black Forest gâteau

**Schwarzwälder Schinken** Black Forest ham

**Schwarzwälder Torte** fruit compote flan with cream

**Schwein** pork

**Schweinebraten** roast pork

**Schweinefleisch** pork

**Schweinehaxe** knuckle of pork

**Schweinekotelett** pork chop

**Schweinsrostbraten** roast pork

**Schwertfisch** swordfish

**Seezunge** sole

**Sekt** sparkling wine like champagne

**Selters(wasser)** sparkling mineral water

**Semmelknödel** whole roll dumpling

**Senf** mustard

**Sesam** sesame

**Scampi** scampi

**Slivovitz** plum schnapps

**Sonnenblumenbrot** wholemeal bread with sunflower seeds

**Soße** sauce

**Spanferkel** suckling pig

**Spargel** asparagus

**Spargelcremesuppe** cream of asparagus soup

**Spargelsalat** asparagus salad

**Spätzle** home-made noodles

**Speck** bacon (fat)

**Spiegelei** fried egg, sunny side up

**Spieß** kebab style

**Spinat** spinach

**Sprudel** sparkling mineral water

**Stachelbeeren** gooseberries

**Stachelbeertorte** gooseberry tart

**Stangl** croissant covered with cheese

**Starkbier** strong beer

**Steinbutt** turbot

**Steinpilze** wild mushroom found in the woods

**Steirischer Selchkäse** ewe's milk cheese

**Steirisches Lammkarree mit Basilikum** lamb baked with basil
**Sterz** Austrian polenta
**Stollen** spiced loaf with candied peel traditionally eaten at Christmas
**Strudel** strudel
**Sulz/Sülze** meat in aspic
**Suppen** soups
**süß** sweet
**süßsauer** sweet-and-sour

# T

**Tafelspitz** boiled beef of various cuts
**Tafelspitzsulz** beef in aspic
**Tagesgericht** dish of the day
**Tee** tea
  **Tee mit Milch** tea with milk
  **Tee mit Zitrone** tea with lemon
**Thunfisch** tuna fish
**Thüringer Rostbratwurst** sausages from Thuringia, grilled or fried
**Tilsiter** savoury cheese with sharpish taste
**Tintenfisch** squid
**Tomaten** tomatoes
  **Tomatensaft** tomato juice
  **Tomatensoße** tomato sauce
**Topf** stew
**Topfen** curd cheese (Austria)

**Topfenknödel** curd cheese dumplings
**Topfennudeln** pasta with cheese
**Topfenstrudel** flaky pastry strudel with curd-cheese filling
**Torte** gateau
**Trauben** grapes
  **Traubensaft** grape juice
**Truthahn** turkey
**Türkischer** Turkish coffee

# U

**überbacken** baked in the oven with cheese on top

# V

**Vollkorn-** wholemeal
**Vollkornbrot** wholemeal bread
**Vorspeisen** starters

# W

**Wacholder** juniper
**Waldpilze** wild mushrooms
**Walnüsse** walnuts
**warm** warm
  **warmer Krautsalat** salad with warm cabbage and crunchy bacon
**Wasser** water
**Weichkäse** cream cheese
**Wein** vine

107

**Weinbrand** brandy
**Weinkarte** wine list
**Weißbrot** wheat bread
**Weiße** golden wheat beer
**Weißkohl** white cabbage
**Weißwein** white wine
**Weißwurst** white sausage (veal and pork with herbs)
**Weizenbier** wheat beer
**Wels** catfish
**Westfälischer Schinken** Westphalian ham
**Wiener** frankfurters
**Wiener Backhendl** roast chicken in breadcrumbs
**Wiener Fischfilets** fish fillets baked in sour cream sauce
**Wiener Hofburgtorte** chocolate gâteau
**Wiener Kartoffelsuppe** potato soup with mushrooms
**Wiener Sachertorte** Viennese chocolate cake
**Wiener Schnitzel** veal escalope fried in breadcrumbs
**Wiener Würstchen** frankfurter
**Wild** game
**Wildbraten** roast venison
**Wildgulasch** game stew
**Wildschwein** wild boar
**Wirsingkohl** Savoy cabbage

**Wurst** sausage
**Würstchen** frankfurter
**Würzfleisch** strips of meat roasted in a spicy sauce

# Z

**Zander** pike-perch
**Ziegenkäse** goat's milk cheese
**Ziegett** mixed milk cheese
**Zigeunerschnitzel** cutlet in paprika sauce
**Zillertaler** cow's cheese from the Zillertal
**Zitrone** lemon
**Zitronentee** lemon tea
**Zopf** braided bread loaf
**Zucchini** courgette
**Zucker** sugar
**Zuger Köteli** baked dace with herbs and wine
**Zunge** tongue
**Zwetschgen** plums
**Zwetschgendatschi** damson tart
**Zwetschgenknödel** plum dumplings
**Zwiebeln** onions
**Zwiebelkuchen** onion flan
**Zwiebelrostbraten** large steak with onions
**Zwiebelsalami** salami with onion
**Zwiebelsuppe** onion soup

# A

a *(with der words)* ein
*(with die words)* eine
*(with das words)* ein

**abbey** die Abtei

**able: to be able** können

**abortion** die Abtreibung

**about** *(concerning)* über
*about 4 o'clock* ungefähr
vier Uhr

**above** *(overhead)* oben
*(higher than)* über

**abroad** im Ausland

**abscess** der Abszess

**accelerator** das Gaspedal

**to accept** akzeptieren

**accident** der Unfall

**accident and emergency
department** die
Notaufnahme

**accommodation** die
Unterkunft

**to accompany** begleiten

**account** *(bill)* die Rechnung
*(in bank)* das Konto

**account number** die
Kontonummer

**to ache: it aches** es tut weh

**acid** die Säure

**actor** der Schauspieler

**adaptor** der Zwischenstecker

**address** die Adresse
*what is the address?* wie
lautet die Adresse?

**address book** das
Adressbuch

**adhesive tape** das
Klebeband

**admission fee** der
Eintrittspreis

**adult** der/die Erwachsene
*for adults* für Erwachsene

**advance: in advance** im
Voraus

**advertisement** *(in paper)*
die Anzeige

**to advise** raten

**A&E** die Notaufnahme

**aeroplane** das Flugzeug

**aerosol** die Spraydose

**afraid: to be afraid of**
Angst haben vor

**after** *(afterwards)* danach
*after lunch* nach dem
Mittagessen

**afternoon** der Nachmittag
*this afternoon* heute
Nachmittag
*tomorrow afternoon*
morgen Nachmittag
*in the afternoon* am
Nachmittag

**aftershave** das Rasierwasser

**again** wieder

**against** gegen

**age** das Alter

**agency** die Agentur

**ago: a week ago** vor einer
Woche

**to agree** vereinbaren

**agreement** die
Vereinbarung

**AIDS** das Aids

# A

**airbag** der Airbag
**airbed** die Luftmatratze
**air conditioning** die Klimaanlage
**air freshener** der Lufterfrischer
**airline** die Fluggesellschaft
**air mail: by air mail** per Luftpost
**airplane** das Flugzeug
**airport** der Flughafen
**airport bus** der Flughafenbus
**air ticket** das Flugticket
**aisle** der Gang
**alarm** die Alarmanlage
**alarm call** der Weckruf
**alarm clock** der Wecker
**alcohol** der Alkohol
**alcohol-free** alkoholfrei
**alcoholic** alkoholisch
**all** alle
**allergic: to be allergic to** allergisch sein gegen
**I'm allergic to...** ich bin allergisch gegen...
**allergy** die Allergie
**to allow** erlauben
**to be allowed** dürfen
**all right** (agreed) in Ordnung
**are you all right?** geht es Ihnen gut?
**almost** fast
**alone** allein
**Alps** die Alpen
**already** schon

**also** auch
**altar** der Altar
**aluminium foil** die Alufolie
**always** immer
**a.m.** vormittags
**am: I am** ich bin
**amber** (traffic lights) das Gelb
**ambulance** der Krankenwagen
**America** Amerika
**American** adj amerikanisch m/f der/die Amerikaner(in)
**amount: total amount** die Gesamtsumme
**anaesthetic** die Narkose
**local anaesthetic** die örtliche Betäubung
**general anaesthetic** die Vollnarkose
**anchor** der Anker
**and** und
**angina** die Angina
**angry** zornig
**animal** das Tier
**ankle** der Knöchel
**anniversary** der Jahrestag
**to announce** bekannt geben
**announcement** die Bekanntmachung
**annual** jährlich
**another** (additional) noch ein/noch eine/noch ein (different) ein anderer/eine andere/ein anderes
**another beer please** noch ein Bier bitte

ENGLISH–GERMAN

**A**

**answer** die Antwort
**to answer** antworten
**answerphone** der Anrufbeantworter
**antacid** das säurebindende Mittel
**antibiotic** das Antibiotikum
**antifreeze** das Frostschutzmittel
**antihistamine** das Antihistamin
**anti-inflammatory** das entzündungs-hemmende Mittel
**antiques** die Antiquitäten
**antique shop** der Antiquitätenladen
**antiseptic** das Antiseptikum
**any** jegliche(r/s)
 *have you any apples?* haben Sie Äpfel?
**anybody** jeder
**anything** irgendetwas
**anywhere** irgendwo
**apartment** das Appartement
**appendicitis** die Blinddarmentzündung
**apple** der Apfel
**appointment** der Termin
 *I have an appointment* ich habe einen Termin
**approximately** ungefähr
**April** der April
**apron** die Schürze
**architect** der/die Architekt(in)

**are** sind ; seid ; bin
**arm** der Arm
**armbands** *(to swim)* die Schwimmflügel
**armchair** der Sessel
**to arrange** vereinbaren
**to arrest** verhaften
**arrival** die Ankunft
**to arrive** ankommen
**art** die Kunst
**art gallery** die Kunsthalle
**arthritis** die Arthritis
**artificial** künstlich
**artist** der/die Künstler(in)
**ashtray** der Aschenbecher
**to ask** *(question)* fragen
 *(for something)* bitten um
**asleep:** *to be asleep* schlafen
 *to fall asleep* einschlafen
**aspirin** das Aspirin
**asthma** das Asthma
 *I have asthma* ich habe Asthma
**at:** *at the hotel* im Hotel
 *at home* zu Hause
 *at 8 o'clock* um acht Uhr
 *at once* sofort
 *at night* am Abend
**to attack** angreifen
**attractive** attraktiv
**auction** die Auktion
**audience** das Publikum
**August** der August
**aunt** die Tante
**au pair** das Au-pair-Mädchen

ENGLISH–GERMAN

111

## A

**Australia** Australien
**Australian** adj australisch m/f der/die Australier(in)
**Austria** Österreich
**Austrian** adj österreichisch m/f der/die Österreicher(in)
**author** der/die Autor(in)
**automatic** automatisch
**automatic car** das Automatikauto
**auto-teller** der Geldautomat
**autumn** der Herbst
**available** erhältlich
**avalanche** die Lawine
**avenue** die Allee
**average** der Durchschnitt
**to avoid** (obstacle) ausweichen (person) meiden
**awake** wach
**away** weg
**awful** schrecklich
**axe** die Axt
**axle** (car) die Achse

## B

**baby** das Baby
**baby food** die Babynahrung
**baby milk** die Babymilch
**baby's bottle** die Babyflasche
**baby seat** (in car) der Kindersitz

**babysitter** der/die Babysitter(in)
**baby wipes** die Babytücher
**back** (of body, hand) der Rücken
**backpack** der Rucksack
**bacon** der Speck
**bad** (weather, news) schlecht (fruit, vegetables) verdorben
**bag** die Tasche
**baggage** das Gepäck
**baggage allowance** das Freigepäck
**baggage reclaim** die Gepäckausgabe
**bait** (for fishing) der Köder
**baked** gebacken
**baker's** die Bäckerei
**balcony** der Balkon
**ball** der Ball
**ballet** das Ballett
**balloon** der Ballon
**Baltic Sea** die Ostsee
**banana** die Banane
**band** (musical) die Band
**bandage** der Verband
**bank** die Bank (river) das Ufer
**bank account** das Bankkonto
**banknote** der Geldschein
**bar** die Bar
**barbecue** der Grill *to have a barbecue* eine Grillparty geben
**barber** der Herrenfriseur

**to bark** bellen

**barn** die Scheune

**basement** das Souterrain

**basket** der Korb

**basketball** der Basketball

**Basle** Basel

**bat** *(racquet)* der Schläger

**bath** das Bad
  **to have a bath** ein Bad nehmen

**bathing cap** die Badekappe

**bathroom** das Badezimmer
  **with bathroom** mit Bad

**battery** die Batterie

**bay** *(along coast)* die Bucht

**B&B** Übernachtung mit Frühstück

**to be** sein

**beach** der Strand
  **private beach** der Privatstrand
  **sandy beach** der Sandstrand
  **nudist beach** der FKK-Strand

**beach hut** der Strandkorb

**beans** die Bohnen

**beard** der Bart

**beautiful** schön

**because** weil

**to become** werden

**bed** das Bett
  **double bed** das Doppelbett
  **single bed** das Einzelbett
  **twin beds** zwei Einzelbetten

**bed and breakfast** Übernachtung mit Frühstück

**bedclothes** die Bettwäsche

**bedroom** das Schlafzimmer

**bee** die Biene

**beef** das Rindfleisch

**beer** das Bier

**before** vor
  **before breakfast** vor dem Frühstück

**to begin** beginnen

**behind** hinter

**beige** beige

**to believe** glauben

**bell** *(church)* die Glocke
  *(door)* die Klingel

**to belong to** gehören zu

**below** unterhalb

**belt** der Gürtel

**bend** *(in road)* die Kurve

**berth** *(train, ship)* die Kabine

**beside** *(next to)* neben

**best: the best** der/die/das beste

**bet** die Wette

**to bet on** wetten auf

**better** besser
  **better than** besser als

**between** zwischen

**bib** *(baby's)* das Lätzchen

**bicycle** das Fahrrad
  **by bicycle** mit dem Fahrrad

**bicycle repair kit** das Fahrradflickzeug

**B**

**big** groß
  *bigger than* größer als
**bike** *(push bike)* das Fahrrad
  *(motorbike)* das Motorrad
**bike lock** das Fahrradschloss
**bikini** der Bikini
**bill** *(account)* die Rechnung
**bin** *(dustbin)* der Mülleimer
**bin liner** der Müllbeutel
**binoculars** das Fernglas
**bird** der Vogel
**biro** der Kugelschreiber
**birth** die Geburt
**birth certificate** die
  Geburtsurkunde
**birthday** der Geburtstag
  *happy birthday!* alles
  Gute zum Geburtstag!
  *my birthday is on...* ich
  habe am ... Geburtstag
**birthday card** die
  Geburtstagskarte
**birthday present** das
  Geburtstagsgeschenk
**biscuits** die Kekse
**bit** *(piece)* das Stück
  *a bit (a little)* ein bisschen
**bite** *(by insect)* der Biss
  *(of food)* der Bissen
**to bite** beißen
  *(insect)* stechen
**bitten** *(by insect)* gestochen
  *I've been bitten* ich bin
  gestochen worden
**bitter** *(taste)* bitter
**black** schwarz

**black ice** das Glatteis
**blanket** die Decke
**bleach** das Bleichmittel
**to bleed** bluten
**blender** der Mixer
**blind** *(person)* blind
**blind** *(for window)* das Rollo
**blister** die Blase
**blocked** *(pipe, road)*
  verstopft
**blond** *(person)* blond
**blood** das Blut
**blood group** die
  Blutgruppe
**blood pressure** der
  Blutdruck
**blood test** der Bluttest
**blouse** die Bluse
**to blow-dry** föhnen
**blue** blau
  *dark blue* dunkelblau
  *light blue* hellblau
**blunt** *(knife, blade)* stumpf
**boar** das Wildschwein
**to board** *(plane, train, etc)*
  einsteigen
**boarding card/pass** die
  Bordkarte
**boarding house** die
  Pension
**boat** *(large)* das Schiff
  *(small)* das Boot
**boat trip** die Bootsfahrt
**body** der Körper
  *(dead)* die Leiche
**to boil** kochen

**boiled** gekocht
**boiler** der Boiler
**bomb** die Bombe
**bone** der Knochen
  *fish bone* die Gräte
**bonfire** das Feuerwerk
**bonnet** *(car)* die
  Motorhaube
**book** das Buch
  *book of tickets* die
  Mehrfahrtenkarte
**to book** buchen
**booking** *(in hotel, train, etc)*
  die Reservierung
**booking office** *(train)* der
  Fahrkartenschalter
**bookshop** die
  Buchhandlung
**boot** *(car)* der Kofferraum
**boots** *(long)* die Stiefel
  *(ankle)* die Schnürschuhe
**border** *(country)* die Grenze
**boring** langweilig
**born: I was born in 1960**
  ich bin neunzehn-
  hundertsechzig geboren
**to borrow** borgen
**boss** der/die Chef(in)
**both** beide
**bottle** die Flasche
  *a bottle of wine* eine
  Flasche Wein
  *a half-bottle* eine kleine
  Flasche
**bottle opener** der
  Flaschenöffner
**bowl** *(soup, etc)* die Schüssel

**bow tie** die Fliege
**box** *(of wood)* die Kiste
  *(of cardboard)* der Karton
**box office** die Kasse
**boy** der Junge
**boyfriend** der Freund
**bra** der BH
**bracelet** das Armband
**to brake** bremsen
**brake fluid** die
  Bremsflüssigkeit
**brake light** das Bremslicht
**brake pads** die Bremsbeläge
**brakes** die Bremsen
**branch** *(of tree)* der Ast
  *(of bank, etc)* die Filiale
**brand** *(make)* die Marke
**brass** das Messing
**brave** mutig
**bread** das Brot
  *brown bread* das
  Schwarzbrot
  *French bread* das
  Baguette
  *sliced bread*
  geschnittenes Brot
  *white bread* das Weißbrot
**bread roll** das Brötchen
**to break** *(object)* zerbrechen
**breakable** zerbrechlich
**breakdown** *(car)* die Panne
**breakdown van** die
  Pannenhilfe
**breakfast** das Frühstück
  *when is breakfast?* wann
  gibt es Frühstück?

**B**

**breast** die Brust
**to breast-feed** stillen
**to breathe** atmen
**brick** der Ziegel
**bride** die Braut
**bridegroom** der Bräutigam
**bridge** die Brücke
**briefcase** die Aktentasche
**to bring** bringen
**Britain** Großbritannien
**British** britisch
**brochure** die Broschüre
**broken** gebrochen
**broken down** (car, etc) kaputt
**bronchitis** die Bronchitis
**bronze** die Bronze
**brooch** die Brosche
**broom** der Besen
**brother** der Bruder
**brother-in-law** der Schwager
**brown** braun
**bruise** der Bluterguss
**brush** die Bürste
  (for floor) der Besen
**bubble bath** das Schaumbad
**bucket** der Eimer
**buffet car** der Speisewagen
**to build** bauen
**building** das Gebäude
**bulb** (electric) die Glühbirne
**bumbag** die Gürteltasche
**bumper** die Stoßstange

**bunch** (flowers) der Blumenstrauß
  (grapes) die Weintraube
**bureau de change** die Wechselstube
**burger** der Hamburger
**burglar** der/die Einbrecher(in)
**burn** die Brandwunde
**to burn** verbrennen
**bus** der Bus
**bus station** der Busbahnhof
**bus stop** die Bushaltestelle
**bus ticket** der Busfahrschein
**bus tour** die Busfahrt
**business** das Geschäft
  *on business* geschäftlich
**business address** die Geschäftsadresse
**business card** die Visitenkarte
**businessman/woman** der Geschäftsmann/ die Geschäftsfrau
**business trip** die Dienstreise
**busy** beschäftigt
**but** aber
**butcher's** die Fleischerei
**butter** die Butter
**button** der Knopf
**to buy** kaufen
**by** (beside) bei
  (via) über
  *by bus* mit dem Bus
  *by car* mit dem Auto

**by ship** mit dem Schiff
**by train** mit dem Zug
**bypass** die Umgehungsstraße

# C

**cab** (taxi) das Taxi
**cabaret** das Varieté
**cabin** (on ship) die Kabine
**cabin crew** die Besatzung
**cable car** die Seilbahn
**café** das Café
  **internet café** das Internet-Café
**cake** der Kuchen
**cake shop** die Konditorei
**calculator** der Taschenrechner
**calendar** der Kalender
**call** (on phone) der Anruf
**to call** (on phone) anrufen
**calm** (person) ruhig
  (weather) windstill
**camcorder** der Camcorder
**camera** die Kamera
**camera shop** das Fotogeschäft
**to camp** campen
**camping gas** das Campinggas
**camping stove** der Campingkocher
**campsite** der Campingplatz
**can** die Dose
**can opener** der Dosenöffner

**can** (to be able) können
  **I can/we can** ich kann/wir können
**Canada** Kanada
**Canadian** adj kanadisch
  m/f der/die Kanadier(in)
**canal** der Kanal
**to cancel** stornieren
**cancellation** die Stornierung
**cancer** der Krebs
**candle** die Kerze
**canoe** das Kanu
**cap** (hat) die Mütze
  (diaphragm) das Pessar
**capital** (city) die Hauptstadt
**car** das Auto
**car alarm** die Autoalarmanlage
**car ferry** die Autofähre
**car hire** die Autovermietung
**car insurance** die Kfz-Versicherung
**car keys** die Autoschlüssel
**car park** der Parkplatz
**car parts** die Ersatzteile
**car radio** das Autoradio
**car seat** (children's) der Kindersitz
**car wash** die Waschanlage
**caravan** der Wohnwagen
**carburettor** der Vergaser
**card** (greetings) die (Glückwunsch)karte
  (playing) die Spielkarte
**cardboard** die Pappe
**cardigan** die Strickjacke

# C

careful vorsichtig
**be careful!** passen Sie auf!

carpet der Teppich

carriage (railway) der Wagen

carrot die Karotte

**to carry** tragen

carton der Karton

case (suitcase) der Koffer

cash das Bargeld

**to cash** (cheque) einlösen

cash desk die Kasse

cash dispenser der Geldautomat

cashier der/die Kassierer(in)

cashpoint der Geldautomat

casino das Kasino

casserole dish die Kasserolle

cassette die Kassette

cassette player der Kassettenrekorder

castle das Schloss
(medieval fortress) die Burg

casualty department die Unfallstation

cat die Katze

cat food das Katzenfutter

catalogue der Katalog

**to catch** (bus, train) nehmen

cathedral der Dom

Catholic katholisch

cave die Höhle

cavity (in tooth) das Loch

CD die CD

CD player der CD-Spieler

ceiling die Decke

cellar der Keller

cellphone das Handy

cemetery der Friedhof

centimetre der Zentimeter

central zentral

central heating die Zentralheizung

central locking (car) die Zentralverriegelung

centre das Zentrum

century das Jahrhundert

ceramic die Keramik

cereal (breakfast) die Cornflakes

certain (sure) sicher

certificate die Bescheinigung

chain die Kette

chair der Stuhl

chairlift der Sessellift

chambermaid das Zimmermädchen

champagne der Champagner

change (money) das Wechselgeld

**to change** (to alter) ändern
(bus, train, etc) umsteigen
**to change money** Geld wechseln
**to change clothes** sich umziehen

changing room die Umkleidekabine

Channel (English) der Kanal

chapel die Kapelle

charcoal die Holzkohle

charge (fee) die Gebühr

**to charge** berechnen
*please charge it to my account* bitte setzen Sie es auf meine Rechnung
**charger** *(for battery, etc)* das Ladegerät
**charter flight** der Charterflug
**cheap** billig
**cheap rate** der Billigtarif
**to check** überprüfen *(passports)* kontrollieren
**to check in** einchecken *(at hotel)* sich an der Rezeption anmelden
**check-in** der Check-in
**cheers!** *(toast)* Prost!
**cheese** der Käse
**chef** der Koch/die Köchin
**chemical toilet** die chemische Toilette
**chemist's** die Drogerie *(for medicines)* die Apotheke
**cheque** der Scheck
**cheque book** das Scheckheft
**cheque card** die Scheckkarte
**chest** *(body)* die Brust
**chewing gum** der Kaugummi
**chicken** das Hühnchen
**chickenpox** die Windpocken
**child** das Kind
**children** die Kinder
*for children* für Kinder
**chimney** der Schornstein

**chin** das Kinn
**china** das Porzellan
**chips** *(french fries)* die Pommes frites
**chocolate** die Schokolade
**chocolates** die Pralinen
**choir** der Chor
**to choose** auswählen
**chopping board** das Küchenbrett
**Christian name** der Vorname
**Christmas** Weihnachten
*merry Christmas!* frohe Weihnachten!
**Christmas card** die Weihnachtskarte
**Christmas Eve** Heiligabend
**church** die Kirche
**cigar** die Zigarre
**cigarette** die Zigarette
**cigarette lighter** das Feuerzeug
**cigarette papers** das Zigarettenpapier
**cinema** das Kino
**circle** *(theatre)* der Rang
**circuit breaker** der Unterbrecher
**cistern** *(of toilet)* der Spülkasten
**city** die Stadt
**city centre** das Stadtzentrum
**class: first class** erste Klasse

**C**

second class zweite Klasse

**clean** sauber

**to clean** säubern

**cleaning lady** die Putzfrau

**clear** klar

**client** der Kunde/die Kundin

**cliff** (along coast) die Klippe (in mountains) der Felsen

**to climb** (mountains) klettern

**climbing boots** die Bergschuhe

**clingfilm®** die Frischhaltefolie

**clinic** die Klinik

**cloakroom** die Garderobe

**clock** die Uhr

**to close** schließen

**closed** geschlossen

**cloth** (rag) der Lappen (fabric) der Stoff

**clothes** die Kleider

**clothes line** die Wäscheleine

**clothes peg** die Wäscheklammer

**clothes shop** das Bekleidungsgeschäft

**cloudy** bewölkt

**club** der Club

**clutch** (car) die Kupplung

**coach** (bus) der Bus

**coach station** der Busbahnhof

**coach trip** die Busreise

**coal** die Kohle

**coast** die Küste

**coastguard** die Küstenwache

**coat** der Mantel

**coat hanger** der Kleiderbügel

**cockroach** die Kakerlake

**cocoa** der Kakao

**code** der Kode

**coffee** der Kaffee
*black coffee* schwarzer Kaffee
*white coffee* Kaffee mit Milch
*decaffeinated coffee* koffeinfreier Kaffee

**coil** (IUD) die Spirale

**coin** die Münze

**Coke®** die Cola

**colander** das Sieb

**cold** kalt
*I'm cold* mir ist kalt
*it's cold* es ist kalt

**cold** (illness) die Erkältung
*I have a cold* ich habe mich erkältet

**cold sore** der Ausschlag

**collar** der Kragen

**collar bone** das Schlüsselbein

**colleague** der Kollege/die Kollegin

**to collect** (person) abholen (something) (etwas) sammeln

**collection** die Sammlung

**Cologne** Köln

**colour** die Farbe

**colour-blind** farbenblind

**colour film** der Farbfilm

**comb** der Kamm

**to come** kommen
*(to arrive)* ankommen

**to come back** zurückkommen

**to come in** hereinkommen
*come in!* herein!

**comedy** die Komödie

**comfortable** bequem

**company** *(firm)* die Firma

**compartment** *(in train)* das Abteil

**compass** der Kompass

**to complain** sich beschweren

**complaint** die Klage

**complete** vollständig

**to complete** vervollständigen

**compulsory** obligatorisch

**computer** der Computer

**computer disk** *(floppy)* die Diskette

**computer game** das Computerspiel

**computer program** das Computerprogramm

**concert** das Konzert

**concert hall** die Konzerthalle

**concession** die Ermäßigung

**concussion** die Gehirnerschütterung

**conditioner** *(hair)* der Conditioner

**condom** das Kondom

**conductor** der Schaffner/ die Schaffnerin

**conference** die Konferenz

**to confirm** bestätigen
*please confirm* bitte bestätigen Sie

**confirmation** *(flight, etc)* die Bestätigung

**confused** verwirrt

**congratulations!** herzlichen Glückwunsch!

**connection** *(train, etc)* die Verbindung

**constipated** verstopft

**consulate** das Konsulat

**to contact** kontaktieren

**contact lens cleaner** der Kontaktlinsenreiniger

**contact lenses** die Kontaktlinsen

**to continue** weitermachen

**contraceptive** das Verhütungsmittel

**contract** der Vertrag

**convenient: is it convenient?** passt es so?

**convulsions** die Krämpfe

**to cook** kochen

**cooked** gekocht

**cooker** der Herd

**cookies** die Kekse

**cool** kühl

**cool-box** *(for picnic)* die Kühlbox

**copy** *(duplicate)* die Kopie

**C**

to **copy** kopieren

**cork** der Korken

**corkscrew** der Korkenzieher

**corner** die Ecke

**cornflakes** die Cornflakes

**corridor** der Flur

**cosmetics** die Kosmetikartikel

**cost** (price) die Kosten

to **cost** kosten
  *how much does it cost?*
  wie viel kostet es?

**costume** (swimming) der Badeanzug

**cot** das Kinderbett

**cottage** das Ferienhäuschen

**cotton** die Baumwolle

**cotton bud** der Wattebausch

**cotton wool** die Watte

**couchette** der Liegewagen

**cough** der Husten

to **cough** husten

**cough sweets** die Hustenbonbons

**counter** (shop, bar) die Theke

**country** das Land

**countryside** die Landschaft

**couple** (two people) das Paar
  *a couple of...* ein paar...

**courier service** der Kurierdienst

**course** (of study) der Kurs
  (of meal) der Gang

**cousin** der Cousin/die Cousine

**cover charge** (in restaurant) die Gedeckkosten

**cow** die Kuh

**crafts** die Kunstgewerbearbeiten

**craftsperson** der Handwerker/die Handwerkerin

**cramps** die Krämpfe

**crash** (collision) der Zusammenstoß

to **crash** einen Unfall haben

**crash helmet** der Sturzhelm

**cream** (lotion) die Creme
  (on milk) die Sahne
  *soured cream* saure Sahne
  *whipped cream* Schlagsahne

**credit card** die Kreditkarte

**crime** das Verbrechen

**crisps** die Chips

to **cross** (road) überqueren

**cross-channel ferry** die Kanalfähre

**cross-country skiing** der Skilanglauf

**crossing** (sea) die Überfahrt

**crossroads** die Kreuzung

**crossword puzzle** das Kreuzworträtsel

**crowd** die Menge

**crowded** überfüllt

**crown** die Krone

**cruise** die Kreuzfahrt

**crutches** die Krücken

to **cry** (weep) weinen

**crystal** das Kristall

**cucumber** die Gurke
**cufflinks** die Manschettenknöpfe
**cul-de-sac** die Sackgasse
**cup** die Tasse
**cupboard** der Schrank
**curlers** die Lockenwickler
**currency** die Währung
**current** *(electric)* der Strom
*(water)* die Strömung
**curtains** die Vorhänge
**cushion** das Kissen
**custom** *(tradition)* der Brauch
**customer** der Kunde/die Kundin
**customs** *(duty)* der Zoll
**cut** die Schnittwunde
**to cut** schneiden
**cutlery** das Besteck
**cutlet** das Schnitzel
**to cycle** Rad fahren
**cycle track** der Radweg
**cycling** das Radfahren
**cyst** die Zyste
**cystitis** die Blasenentzündung

# D

**daily** *(each day)* täglich
**dairy products** die Milchprodukte
**dam** der Damm
**damage** der Schaden
**damp** feucht
**dance** der Tanz

**to dance** tanzen
**danger** die Gefahr
**dangerous** gefährlich
**dark** dunkel
*after dark* nach Einbruch der Dunkelheit
**date** das Datum
**date of birth** das Geburtsdatum
**daughter** die Tochter
**daughter-in-law** die Schwiegertochter
**dawn** die Morgendämmerung
**day** der Tag
*every day* jeden Tag
*per day* pro Tag
**dead** tot
**deaf** taub
**dear** *(in letter)* liebe(r/s)
*(expensive)* teuer
**debts** die Schulden
**decaffeinated coffee** der koffeinfreie Kaffee
**December** der Dezember
**deckchair** der Liegestuhl
**to declare** erklären
*nothing to declare* nichts zu verzollen
**deep** tief
**deep freeze** die Tiefkühltruhe
**deer** das Reh
**to defrost** entfrosten
**to de-ice** enteisen
**delay** die Verspätung

**D**

**delayed** verspätet

**delicatessen** das Feinkostgeschäft

**delicious** köstlich

**demonstration** die Demonstration

**dental floss** die Zahnseide

**dentist** der Zahnarzt/die Zahnärztin

**dentures** das Gebiss

**deodorant** das Deo

**to depart** abfahren

**department** die Abteilung

**department store** das Kaufhaus

**departure** die Abfahrt *(plane)* der Abflug

**departure lounge** die Abflughalle

**deposit** die Anzahlung

**to describe** beschreiben

**description** die Beschreibung

**desk** der Schreibtisch

**dessert** der Nachtisch

**details** die Details

**detergent** das Waschmittel

**detour** der Umweg

**to develop** *(photos)* entwickeln

**diabetes** der Diabetes

**diabetic person** der Diabetiker/die Diabetikerin

**to dial** wählen

**dialling code** die Vorwahl

**dialling tone** der Wählton

**diamond** der Diamant

**diarrhoea** der Durchfall

**diapers** die Windeln

**diaphragm** *(contraception)* das Pessar

**diary** der Terminkalender

**dice** der Würfel

**dictionary** das Wörterbuch

**to die** sterben

**diesel** der Diesel

**diet** die Diät
*I'm on a diet* ich muss eine Diät einhalten
*special diet* spezielle Diät

**different** verschieden

**difficult** schwierig

**to dilute** verdünnen

**dinghy** *(rubber)* das Schlauchboot

**dining room** das Esszimmer

**dinner** *(evening meal)* das Abendessen
*to have dinner* zu Abend essen

**diplomat** der Diplomat/die Diplomatin

**direct** *(route)* direkt
*(train, etc)* durchgehend

**directions: to ask for directions** nach dem Weg fragen

**directory** *(phone)* das Telefonbuch

**directory enquiries** die Auskunft

**dirty** schmutzig
**disability** die Behinderung
**disabled** *(person)* behindert
**to disagree** nicht zustimmen
**to disappear** verschwinden
**disco** die Disko
**discount** der Rabatt
**to discover** entdecken
**disease** die Krankheit
**dish** die Schale
*(food)* das Gericht
**dishtowel** das Geschirrtuch
**dishwasher** die Geschirrspülmaschine
**disinfectant** das Desinfektionsmittel
**disk** die Diskette
**to dislocate** auskugeln
**disposable** wegwerfbar
**distance** die Entfernung
**distilled water** das destillierte Wasser
**district** der Bezirk
**to disturb** stören
**to dive** tauchen
**diversion** die Umleitung
**diving** das Tauchen
**divorced** geschieden
**DIY shop** der Baumarkt
**dizzy** schwindelig
**to do** machen
**doctor** der Arzt/die Ärztin
**documents** die Dokumente
**dog** der Hund

**dog food** das Hundefutter
**dog lead** die Hundeleine
**doll** die Puppe
**dollar** der Dollar
**domestic** *(flight)* Inlands-
**donor card** der Organspenderausweis
**door** die Tür
**doorbell** die Klingel
**double** Doppel-
**double bed** das Doppelbett
**double room** das Doppelzimmer
**doughnut** der Berliner
**down: to go down** nach unten gehen
**downstairs** unten
**drain** der Abfluss
**draught** *(of air)* der Durchzug
*there's a draught* hier zieht es
**draught lager** das Fassbier
**drawer** die Schublade
**drawing** die Zeichnung
**dress** das Kleid
**to dress** *(get dressed)* sich anziehen
**dressing** *(for food)* die Soße
*(for wound)* das Verbandsmaterial
**dressing gown** der Morgenmantel
**drill** *(tool)* der Bohrer
**drink** das Getränk
**to drink** trinken

125

**D**

**drinking water** das Trinkwasser

**to drive** fahren

**driver** *(of car)* der Fahrer/die Fahrerin

**driving licence** der Führerschein

**to drown** ertrinken

**drug** das Medikament *(narcotic)* die Droge

**drunk** betrunken

**dry** trocken

**to dry** trocknen

**dry cleaner's** die Reinigung

**dryer** der Wäschetrockner

**due: when's it due?** wann soll er ankommen?

**dummy** *(for baby)* der Schnuller

**during** während

**dust** der Staub

**duster** das Staubtuch

**dustpan and brush** Schaufel und Handfeger

**duty-free** zollfrei

**duvet** die Bettdecke

**duvet cover** der Bettbezug

**to dye** färben

**dynamo** die Lichtmaschine

**E**

**each** jede(r/s)

**ear** das Ohr

**earache** die Ohrenschmerzen

*I have earache* ich habe Ohrenschmerzen

**earlier** früher

**early** früh

**to earn** verdienen

**earphones** die Kopfhörer

**earrings** die Ohrringe

**earth** die Erde

**earthquake** das Erdbeben

**east** der Osten

**Easter** Ostern

**easy** leicht

**to eat** essen

**economy class** die Touristenklasse

**egg** das Ei
*fried egg* das Spiegelei
*hard-boiled egg* das hart gekochte Ei
*scrambled egg* das Rührei
*soft-boiled egg* das weich gekochte Ei

**either ... or** entweder ... oder

**elastic band** das Gummiband

**Elastoplast®** das Pflaster

**elbow** der Ellbogen

**electric** elektrisch

**electric blanket** die Wärmedecke

**electric razor** der Elektrorasierer

**electric shock** der elektrische Schlag

**electrician** der Elektriker

**electricity meter** der Stromzähler

**elevator** der Fahrstuhl

**e-mail** die E-Mail

**to e-mail** e-mailen

**e-mail address** die E-Mail-Adresse

**embassy** die Botschaft

**emergency** der Notfall

**emergency exit** der Notausgang

**emery board** die Nagelfeile

**empty** leer

**end** das Ende

**engaged** (to marry) verlobt (toilet, telephone) besetzt

**engine** der Motor

**engineer** der Ingenieur/die Ingenieurin

**England** England

**English** adj englisch

**Englishman/woman** der Engländer/die Engländerin

**to enjoy** (to like) mögen *enjoy your meal!* guten Appetit!

**enough** genug *that's enough* das reicht

**enquiry desk** die Auskunft

**to enter** eintreten

**entertainment** das Entertainment

**entrance** der Eingang

**entrance fee** der Eintrittpreis

**envelope** der Umschlag

**epileptic** der Epileptiker/die Epileptikerin

**epileptic fit** der epileptische Anfall

**equal** gleich

**equipment** die Ausrüstung

**eraser** der Radiergummi

**error** der Fehler

**escalator** die Rolltreppe

**to escape** entkommen

**essential** wesentlich

**estate agent's** der Grundstücksmakler

**euro** der Euro

**Europe** Europa

**European** europäisch

**European Union** die Europäische Union

**evening** der Abend *this evening* heute Abend *tomorrow evening* morgen Abend *in the evening* am Abend

**evening dress** das Abendkleid

**evening meal** das Abendessen

**every** (each) jede(r/s)

**everyone** jeder

**everything** alles

**everywhere** überall

**examination** *(medical)* die Untersuchung *(school)* die Prüfung

**example: for example** zum Beispiel

**excellent** ausgezeichnet

**except** außer

**excess baggage** das Übergewicht

**exchange** der Austausch

**to exchange** tauschen *(money)* wechseln

**exchange rate** der Wechselkurs

**exciting** aufregend

**excursion** der Ausflug

**excuse me!** *(sorry)* Entschuldigung!!

**exhaust** der Auspuff

**exhibition** die Ausstellung

**exit** der Ausgang

**expense Account** das Spesenkonto

**expenses** die Spesen

**expensive** teuer

**expert** der Experte/die Expertin

**to expire** *(ticket, etc)* ungültig werden

**to explain** erklären

**explanation** die Erklärung

**explosion** die Explosion

**export** der Export

**to export** exportieren

**express** *(train)* der Schnellzug

**express** *(parcel, etc)* per Express

**extension lead** das Verlängerungskabel

**extra** *(spare)* übrig *(more)* noch ein(e) **an extra towel** ein zusätzliches Handtuch

**eye** das Auge

**eyebrows** die Augenbrauen

**eye drops** die Augentropfen

**eye liner** der Eyeliner

**eye shadow** der Lidschatten

# F

**fabric** der Stoff

**face** das Gesicht

**face cloth** der Waschlappen

**facial** die Gesichtspflege

**facilities** die Einrichtungen

**factory** die Fabrik

**to faint** ohnmächtig werden

**fainted** ohnmächtig

**fair** *(hair)* blond *(just)* gerecht

**fair** *(trade fair)* die Messe *(funfair)* die Kirmes

**fake** unecht

**fall** *(autumn)* der Herbst

**to fall** fallen **I have fallen** ich bin hingefallen

**false teeth** das Gebiss

**family** die Familie

**famous** berühmt

**fan** *(electric)* der Ventilator
*(football, music)* der Fan

**fan belt** der Keilriemen

**fancy dress** die Verkleidung

**far** weit
*how far is it?* wie weit ist es?

**fare** *(train, bus, etc)* der Fahrpreis

**farm** der Bauernhof

**farmer** der Bauer/die Bäuerin

**farmhouse** das Bauernhaus

**fashionable** modern

**fast** schnell
*too fast* zu schnell

**to fasten:** *to fasten the seatbelt* sich anschnallen

**fat** *(big)* dick

**fat** das Fett
*saturated fat* gesättigte Fettsäuren
*unsaturated fat* ungesättigte Fettsäuren

**father** der Vater

**father-in-law** der Schwiegervater

**fault** *(defect)* der Fehler
*it wasn't my fault* das war nicht meine Schuld

**favour** der Gefallen

**favourite** Lieblings-

**fax** das Fax
*by fax* per Fax

**to fax** faxen

**fax number** die Faxnummer

**February** der Februar

**to feed** füttern

**feeding bottle** die Babyflasche

**to feel** fühlen
*I don't feel well* ich fühle mich nicht wohl
*I feel sick* mir ist schlecht

**feet** die Füße

**female** weiblich

**ferry** die Fähre

**festival** das Fest

**to fetch** *(bring)* holen

**fever** das Fieber

**few:** *a few* ein paar

**fiancé(e)** der/die Verlobte

**field** das Feld

**to fight** kämpfen

**file** *(nail)* die Feile
*(computer)* die Datei
*(for papers)* der Ordner

**to fill** füllen

**to fill in** *(form)* ausfüllen

**to fill up** *(tank)* voll tanken

**fillet** das Filet

**filling** *(in tooth)* die Plombe

**film** der Film

**Filofax®** der Terminkalender

**filter** der Filter

**to find** finden

**fine** *(to be paid)* die Geldstrafe

**finger** der Finger

**to finish** beenden

**F**

**fire** das Feuer
**fire alarm** der Feuermelder
**fire brigade** die Feuerwehr
**fire engine** das Feuerwehrauto
**fire escape** die Feuertreppe
**fire exit** der Notausgang
**fire extinguisher** der Feuerlöscher
**fireplace** der Kamin
**fireworks** das Feuerwerk
**firm** (company) die Firma
**first** erste(r/s)
**first aid** die erste Hilfe
**first class** (travel) erste Klasse
**first name** der Vorname
**fish** der Fisch
**to fish** angeln
**fishing permit** der Angelschein
**fishing rod** die Angel
**fishmonger's** die Fischhandlung
**fit** (seizure) der Anfall
**to fit** passen
  *it doesn't fit* es passt nicht
**to fix** reparieren
  *can you fix it?* können Sie es reparieren?
**fizzy** sprudelnd
**flag** die Fahne

**flames** die Flammen
**flash** das Blitzlicht
**flashlight** die Taschenlampe
**flask** (thermos) die Thermosflasche
**flat** (level) flach
**flat** die Wohnung
**flat battery** die leere Batterie
**flat tyre** die Reifenpanne
**flavour** der Geschmack
  *what flavour?* welchen Geschmack?
**flaw** der Mangel
**fleas** die Flöhe
**flesh** das Fleisch
**flex** die Verlängerungsschnur
**flight** der Flug
**flip-flops** die Badelatschen
**flippers** die Schwimmflossen
**flood** die Flut
  *flash flood* die Überschwemmung
**floor** (of building) die Etage
  (of room) der Boden
  *which floor?* auf welcher Etage?
  *on the ground floor* im Erdgeschoss
  *on the first floor* in der ersten Etage
**floorcloth** der Scheuerlappen
**flour** das Mehl

**flowers** die Blumen
**flu** die Grippe
**fly** die Fliege
**to fly** fliegen
**fly sheet** das Überzelt
**fog** der Nebel
**foggy** neblig
**foil** die Folie
**to fold** falten
**to follow** folgen
**food** das Essen
**food poisoning** die Lebensmittelvergiftung
**foot** der Fuß
  *on foot* zu Fuß
**football** der Fußball
**football match** das Fußballspiel
**football player** der Fußballer
**footpath** der Fußweg
**for** für
  *for me* für mich
  *for him/her* für ihn/sie
**forbidden** verboten
**forehead** die Stirn
**foreign** ausländisch
**foreigner** der Ausländer/die Ausländerin
**forest** der Wald
**forever** für immer
**to forget** vergessen
**fork** *(for eating)* die Gabel
  *(in road)* die Gabelung
**form** *(document)* das Formular

**fortnight** zwei Wochen
**forward** vorwärts
**fountain** der Brunnen
**fox** der Fuchs
**fracture** der Bruch
**fragile** zerbrechlich
**fragrance** das Parfüm
**frame** *(picture)* der Rahmen
**France** Frankreich
**free** *(not occupied)* frei
  *(costing nothing)* umsonst
**freezer** die Tiefkühltruhe
**French** *adj* französisch
**French fries** die Pommes frites
**Frenchman/woman** der Franzose/die Französin
**frequent** häufig
**fresh** frisch
**fresh water** das frische Wasser
**Friday** der Freitag
**fridge** der Kühlschrank
**fried** gebraten
**friend** der Freund/die Freundin
**friendly** freundlich
**frog** der Frosch
**from** von
  *from Scotland* aus Schottland
  *from England* aus England
**front** die Vorderseite
  *in front of* vor
**front door** die Eingangstür

**F**

**frost** der Frost
**frozen** gefroren
**fruit** das Obst
   *dried fruit* das Trockenobst
**fruit juice** der Fruchtsaft
**to fry** braten
**frying pan** die Bratpfanne
**fuel** *(petrol)* der Treibstoff
**fuel gauge** die Tankanzeige
**fuel pump** *(in car)* die Benzinpumpe
   *(at petrol station)* die Zapfsäule
**fuel tank** der Tank
**full** voll
   *(occupied)* besetzt
**full board** die Vollpension
**fumes** die Abgase
**fun** der Spaß
**funeral** die Beerdigung
**funfair** die Kirmes
**funny** *(amusing)* komisch
**fur** der Pelz
**furnished** möbliert
**furniture** die Möbel
**fuse** die Sicherung
**fuse box** der Sicherungskasten
**future** die Zukunft

# G

**gallery** die Galerie
**game** das Spiel
   *(meat)* das Wild

**garage** *(private)* die Garage
   *(for repairs)* die Werkstatt
   *(petrol station)* die Tankstelle
**garden** der Garten
**garlic** der Knoblauch
**gas** das Gas
**gas cooker** der Gasherd
**gastritis** die Gastritis
**gate** *(airport)* das Gate
**gay** *(person)* der/die Homosexuelle
**gearbox** das Getriebe
**gears** das Getriebe
   *first gear* der erste Gang
   *second gear* der zweite Gang
   *third gear* der dritte Gang
   *fourth gear* der vierte Gang
   *neutral* der Leerlauf
   *reverse* der Rückwärtsgang
**generous** großzügig
**gents'** *(toilet)* die Herrentoilette
**genuine** echt
**German** *adj* deutsch
   *m/f* der/die Deutsche
**German measles** die Röteln
**Germany** Deutschland
**to get** *(to obtain)* bekommen
   *(to fetch)* holen
**to get in(to)** *(bus, etc)* einsteigen
**to get off** *(bus, etc)* aussteigen

ENGLISH-GERMAN

**gift** das Geschenk

**gift shop** der Geschenkeladen

**girl** das Mädchen

**girlfriend** die Freundin

**to give** geben

**to give back** zurückgeben

**glacier** der Gletscher

**glass** das Glas
*a glass of water* ein Glas Wasser

**glasses** *(spectacles)* die Brille

**glasses case** das Brillenetui

**gloves** die Handschuhe

**glue** der Klebstoff

**to go** *(on foot)* gehen
*(in car)* fahren
*I'm going to...* ich fahre nach...
*we're going to...* wir fahren nach...
*to go home* nach Hause fahren
*to go on foot* zu Fuß gehen

**to go back** zurückgehen

**to go in** hineingehen

**to go out** ausgehen

**God** Gott

**goggles** *(swimming)* die Taucherbrille
*(skiing)* die Schneebrille

**gold** das Gold

**golf** das Golf

**golf ball** der Golfball

**golf clubs** die Golfschläger

**golf course** der Golfplatz

**good** gut
*(pleasant)* schön

**good afternoon** guten Tag

**goodbye** auf Wiedersehen

**good day** guten Tag

**good evening** guten Abend

**good morning** guten Morgen

**good night** gute Nacht

**goose** die Gans

**grandchild** das Enkelkind

**granddaughter** die Enkelin

**grandfather** der Großvater

**grandmother** die Großmutter

**grandparents** die Großeltern

**grandson** der Enkel

**grapes** die Trauben

**grass** das Gras

**grated** *(cheese)* gerieben

**gram** das Gramm

**grater** die Reibe

**great** *(big)* groß
*(wonderful)* großartig

**Great Britain** Großbritannien

**green** grün

**greengrocer's** der Gemüseladen

**greetings card** die Grußkarte

**grey** grau

**grill** der Grill

**to grill** grillen
**grilled** gegrillt
**grocer's** der Lebensmittelladen
**ground** der Boden
**ground floor** das Erdgeschoss
*on the ground floor* im Erdgeschoss
**groundsheet** der Zeltboden
**group** die Gruppe
**guarantee** die Garantie
**guard** m/f (on train) der Schaffner/die Schaffnerin
**guest** der Gast
**guesthouse** die Pension
**guide** m/f (tour guide) der Fremdenführer/ die Fremdenführerin
**guidebook** der Reiseführer
**guided tour** die Führung
**guitar** die Gitarre
**gun** die Waffe
**gym** das Fitnesscenter
**gym shoes** die Turnschuhe

**haemorrhoids** die Hämorrhoiden
**hail** der Hagel
**hair** die Haare
**hairbrush** die Haarbürste
**haircut** der Haarschnitt
**hairdresser** der Friseur
**hairdryer** der Föhn

**hair dye** die Tönung
**hair gel** das Haargel
**hairgrip** die Haarklemme
**hair spray** das Haarspray
**half** halb
*a half bottle* eine kleine Flasche
*half an hour* eine halbe Stunde
**half board** die Halbpension
**half fare** der halbe Fahrpreis
**half price** der halbe Preis
**ham** der Schinken
(cooked) Kochschinken
(cured) geräucherter Schinken
**hamburger** der Hamburger
**hammer** der Hammer
**hand** die Hand
**handbag** die Handtasche
**hand-made** handgearbeitet
**handicapped** behindert
**handkerchief** das Taschentuch
**handle** der Griff
**handlebars** der Lenker
**hand luggage** das Handgepäck
**hands-free phone** das Telefon mit Freisprechanlage
**handsome** gut aussehend
**hang gliding** das Drachenfliegen
**hangover** der Kater
**to hang up** auflegen

**to happen** passieren
  **what happened?** was ist passiert?
**happy** glücklich
  **happy birthday!** alles Gute zum Geburtstag!
**harbour** der Hafen
**hard** (difficult) schwierig
  (not soft) hart
**hardware shop** die Eisenwarenhandlung
**to harm** schädigen
**harvest** die Ernte
**hat** der Hut
**to have** haben
  **I have...** ich habe...
  **we have...** wir haben...
  **do you have...?** haben Sie...?
**to have to** müssen
**hay fever** der Heuschnupfen
**he** er
**head** der Kopf
**headache** die Kopfschmerzen
  **I have a headache** ich habe Kopfschmerzen
**headlights** die Scheinwerfer
**headphones** die Kopfhörer
**health** die Gesundheit
**health food shop** das Reformhaus
**healthy** gesund
**to hear** hören
**hearing aid** das Hörgerät
**heart** das Herz

**heart attack** der Herzanfall
**heartburn** das Sodbrennen
**to heat up** (food, milk) aufwärmen
**heater** das Heizgerät
**heating** die Heizung
**heavy** schwer
**heel** der Absatz
**heel bar** die Absatzbar
**height** die Höhe
**helicopter** der Helikopter
**hello** hallo
**helmet** (for bike) der Schutzhelm
**help!** Hilfe!
**to help** helfen
**hem** der Saum
**hepatitis** die Hepatitis
**her** (with der words) ihr
  (with das words) ihr
  (with die words) ihre
  **to her** zu ihr
**herbal tea** der Kräutertee
**herbs** die Kräuter
**here** hier
  **here is...** hier ist...
**hernia** der Eingeweidebruch
**hi!** hallo!
**to hide** verstecken
**high** hoch
  (number, speed) groß
**high blood pressure** der hohe Blutdruck
**high chair** der Kinderstuhl
**high tide** die Flut

**hill** der Hügel
**hill-walking** das Bergwandern
**him** ihm
**hip** die Hüfte
**hip replacement** die künstliche Hüfte
**hire** die Vermietung
  *car hire* die Autovermietung
  *bike hire* die Fahrradvermietung
  *boat hire* der Bootsverleih
  *ski hire* der Skiverleih
**to hire** mieten
**hire car** das Mietauto
**his** *(with the words)* sein
  *(with das words)* sein
  *(with die words)* seine
**historic** historisch
**history** die Geschichte
**to hit** schlagen
**to hitchhike** trampen
**hobby** das Hobby
**to hold** halten
  *(to contain)* enthalten
**hold-up** *(traffic jam)* der Stau
**hole** das Loch
**holiday** der Feiertag
  *holidays* der Urlaub
  *on holiday* in den Ferien
**home** das Zuhause
  *at home* zu Hause
**homesick** *(to be)* Heimweh haben
  *I'm homesick* ich habe Heimweh

**homosexual** homosexuell
**honest** ehrlich
**honey** der Honig
**honeymoon** die Flitterwochen
**hood** *(of jacket)* die Kapuze
**hook** der Haken
**to hope** hoffen
  *I hope so* hoffentlich
  *I hope not* hoffentlich nicht
**horn** *(car)* die Hupe
**hors d'œuvre** die Vorspeise
**horse** das Pferd
**horse racing** das Pferderennen
**to horse ride** reiten
**hosepipe** der Schlauch
**hospital** das Krankenhaus
**hostel** das Wohnheim
**hot** heiß
  *I'm hot* mir ist heiß
  *it's hot (weather)* es ist heiß
**hot-water bottle** die Wärmflasche
**hotel** das Hotel
**hour** die Stunde
  *1 hour* eine Stunde
  *2 hours* zwei Stunden
  *half an hour* eine halbe Stunde
**house** das Haus
**housewife/husband** die Hausfrau/der Hausmann
**house wine** der Hauswein
**housework** die Hausarbeit

**how** wie
*how much?* wie viel?
*how many?* wie viele?
*how are you?* wie geht
es Ihnen?

**hungry** *(to be)* hungrig

**to hunt** jagen

**hunting permit** die
Jagderlaubnis

**hurry:** *I'm in a hurry* ich
habe es eilig

**to hurt** *(be painful)* weh tun
*my back hurts* mir tut der
Rücken weh
*that hurts* das tut weh

**husband** der Mann

**hut** *(beach)* der Strandkorb
*(mountain)* die Hütte

**hypodermic needle** die
Spritze

# I

**I** ich

**ice** das Eis
*with/without ice* mit/ohne
Eis

**ice box** die Kühlbox

**ice cream** das Eis

**ice cube** der Eiswürfel

**ice rink** die Eisbahn

**to ice-skate** Schlittschuh
laufen

**ice skates** die Schlittschuhe

**iced:** *iced coffee* der
Eiskaffee
*iced tea* der Eistee

**idea** die Idee

**identity card** der
Personalausweis

**if** wenn

**ignition** die Zündung

**ignition key** der
Zündschlüssel

**ill** krank
*I'm ill* ich bin krank

**illness** die Krankheit

**immediately** sofort

**immersion heater** der
Boiler

**immunisation** die
Immunisierung

**to import** importieren

**important** wichtig

**impossible** unmöglich

**to improve** verbessern

**in** in
*in 2 hours* in zwei Stunden
*in Vienna* in Wien

**in front of** vor

**included** inbegriffen

**inconvenient** unpassend

**to increase** vergrößern

**indicator** *(in car)* der Blinker

**indigestion** die
Magenverstimmung

**indigestion tablets** die
Magentabletten

**indoors** drinnen

**infection** die Infektion

**infectious** ansteckend

**information** die Auskunft

**information desk** der Informationsschalter

**information office** das Informationsbüro

**ingredients** die Zutaten

**inhaler** *(for medication)* der Inhalationsapparat

**injection** die Spritze

**to injure** verletzen

**injured** *(person)* verletzt

**injury** die Verletzung

**ink** die Tinte

**inn** das Gasthaus

**inner tube** der Schlauch

**inquiries** die Auskunft

**inquiry desk** der Auskunftsschalter

**insect** das Insekt

**insect bite** der Insektenstich

**insect repellent** das Insektenschutzmittel

**inside** in

**instant coffee** der Pulverkaffee

**instead of** anstelle von

**insulin** das Insulin

**insurance** die Versicherung

**to insure** versichern

**insured** versichert

**to intend to** vorhaben

**interesting** interessant

**international** international *(arrivals, departures)* Ausland

**internet** das Internet

**internet café** das Internet-Café

**interpreter** der Dolmetscher/die Dolmetscherin

**interval** die Pause

**into** in
*into town* in die Stadt
*into the centre* ins Zentrum

**to introduce** vorstellen

**invitation** die Einladung

**to invite** einladen

**invoice** die Rechnung

**Ireland** Irland

**Irish** *adj* irisch

**Irishman/woman** der Ire/die Irin

**iron** *(for clothes)* das Bügeleisen
*(metal)* das Eisen

**to iron** bügeln

**ironing board** das Bügelbrett

**ironmonger's** die Eisenwarenhandlung

**is** ist

**island** die Insel

**it** er/sie/es

**Italian** *adj* italienisch
*m/f* der Italiener/die Italienerin

**Italy** Italien

**to itch** jucken

**item** das Ding

**jack** (for car) der Wagenheber
**jacket** die Jacke
**jacuzzi** der Whirlpool
**jam** (food) die Marmelade
**jammed** blockiert
**January** der Januar
**jar** (honey, jam, etc) das Glas
**jaundice** die Gelbsucht
**jaw** der Kiefer
**jealous** eifersüchtig
**jeans** die Jeans
**jellyfish** die Qualle
**jet ski** das Wassermotorrad
**jetty** die Mole
**Jew** der Jude/die Jüdin
**jeweller's** der Juwelier
**jewellery** der Schmuck
**Jewish** jüdisch
**job** (employment) die Stelle
**to jog** joggen
**to join** (club) beitreten
**to join in** mitmachen
**joint** (of body) das Gelenk
**to joke** scherzen
**joke** der Witz
**journalist** der Journalist/die Journalistin
**journey** die Reise
**judge** der Richter/die Richterin
**jug** der Krug

**juice** der Saft
  **carton of juice** der Saftkarton
**July** der Juli
**to jump** springen
**jumper** der Pullover
**jump leads** (for car) das Starthilfekabel
**junction** (road) die Kreuzung
**June** der Juni
**just:** *just two* nur zwei
  *I've just arrived* ich bin gerade angekommen

# K

**to keep** (retain) behalten
**kettle** der Wasserkocher
**key** der Schlüssel
**keyring** der Schlüsselring
**to kick** (ball) schießen
  (person) treten
**kidneys** die Nieren
**to kill** töten
**kilo** das Kilo
**kilometre** der Kilometer
**kind** (person) nett
**kind** (sort) die Art
**kiosk** der Kiosk
**kiss** der Kuss
**to kiss** küssen
**kitchen** die Küche
**kitchen paper** das Küchenpapier
**kite** der Drachen

**K**

**knee** das Knie
**kneehighs** die Kniestrümpfe
**knickers** der Slip
**knife** das Messer
**to knit** stricken
**to knock** stoßen
**to knock down** *(in car)* überfahren
**to knock over** *(object)* umstoßen
**knot** der Knoten
**to know** *(facts)* wissen *(be acquainted with)* kennen
  *I don't know* ich weiß nicht
**to know how to** können
**kosher** koscher

**L**

**label** das Schild
**lace** *(shoe)* der Schnürsenkel
**ladder** die Leiter
**ladies'** *(toilet)* die Damentoilette
**lady** die Dame
**lager** das helle Bier
  *bottled lager* das Flaschenbier
  *draught lager* das Fassbier
**lake** der See
**lamb** das Lammfleisch
**lamp** *(for table)* die Lampe
**to land** landen
**landlady** die Vermieterin
**landlord** der Vermieter
**landslide** der Erdrutsch

**lane** die Gasse
  *(of motorway/road)* die Spur
**language** die Sprache
**language school** die Sprachenschule
**laptop** der Laptop
**large** groß
**last** *(final)* letzte(r/s)
  *the last bus* der letzte Bus
  *last night* gestern Abend
  *last time* letztes Mal
**late** spät
  *the train is late* der Zug hat Verspätung
**later** später
**to laugh** lachen
**launderette** der Waschsalon
**laundry service** der Wäschereiservice
**lavatory** die Toilette
**law** das Gesetz
**lawn** der Rasen
**lawyer** der Rechtsanwalt/ die Rechtsanwältin
**laxative** das Abführmittel
**layby** die Haltebucht
**lazy** faul
**lead** *(metal)* das Blei
**to lead** führen
**lead-free** bleifrei
**leaf** das Blatt
**leak** *(of gas, liquid)* das Leck
**to leak:** *it's leaking* es hat ein Leck
**to learn** lernen

**lease** (rental) der Mietvertrag

**leather** das Leder

**to leave** (a place) weggehen/wegfahren
*when does the train leave?* wann fährt der Zug ab?

**left:** on the left links
to the left nach links

**left-luggage locker** das Schließfach

**left-luggage office** die Gepäckaufbewahrung

**leg** das Bein

**lemon** die Zitrone

**lemon tea** der Zitronentee

**lemonade** die Limonade

**to lend** leihen

**length** (size) die Länge
(duration) die Dauer

**lens** die Linse

**lenses** (contact) die Kontaktlinsen

**lesbian** lesbisch

**less** weniger
*less than* weniger als

**lesson** die Unterrichtsstunde

**to let** (to allow) erlauben
(room, house) vermieten

**letter** (written) der Brief
(of alphabet) der Buchstabe

**letterbox** der Briefkasten

**lettuce** der Kopfsalat

**library** die Bibliothek

**lid** der Deckel

**lie** (untruth) die Lüge

**to lie down** sich hinlegen

**lifebelt** der Rettungsring

**lifeboat** das Rettungsboot

**lifeguard** der Rettungsschwimmer/ die Rettungsschwimmerin

**life insurance** die Lebensversicherung

**life jacket** die Schwimmweste

**life raft** die Rettungsinsel

**lift** (elevator) der Aufzug
*can I have a lift?* können Sie mich mitnehmen?

**lift pass** der Liftpass

**light** (not heavy) leicht

**light** das Licht
*have you a light?* haben Sie Feuer?

**light bulb** die Glühbirne

**lighter** das Feuerzeug

**lighthouse** der Leuchtturm

**lightning** der Blitz

**like** (preposition) wie

**to like** mögen
*I like coffee* ich trinke gern Kaffee
*I don't like...* ich mag ... nicht
*we'd like...* wir möchten...

**lilo®** die Luftmatratze

**lime** (fruit) die Limone

**line** (row, of railway) die Linie
(telephone) die Leitung

**linen** das Leinen

**lingerie** die Unterwäsche

**lips** die Lippen

**L**

**lip-reading** das Lippenlesen

**lipstick** der Lippenstift

**liqueur** der Likör

**list** die Liste

**to listen to** zuhören

**litre** der Liter
 *litre of milk* ein Liter Milch

**litter** (rubbish) der Abfall

**little** (small) klein
 *a little...* ein bisschen...

**to live** (exist) leben
 (reside) wohnen
 *I live in London* ich
 wohne in London

**liver** die Leber

**living room** das Wohnzimmer

**loaf of bread** das Brot

**local** (wine, speciality) hiesig

**lock** das Schloss

**to lock** zuschließen

**locker** (luggage) das
 Schließfach

**locksmith** der Schlosser

**log** (for fire) der Holzscheit

**log book** (car) die Zulassung

**long** lang
 *for a long time* lange Zeit

**long-sighted** weitsichtig

**to look after** sich kümmern
 um

**to look at** anschauen

**to look for** suchen

**loose** (screw, tooth) locker
 *it's come loose* es hat sich
 gelockert

**lorry** der Lastwagen

**to lose** verlieren

**lost** (object) verloren
 *I've lost my wallet* ich
 habe meine Brieftasche
 verloren
 *I'm lost (on foot)* ich habe
 mich verlaufen
 *I'm lost (in car)* ich habe
 mich verfahren

**lost property office** das
 Fundbüro

**lot: a lot** viel

**lotion** die Lotion

**lottery** das Lotto

**loud** laut

**lounge** (hotel/airport) die
 Lounge
 (in house) das Wohnzimmer

**love** die Liebe

**to love** lieben
 *I love you* ich liebe dich
 *I love swimming* ich
 schwimme gern

**lovely** schön

**low** niedrig

**low-alcohol** alkoholarm

**low-fat** fettarm

**low tide** die Ebbe

**luck** das Glück

**lucky** glücklich

**luggage** das Gepäck

**luggage rack** die
 Gepäckablage

**luggage tag** der
 Kofferanhänger

**luggage trolley** der
 Gepäckwagen

**lump** *(swelling)* die Beule

**lunch** das Mittagessen

**lunch break** die Mittagspause

**lung** die Lunge

**luxury** der Luxus

# M

**machine** die Maschine

**mad** verrückt

**magazine** die Zeitschrift

**magnet** der Magnet

**magnifying glass** die Lupe

**maid** *(in hotel)* das Zimmermädchen

**maiden name** der Mädchenname

**mail** die Post
*by mail* per Post

**main** *(principal)* Haupt-

**main course** *(of meal)* das Hauptgericht

**main road** die Hauptstraße

**to make** machen
*(meal)* zubereiten

**make-up** das Make-up

**male** männlich

**man** der Mann
*men* die Männer

**manager** der Geschäftsführer/ die Geschäftsführerin

**manual** *(gear change)* das Schaltgetriebe

**many** viele

**map** die Karte
*(of region, country)* die Landkarte
*(of town)* der Stadtplan

**March** der März

**margarine** die Margarine

**marina** der Jachthafen

**mark** *(stain)* der Fleck

**market** der Markt

**market place** der Marktplatz

**marmalade** die Orangenmarmelade

**married** verheiratet
*I'm married* ich bin verheiratet
*are you married?* sind Sie verheiratet?

**to marry** heiraten

**mascara** die Wimperntusche

**mass** *(in church)* die Messe

**mast** der Mast

**matches** die Streichhölzer

**material** das Material

**matter:** *it doesn't matter* das macht nichts
*what's the matter?* was ist los?

**mattress** die Matratze

**May** der Mai

**mayonnaise** die Mayonnaise

**maximum** das Maximum

**me** *(direct object)* mich
*(indirect object)* mir

**meal** das Essen

**to mean** bedeuten
*what does this mean?*
was bedeutet das?

**measles** die Masern

**to measure** messen

**meat** das Fleisch
*I don't eat meat* ich esse
kein Fleisch

**mechanic** der Mechaniker/
die Mechanikerin

**medical insurance** die
Krankenversicherung

**medical treatment** die
medizinische Behandlung

**medicine** die Medizin

**medieval** mittelalterlich

**medium rare** *(meat)* halb
durch

**to meet** *(by chance)* treffen
*(arranged)* sich treffen mit
*pleased to meet you!*
sehr erfreut!

**meeting** das Treffen

**to melt** schmelzen

**member** *(of club, etc)* das
Mitglied

**memory** das Gedächtnis

**men** die Männer

**to mend** reparieren

**meningitis** die
Hirnhautentzündung

**menu** die Speisekarte
*set menu* die Tageskarte

**message** die Nachricht

**metal** das Metall

**meter** der Zähler

**metre** der Meter

**metro** die U-Bahn

**metro station** die U-Bahn-
Station

**microwave oven** die
Mikrowelle

**midday** der Mittag
*at midday* am Mittag

**middle** die Mitte

**middle-aged** in den
mittleren Jahren

**midge** die Mücke

**midnight** die Mitternacht
*at midnight* um
Mitternacht

**migraine** die Migräne
*I have a migraine* ich
habe Migräne

**mile** die Meile

**milk** die Milch
*fresh milk* frische Milch
*full cream milk* Vollfettmilch
*hot milk* heiße Milch
*long-life milk* H-Milch
*powdered milk* das
Milchpulver
*semi-skimmed milk*
Halbfettmilch
*skimmed milk* Magermilch
*soya milk* die Sojamilch
*with/without milk*
mit/ohne Milch

**millimetre** der Millimeter

**mince** *(meat)* das Hackfleisch

**mind:** *do you mind if…?*
haben Sie etwas dagegen,
wenn…?
*I don't mind* es ist mir egal

**mineral water** das Mineralwasser

**minibar** die Minibar

**minimum** das Minimum

**minister** *(church)* der Pfarrer/die Pfarrerin *(political)* der Minister/die Ministerin

**mint** *(herb)* die Minze *(sweet)* das Pfefferminzbonbon

**minute** die Minute

**mirror** der Spiegel

**miscarriage** die Fehlgeburt

**to miss** *(train, etc)* verpassen

**Miss** Fräulein

**missing** *(object)* verschwunden
*my son's missing* mein Sohn ist weg

**mistake** der Fehler

**misty** dunstig

**misunderstanding** das Missverständnis

**to mix** mischen

**mixer** der Mixer

**mobile phone** das Handy

**modem** das Modem

**modern** modern

**moisturizer** die Feuchtigkeitscreme

**mole** *(on skin)* das Muttermal

**moment:** *just a moment* einen Moment, bitte

**monastery** das Kloster

**Monday** der Montag

**money** das Geld
*I have no money* ich habe kein Geld

**moneybelt** die Gürteltasche

**money order** die Postanweisung

**month** der Monat
*this month* diesen Monat
*last month* letzten Monat
*next month* nächsten Monat

**monthly** monatlich

**monument** das Denkmal

**moon** der Mond

**mooring** der Anlegeplatz

**mop** *(floor)* der Mopp

**moped** das Moped

**more** mehr
*more than* mehr als
*more wine* noch etwas Wein

**morning** der Morgen
*in the morning* am Morgen
*this morning* heute Morgen

**morning-after pill** die Pille danach

**mosque** die Moschee

**mosquito** die Stechmücke

**mosquito net** das Moskitonetz

**mosquito repellent** das Insektenschutzmittel

**most:** *most of* das meiste von

**moth** *(clothes)* die Motte

145

**M**

mother die Mutter
mother-in-law die Schwiegermutter
motor der Motor
motorbike das Motorrad
motorboat das Motorboot
motorway die Autobahn
mould der Schimmel
mountain der Berg
mountain bike das Mountainbike
mountain rescue die Bergwacht
mountaineering das Bergsteigen
mouse die Maus
moustache der Schnurrbart
mouth der Mund
to move bewegen
  *it isn't moving* es bewegt sich nicht
movie der Kinofilm
to mow mähen
Mr Herr
Mrs Frau
Ms Frau
much viel
  *too much* zu viel
muddy schlammig
mugging der Überfall
mumps der Mumps
Munich München
muscle der Muskel
museum das Museum
mushrooms die Pilze

music die Musik
musical das Musical
mussel die Muschel
must müssen
  *I must* ich muss
  *we must* wir müssen
  *you mustn't* du darfst nicht
mustard der Senf
my *(with der words)* mein
  *(with das words)* mein
  *(with die words)* meine

**N**

nail *(fingernail)* der Fingernagel
  *(metal)* der Nagel
nailbrush die Nagelbürste
nail file die Nagelfeile
nail polish/varnish der Nagellack
nail polish remover der Nagellackentferner
nail scissors die Nagelschere
name der Name
  *what is your name?* wie ist Ihr Name?
nanny das Kindermädchen
napkin die Serviette
nappy die Windel
narrow eng
national national
nationality die Nationalität
natural natürlich
nature die Natur
nature reserve das Naturschutzgebiet

**navy blue** marineblau

**near** *(place, time)* nahe
*near the bank* in der Nähe der Bank
*is it near?* ist es in der Nähe?

**necessary** notwendig

**neck** der Hals

**necklace** die Halskette

**nectarine** die Nektarine

**to need** brauchen
*I need...* ich brauche...
*we need...* wir brauchen...
*I need to go* ich muss gehen

**needle** die Nadel
*needle and thread* Nadel und Faden

**neighbour** der Nachbar/die Nachbarin

**nephew** der Neffe

**net** das Netz
*the Net* das Internet

**never** nie
*I never drink wine* Wein trinke ich nie

**new** neu

**news** die Nachrichten

**newsagent's** der Zeitungsladen

**newspaper** die Zeitung

**newsstand** der Zeitungskiosk

**New Year (1 Jan)** Neujahr
*happy New Year!* ein gutes neues Jahr!

**New Year's Eve** Silvester

**New Zealand** Neuseeland

**next** nächste(r/s)
*next to* neben
*next week* nächste Woche
*the next bus* der nächste Bus

**nice** *(person)* nett
*(place, holiday)* schön

**niece** die Nichte

**night** die Nacht
*at night* am Abend
*last night* gestern Abend
*per night* pro Nacht
*tonight* heute Abend

**night club** der Nachtklub

**nightdress** das Nachthemd

**no** nein
*no thanks* nein danke
*no problem* kein Problem
*(without)* ohne
*no sugar* ohne Zucker
*no ice* ohne Eis

**nobody** niemand

**noise** der Lärm

**noisy** laut
*it's very noisy* es ist sehr laut

**non-alcoholic** alkoholfrei

**none** keine(r/s)

**non-smoker** der Nichtraucher

**non-smoking** Nichtraucher-

**north** der Norden

**Northern Ireland** Nordirland

**North Sea** die Nordsee

**nose** die Nase

**N**

**not** nicht
 *I do not know* ich weiß nicht
**note** *(banknote)* der Geldschein
 *(written)* die Notiz
**note pad** der Notizblock
**nothing** nichts
 *nothing else* nichts weiter
**notice** *(sign)* das Schild
**novel** der Roman
**November** der November
**now** jetzt
**nowhere** nirgends
**nuclear** nuklear
**nudist beach** der FKK-Strand
**number** die Zahl
**number plate** das Nummernschild
**nurse** die Krankenschwester/ der Krankenpfleger
**nursery** die Kinderbetreuung
**nursery school** die Vorschule
**nut** *(to eat)* die Nuss
 *(for bolt)* die Schraubenmutter

**O**

**oar** das Ruder
**oats** der Hafer
**to obtain** erhalten
**occupation** *(work)* der Beruf
**ocean** der Ozean
**October** der Oktober

**odd** *(strange)* seltsam
**of** von
 *a glass of water* ein Glas Wasser
 *made of...* aus...
**off** *(light, radio, etc)* aus
 *(rotten)* schlecht
**office** das Büro
**often** oft
 *how often?* wie oft?
**oil** das Öl
**oil filter** der Ölfilter
**ointment** die Salbe
**OK** okay
**old** alt
 *how old are you?* wie alt sind Sie?
 *I'm... years old* ich bin... Jahre alt
**old age pensioner** der Rentner/die Rentnerin
**on** *(light, radio, etc)* an
**on** auf
 *on the table* auf dem Tisch
 *on time* pünktlich
**once** einmal
 *at once* sofort
**onion** die Zwiebel
**only** nur
**open** geöffnet
**to open** öffnen
**opera** die Oper
**operation** *(surgical)* die Operation
**operator** *(phone)* die Vermittlung
**opposite** gegenüber

*opposite the bank*
gegenüber der Bank
*quite the opposite* ganz
im Gegenteil

**optician's** der Optiker

**or** oder

**orange** *(colour)* orange

**orange** *(fruit)* die Orange

**orange juice** der Orangensaft

**orchestra** das Orchester

**order** *(in restaurant)* die
Bestellung

**to order** *(food)* bestellen

**organic** organisch

**to organize** organisieren

**other:** *the other one*
der/die/das andere
*have you got any others?*
haben Sie noch andere?

**our** *(with der words)* unser
*(with das words)* unser
*(with die words)* unsere

**out** *(light, etc)* aus
*she's out* sie ist nicht da

**out of order** kaputt

**outdoor** *(pool, etc)* im Freien

**outside** draußen

**oven** der Herd

**ovenproof dish** die
feuerfeste Form

**over** *(on top of, above)* über

**to overbook** überbuchen

**to overcharge** zu viel
berechnen

**overdone** *(food)* verkocht

**overdose** die Überdosis

**to overheat** überhitzen

**to overload** überladen

**to oversleep** verschlafen

**to overtake** überholen

**to owe** schulden
*I owe you...* ich schulde
Ihnen...
*you owe me...* Sie
schulden mir...

**owner** der Besitzer/die
Besitzerin

**oxygen** der Sauerstoff

# P

**pace** das Tempo

**pacemaker** der
Herzschrittmacher

**to pack** *(luggage)* packen

**package** das Paket

**package tour** die
Pauschalreise

**packet** das Paket

**padded envelope** der
gefütterte Umschlag

**paddling pool** das
Planschbecken

**padlock** das Vorhängeschloss

**page** die Seite

**paid** bezahlt
*I've paid* ich habe bezahlt

**pain** der Schmerz

**painful** schmerzhaft

**painkiller** das Schmerzmittel

**to paint** malen

**painting** *(picture)* das Bild

**P**

**pair** das Paar
**palace** der Palast
**pale** blass
**pan** (saucepan) der Kochtopf
(frying pan) die Bratpfanne
**pancake** der Pfannkuchen
**panniers** (for bike) die
Satteltaschen
**panties** die Unterhose
**pants** (underwear) der Slip
**panty liner** die Slipeinlage
**paper** das Papier
**paper hankies** die
Papiertaschentücher
**paper napkins** die
Papierservietten
**paralysed** gelähmt
**parcel** das Paket
**pardon?** wie bitte?
*I beg your pardon!*
Entschuldigung!
**parents** die Eltern
**park** der Park
**to park** parken
**parking disk** die Parkscheibe
**parking fine** der Strafzettel
**parking meter** die Parkuhr
**parking ticket** (fine) der
Strafzettel
(to display) der Parkschein
**partner** (business) der
Geschäftspartner/ die
Geschäftspartnerin
(boy/girlfriend) der Partner/
die Partnerin

**party** (celebration) die Party
(political) die Partei
**pass** der Pass
**passenger** der Passagier
**passport** der Reisepass
**passport control** die
Passkontrolle
**pasta** die Nudeln
**pastry** der Teig
(cake) das Gebäck
**path** der Weg
**patient** (in hospital) der
Patient/die Patientin
**pavement** der Bürgersteig
**to pay** zahlen
*I'd like to pay* ich möchte
zahlen
*where do I pay?* wo kann
ich bezahlen?
**payment** die Bezahlung
**payphone** das Münztelefon
**peace** der Frieden
**peach** der Pfirsich
**peak rate** der Höchsttarif
**peanut allergy** die
Erdnussallergie
**pear** die Birne
**pearls** die Perlen
**peas** die Erbsen
**pedal** das Pedal
**pedalo** der Wassertreter
**pedestrian** der Fußgänger/
die Fußgängerin
**pedestrian crossing** der
Fußgängerübergang
**to pee** austreten

**to peel** *(fruit)* schälen

**peg** *(clothes)* die Wäscheklammer *(tent)* der Hering

**pen** der Füller

**pencil** der Bleistift

**penfriend** der Brieffreund/ die Brieffreundin

**penicillin** das Penizillin

**penis** der Penis

**penknife** das Taschenmesser

**pension** die Rente

**pensioner** der Rentner/die Rentnerin

**people** die Leute

**pepper** *(spice)* der Pfeffer die Paprikaschote

**per** pro
*per day* pro Tag
*per hour* pro Stunde
*per person* pro Person

**perfect** perfekt

**performance** die Vorstellung

**perfume** das Parfüm

**perhaps** vielleicht

**period** *(menstruation)* die Periode

**perm** die Dauerwelle

**permit** die Genehmigung

**person** die Person

**personal organizer** der Terminplaner

**personal stereo** der Walkman®

**pet** das Haustier

**pet food** das Tierfutter

**pet shop** die Zoohandlung

**petrol** das Benzin
*4-star petrol* Superbenzin
*unleaded petrol* bleifreies Benzin

**petrol cap** der Tankdeckel

**petrol pump** *(at petrol station)* die Tanksäule *(in car)* die Benzinpumpe

**petrol station** die Tankstelle

**petrol tank** der Tank

**pharmacy** die Apotheke

**to phone** telefonieren

**phone** das Telefon
*by phone* per Telefon

**phonebook** das Telefonbuch

**phonebox** die Telefonzelle

**phone call** der Anruf

**phonecard** die Telefonkarte

**photocopy** die Fotokopie
*I need a photocopy* ich brauche eine Fotokopie

**to photocopy** fotokopieren

**photograph** das Foto
*to take a photograph* fotografieren

**phrase book** der Sprachführer

**piano** das Klavier

**to pick** *(choose)* auswählen *(pluck)* pflücken

**pickpocket** der Taschendieb

**picnic** das Picknick
*to have a picnic* ein Picknick machen

**picture** *(painting)* das Bild *(photo)* das Foto

**P**

pie *(sweet)* der Obstkuchen *(savoury)* die Pastete

piece das Stück

pier die Pier

pig das Schwein

pill die Pille
 **to be on the Pill** die Pille nehmen

pillow das Kopfkissen

pillowcase der Kopfkissenbezug

pilot der Pilot/die Pilotin

pin die Stecknadel

pink rosa

pipe *(smoker's)* die Pfeife *(drain, etc)* das Rohr

pity: **what a pity** wie schade

pizza die Pizza

place der Platz

place of birth der Geburtsort

plain *(unflavoured)* einfach

plait der Zopf

plane *(airplane)* das Flugzeug

plant die Pflanze

plaster *(sticking)* das Pflaster *(for broken limb)* der Gips

plastic *(made of)* Plastik-

plastic bag der Plastikbeutel

plate der Teller

platform *(at station)* der Bahnsteig
 **which platform?** welcher Bahnsteig?

play *(theatre)* das Stück

to play spielen

play area die Spielecke

playground der Spielplatz

play park der Spielplatz

playroom das Spielzimmer

please bitte

pleased erfreut
 **pleased to meet you** sehr erfreut

pliers die Zange

plug *(electrical)* der Stecker *(in sink)* der Stöpsel

to plug in einstecken

plum die Pflaume

plumber der Klempner

plumbing die Installationen

p.m. nachmittags

poached *(egg, fish)* pochiert

pocket die Tasche

points *(in car)* die Unterbrecherkontakte

poison das Gift

poisonous giftig

police *(force)* die Polizei

policeman/woman der Polizist/die Polizistin

police station das Polizeirevier

polish *(shoe)* die Schuhcreme *(furniture)* die Möbelpolitur

pollen der Pollen

polluted verschmutzt

pony das Pony

**pony trekking** das Ponyreiten
**pool** der Swimmingpool
**pool attendant** der Bademeister
**poor** arm
**pop socks** die Kniestrümpfe
**popular** beliebt
**pork** das Schweinefleisch
**port** *(seaport)* der Hafen
**porter** *(for door)* der Portier *(station)* der Gepäckträger
**portion** die Portion
**portrait** das Portrait
**possible** möglich
**post: by post** per Post
**to post** aufgeben
**postbox** der Briefkasten
**postcard** die Ansichtskarte
**postcode** die Postleitzahl
**postman** der Briefträger/ die Briefträgerin
**post office** das Postamt
**poster** das Poster
**to postpone** verschieben
**pot** *(cooking)* der Topf
**potato** die Kartoffel
 *baked potato* die Folienkartoffel
 *boiled potatoes* die Salzkartoffeln
 *fried potatoes* die Bratkartoffeln
 *mashed potatoes* das Kartoffelpüree

*roast potatoes* die Bratkartoffeln
*sautéed potatoes* die Röstkartoffeln
**potato peeler** der Kartoffelschäler
**potato salad** der Kartoffelsalat
**pothole** das Schlagloch
**pottery** die Töpferwaren
**pound** das Pfund
**to pour** eingießen
**powder: in powder form** pulverförmig
**powdered milk** die Trockenmilch
**power** *(electricity)* der Strom
**power cut** der Stromausfall
**pram** der Kinderwagen
**to pray** beten
**to prefer** vorziehen
**pregnant** schwanger
 *I'm pregnant* ich bin schwanger
**to prepare** vorbereiten
**to prescribe** verschreiben
**prescription** das Rezept
**present** *(gift)* das Geschenk
**president** der Präsident
**pressure: tyre pressure** der Reifendruck
 *blood pressure* der Blutdruck
**pretty** hübsch
**price** der Preis
**price list** die Preisliste

153

**P**

**priest** der Priester
**print** *(photo)* der Abzug
**printer** der Drucker
**prison** das Gefängnis
**private** privat
**prize** der Preis
**probably** wahrscheinlich
**problem** das Problem
**professor** der Professor/
die Professorin
**programme** das Programm
**prohibited** verboten
**to promise** versprechen
**to pronounce** aussprechen
*how's it pronounced?*
wie spricht man das aus?
**protein** das Eiweiß
**Protestant** protestantisch
**to provide** zur Verfügung
stellen
**public** öffentlich
**public holiday** der
gesetzliche Feiertag
**pudding** die Nachspeise
**to pull** ziehen
*to pull a muscle* sich
einen Muskel verziehen
**to pull over** *(car)* anhalten
**pullover** der Pullover
**pump** *(bike, etc)* die
Luftpumpe
*(in petrol station)* die
Tanksäule
**puncture** die Reifenpanne
**puncture repair kit** das
Reifenflickzeug

**puppet** die Puppe
**puppet show** das
Puppenspiel
**purple** violett
**purpose** der Zweck
*on purpose* absichtlich
**purse** der Geldbeutel
**to push** stoßen
**pushchair** die Kinderkarre
**to put** *(place)* stellen
**to put back** verschieben
**pyjamas** der Pyjama

**Q**

**quality** die Qualität
**quantity** die Quantität
**quarantine** die Quarantäne
**to quarrel** streiten
**quarter** das Viertel
**quay** der Kai
**queen** die Königin
**query** die Frage
**question** die Frage
**queue** die Schlange
**to queue** anstehen
**quick(ly)** schnell
**quiet** ruhig
**quilt** die Bettdecke
**quite** *(rather)* ziemlich
*it's quite good* es ist ganz
gut
*it's quite expensive* es ist
ziemlich teuer
**quiz show** das Quiz

# R

**rabbit** das Kaninchen
**rabies** die Tollwut
**race** das Rennen
**race course** die Rennbahn
**racquet** der Schläger
**radiator** *(car)* der Kühler
*(heater)* der Heizkörper
**radio** das Radio
**railcard** die Bahncard
**railway** die Eisenbahn
**railway station** der
Bahnhof
**rain** der Regen
**to rain** regnen
*it's raining* es regnet
**raincoat** der Regenmantel
**raisins** die Rosinen
**rake** die Harke
**rape** die Vergewaltigung
**to rape** vergewaltigen
**rare** *(unique)* selten
*(steak)* blutig
**rash** *(skin)* der Ausschlag
**rate** *(price)* der Preis
**rate of exchange** der
Wechselkurs
**raw** roh
**razor** der Rasierapparat
**razor blades** die
Rasierklingen
**to read** lesen
**ready** fertig
*to get ready* sich fertig
machen

**real** echt
**to realize** erkennen
**rearview mirror** der
Rückspiegel
**receipt** die Quittung
**receiver** der Hörer
**reception** *(desk)* der
Empfang
**receptionist** der
Empfangschef/
die Empfangsdame
**to recharge** *(battery)* wieder
aufladen
**recipe** das Rezept
**to recognize** erkennen
**to recommend** empfehlen
**to record** aufnehmen
**to recover** genesen
**to recycle** recyceln
**red** rot
**to reduce** reduzieren
**reduction** die Ermäßigung
**refund** die Rückerstattung
**to refund** rückerstatten
**to refuse** ablehnen
**region** das Gebiet
**to register** *(at hotel)* sich
anmelden
**registered letter** das
Einschreiben
**registration form** das
Anmeldeformular
**to reimburse** entschädigen
**relation** *(family)* der/die
Verwandte
**to remain** *(to stay)* bleiben

**R**

**to remember** sich erinnern
   *I don't remember* ich
   kann mich nicht erinnern
**remote control** die
   Fernbedienung
**to remove** entfernen
**rent** die Miete
**to rent** mieten
**repair** die Reparatur
**to repair** reparieren
**to repeat** wiederholen
**to reply** antworten
**report** der Bericht
**to report** berichten
**request** die Bitte
**to request** erbitten
**to require** benötigen
**to rescue** retten
**reservation** die
   Reservierung ; die Buchung
**to reserve** reservieren ;
   buchen
**reserved** reserviert
**rest** *(repose)* die Ruhe
   *(remainder)* der Rest
**to rest** ruhen
**restaurant** das Restaurant
**restaurant car** der
   Speisewagen
**retired** pensioniert
**to return** *(in car)*
   zurückfahren
   *(on foot)* zurückgehen
   *(return something)*
   zurückgeben

**return ticket** *(train)* die
   Rückfahrkarte
   *(plane)* das Rückflugticket
**to reverse** *(car)* rückwärts
   fahren
**to reverse the charges** ein
   R-Gespräch führen
**reverse charge call** das R-
   Gespräch
**reverse gear** der
   Rückwärtsgang
**rheumatism** der
   Rheumatismus
**rib** die Rippe
**ribbon** das Band
**rice** der Reis
**rich** *(person)* reich
   *(food)* reichhaltig
**to ride** *(horse)* reiten
**right** *(correct)* richtig
**right: on the right** rechts
   *to the right* nach rechts
**right of way** die Vorfahrt
**ring** der Ring
**to ring** klingeln
   *it's ringing* es klingelt
   *to ring s.o.* jemanden
   anrufen
**ripe** reif
**river** der Fluss
**road** die Straße
**road map** die Straßenkarte
**road sign** das Straßenschild
**roast** Rost-
**roll** *(bread)* das Brötchen

**roller blades** die Rollerblades

**romantic** romantisch

**roof** das Dach

**roof-rack** der Dachgepäckträger

**room** (in house, hotel) das Zimmer
*(space)* der Platz
*double room* das Doppelzimmer
*family room* das Familienzimmer
*single room* das Einzelzimmer

**room number** die Zimmernummer

**room service** der Zimmerservice

**root** die Wurzel

**rope** das Seil

**rose** (flower) die Rose

**rotten** (fruit, etc) verfault

**round** rund

**roundabout** (traffic) der Kreisverkehr

**row** (in theatre, etc) die Reihe

**to row** (boat) rudern

**rowing** (sport) das Rudern

**rubber** (eraser) der Radiergummi
*(material)* das Gummi

**rubber gloves** die Gummihandschuhe

**rubbish** der Abfall

**rubella** die Röteln

**rucksack** der Rucksack

**ruin** (eg castle) die Ruine

**ruler** (measuring) das Lineal

**to run** rennen

**rush hour** die Rushhour

**rusty** rostig

**rye bread** das Roggenbrot

# S

**sad** traurig

**saddle** der Sattel

**safe** (for valuables) der Safe

**safe** ungefährlich
*is it safe?* ist das ungefährlich?

**safety** die Sicherheit

**safety belt** der Sicherheitsgurt

**safety pin** die Sicherheitsnadel

**sail** das Segel

**to sail** segeln

**sailboard** das Segelbrett

**sailing** (sport) das Segeln

**sailing boat** das Segelboot

**salad** der Salat
*green salad* grüner Salat
*mixed salad* gemischter Salat
*potato salad* Kartoffelsalat
*tomato salad* Tomatensalat

**salad dressing** die Salatsoße

**salary** das Gehalt

**sale** (in general) der Verkauf (seasonal bargains) der Schlussverkauf

**salesperson** der Verkäufer/ die Verkäuferin

**salt** das Salz

**salt water** das Salzwasser

**salty** salzig

**same** gleich

**sand** der Sand

**sandals** die Sandalen

**sandwich** das Sandwich

**sanitary pads** die Damenbinden

**satellite dish** die Satellitenschüssel

**satellite TV** das Satellitenfernsehen

**Saturday** der Samstag

**sauce** die Soße
*tomato sauce* die Tomatensoße

**saucepan** der Kochtopf

**sauna** die Sauna

**sausage** die Wurst

**to save** (person) retten (money) sparen

**savoury** pikant

**to say** sagen

**scales** die Waage

**scarf** (headscarf) das Kopftuch
(round neck) das Halstuch

**scenery** die Landschaft

**schedule** der Plan

**school** die Schule
*primary school* die Grundschule
*secondary school* die Oberschule

**scissors** die Schere

**score** der Endstand

**Scot** der Schotte/die Schottin

**Scotland** Schottland

**Scottish** schottisch

**screen** der Bildschirm

**screen wash** das Scheibenputzmittel

**screw** die Schraube

**screwdriver** der Schraubenzieher

**sedative** das Beruhigungsmittel

**to see** sehen

**self-catering** für Selbstversorger

**self-employed** freiberuflich

**self-service** die Selbstbedienung

**to sell** verkaufen
*do you sell...?* verkaufen Sie...?

**sell-by date** das Haltbarkeitsdatum

**Sellotape®** der Tesafilm®

**to send** schicken

**senior citizen** der Rentner/die Rentnerin

**separated** (couple) getrennt

**September** der September

**septic tank** die Klärgrube
**serious** schlimm
**to serve** (dish) servieren
**service** (in shop, etc) die Bedienung
  **is service included?** ist die Bedienung inbegriffen?
**service station** die Raststätte
**set menu** die Tageskarte
**settee** das Sofa
**several** verschiedene
**to sew** nähen
**sex** das Geschlecht
  (intercourse) der Sex
**shade** der Schatten
  **in the shade** im Schatten
**to shake** schütteln
**shallow** (water) seicht
**shampoo** das Shampoo
**shampoo and set** Waschen und Föhnen
**to share** teilen
**sharp** scharf
**to shave** rasieren
**she** sie
**sheep** das Schaf
**sheet** (on bed) das Betttuch
**shell** (seashell) die Muschel
  (egg, nut) die Schale
**sheltered** geschützt
**to shine** scheinen
**shingles** die Gürtelrose
**ship** das Schiff
**shirt** das Hemd

**shock** der Schock
**shock absorber** der Stoßdämpfer
**shoe** der Schuh
**shoelaces** die Schnürsenkel
**shoe polish** die Schuhcreme
**shoe shop** der Schuhladen
**shop** der Laden
**to shop** einkaufen
**shop assistant** der Verkäufer/die Verkäuferin
**shopping** das Einkaufen
  **to go shopping** einkaufen gehen
**shopping centre** das Einkaufszentrum
**shore** das Ufer
**short** kurz
**shortage** der Mangel
**short circuit** der Kurzschluss
**short cut** die Abkürzung
**shorts** die Shorts
**short-sighted** kurzsichtig
**shoulder** die Schulter
**to shout** rufen
**show** (theatrical) die Aufführung
**to show** zeigen
**shower** (bath) die Dusche
  (of rain) der Schauer
**shower cap** die Duschhaube
**shower gel** das Duschgel
**to shrink** einlaufen
**shut** (closed) geschlossen

**S** **to shut** schließen
**shutter** *(on window)* der Fensterladen
**sick** *(ill)* krank
*(nauseous)* übel
**I feel sick** mir ist schlecht
**side** die Seite
**side dish** die Beilage
**sidelight** das Standlicht
**sidewalk** der Bürgersteig
**sight** die Sehenswürdigkeit
**sightseeing tour** die Besichtigungstour
**sign** *(notice)* das Schild
**to sign** unterschreiben
**signature** die Unterschrift
**signpost** der Wegweiser
**silk** die Seide
**silver** das Silber
**to sing** singen
**single** *(unmarried)* ledig
*(not double)* Einzel-
*(ticket)* einfach
**single bed** das Einzelbett
**single room** das Einzelzimmer
**sink** *(kitchen)* das Spülbecken
**sister** die Schwester
**sister-in-law** die Schwägerin
**to sit** sitzen
**sit down please!** bitte setzen Sie sich!
**size** *(clothes, shoes)* die Größe
**to skate** *(on ice)* Schlittschuh laufen

**skates** *(ice)* die Schlittschuhe
*(roller)* die Rollschuhe
**skateboard** das Skateboard
**skating rink** die Eisbahn
**ski** der Ski
**to ski** Ski fahren
**ski boots** die Skistiefel
**skiing** das Skilaufen
**ski instructor** der Skilehrer/die Skilehrerin
**ski jump** die Sprungschanze
**ski lift** der Skilift
**ski pants** die Skihose
**ski pass** der Skipass
**ski run/piste** die Abfahrt
**ski stick/pole** der Skistock
**ski suit** der Skianzug
**skin** die Haut
**skirt** der Rock
**sky** der Himmel
**sledge** der Schlitten
**to sleep** schlafen
**to sleep in** verschlafen
**sleeper** *(on train)* der Schlafwagen
**sleeping bag** der Schlafsack
**sleeping car** der Schlafwagen
**sleeping pills** die Schlaftabletten
**slice** die Scheibe
**slide** *(photograph)* das Dia
**to slip** rutschen
**slippers** die Hausschuhe

**slow(ly)** langsam

**to slow down** langsamer werden

**small** klein

**smaller than** kleiner als

**smell** der Geruch *(unpleasant)* der Gestank

**to smell** riechen

**smile** das Lächeln

**to smile** lächeln

**smoke** der Rauch

**to smoke** rauchen
*I don't smoke* ich bin Nichtraucher(in)

**smoke alarm** der Feuermelder

**smoked** *(food)* geräuchert

**smokers** *(sign)* Raucher

**smooth** weich

**snack** der Snack
*to have a snack* einen Imbiss essen

**snack bar** die Snackbar

**snake** die Schlange

**snake bite** der Schlangenbiss

**to sneeze** niesen

**snorkel** der Schnorchel

**snow** der Schnee

**to snow:** *it's snowing* es schneit

**to snowboard** Snowboard fahren

**snow chains** die Schneeketten

**snow tyres** die Winterreifen

**snowed up** eingeschneit

**soap** die Seife

**soap powder** das Waschmittel

**socket** die Steckdose

**socks** die Socken

**soda water** das Soda

**sofa** das Sofa

**sofa bed** das Sofabett

**soft** weich

**soft drink** das alkoholfreie Getränk

**soldier** der Soldat

**sole** *(of shoe)* die Sohle

**soluble** löslich

**some** einige

**someone** irgendjemand

**something** etwas

**son** der Sohn

**son-in-law** der Schwiegersohn

**song** das Lied

**soon** bald
*as soon as possible* so bald wie möglich

**sore throat** die Halsschmerzen

**sorry: I'm sorry!** tut mir leid!

**sort** die Sorte
*what sort?* welche Sorte?

**soup** die Suppe

**sour** sauer

**soured cream** die saure Sahne

**south** der Süden

**souvenir** das Souvenir

**spa** das Bad

**space** der Platz

**spade** der Spaten

**Spain** Spanien

**Spanish** adj spanisch

**spanner** der Schraubenschlüssel

**spare parts** die Ersatzteile

**spare room** das Gästezimmer

**spare tyre** der Ersatzreifen

**spare wheel** das Ersatzrad

**sparkling** perlend
*sparkling water* das Sprudelwasser
*sparkling wine* der Schaumwein

**spark plugs** die Zündkerzen

**to speak** sprechen
*do you speak English?* sprechen Sie Englisch?

**special** speziell

**specialist** der Spezialist/die Spezialistin

**speciality** die Spezialität

**speed** die Geschwindigkeit

**speed limit** die Geschwindigkeitsbegrenzung
*to exceed the speed limit* die Geschwindigkeitsbegrenzung überschreiten

**speedometer** der Tachometer

**to spell:** *how's it spelt?* wie buchstabiert man das?

**to spend** ausgeben

**spice** das Gewürz

**spicy** würzig

**to spill** verschütten

**spinach** der Spinat

**spin dryer** die Wäscheschleuder

**spine** das Rückgrat

**splinter** der Splitter

**spoilt** verdorben

**sponge** der Schwamm

**spoon** der Löffel

**sport** der Sport

**sports centre** das Fitnesscenter

**sports shop** das Sportgeschäft

**spot** der Fleck

**sprain** die Verstauchung

**spring** *(season)* der Frühling
*(metal)* die Feder

**square** *(in town)* der Platz

**stadium** das Stadion

**staff** das Personal

**stain** der Fleck

**stairs** die Treppe

**stale** *(bread)* trocken

**stalls** *(in theatre)* das Parkett

**stamp** die Briefmarke

**to stand** stehen

**star** der Stern
*(film)* der Star

**to start** *(begin)* anfangen

**starter** *(in meal)* die Vorspeise
*(in car)* der Anlasser

**station** der Bahnhof

**stationer's** die Schreibwarenhandlung

**statue** die Statue

**stay** der Aufenthalt
*enjoy your stay!* angenehmen Aufenthalt!

**to stay** *(to remain)* bleiben

**steak** das Steak

**to steal** stehlen

**steamed** gedünstet

**steel** der Stahl

**steep** steil

**steeple** der Kirchturm

**step** der Schritt

**stepdaughter** die Stieftochter

**stepfather** der Stiefvater

**stepmother** die Stiefmutter

**stepson** der Stiefsohn

**stereo** die Stereoanlage

**sterling** das Pfund Sterling

**steward/stewardess** der Steward/die Stewardess

**to stick** *(with glue)* kleben

**sticking plaster** das Heftpflaster

**still** *(yet)* noch
*(motionless)* still
*still water* stilles Wasser

**sting** der Stachel

**to sting** stechen

**stitches:** *the wound needs stitches* die Wunde muss genäht werden

**stockings** die Strümpfe

**stolen** gestohlen

**stomach** der Magen

**stomach ache** die Magenschmerzen

**stone** der Stein

**stop** *(sign)* das Stoppschild

**to stop** halten

**store** *(shop)* das Geschäft

**storey** das Geschoss

**storm** der Sturm

**story** die Geschichte

**straight away** sofort

**straight on** geradeaus

**strange** *(odd)* seltsam

**straw** *(for drinking)* der Strohhalm

**strawberries** die Erdbeeren

**stream** der Bach

**street** die Straße

**street map** der Stadtplan

**strength** die Stärke

**stress** der Stress

**strike** *(of workers)* der Streik

**string** die Schnur

**striped** gestreift

**stroke** der Schlaganfall
*to have a stroke* einen Schlaganfall haben

**strong** stark
*strong coffee* starker Kaffee
*strong tea* starker Tee

**stuck:** *it's stuck* es klemmt
**student** der Student/die Studentin
**student discount** die Studentenermäßigung
**stuffed** gefüllt
**stung** gestochen
**stupid** dumm
**subscription** *(fee)* der Beitrag
**subtitles** die Untertitel
**subway** die Unterführung
**suddenly** plötzlich
**suede** das Wildleder
**sugar** der Zucker
**sugar-free** zuckerfrei
**to suggest** vorschlagen
**suit** *(man's)* der Anzug *(woman's)* das Kostüm
**suitcase** der Koffer
**sum** die Summe
**summer** der Sommer
**summer holidays** die Sommerferien
**summit** der Gipfel
**sun** die Sonne
**to sunbathe** sonnenbaden
**sunblock** die Sonnencreme
**sunburn** der Sonnenbrand
**Sunday** der Sonntag
**sunglasses** die Sonnenbrille
**sunny** sonnig
**sunrise** der Sonnenaufgang
**sunroof** das Sonnendach

**sunscreen** das Sonnenschutzmittel
**sunset** der Sonnenuntergang
**sunshade** der Sonnenschirm
**sunstroke** der Sonnenstich
**suntan** die Sonnenbräune
**suntan lotion** das Sonnenöl
**supermarket** der Supermarkt
**supper** das Abendessen
**supplement** *(to pay)* der Zuschlag
**to supply** zur Verfügung stellen
**sure:** *I'm sure* ich bin mir sicher
**to surf** surfen
   *to surf the Net* im Internet surfen
**surfboard** das Surfbrett
**surgery** die Operation
**surname** der Nachname
**surprise** die Überraschung
**to survive** überleben
**suspension** *(in car)* die Aufhängung
**to swallow** verschlucken
**to sweat** schwitzen
**sweater** der Pullover
**sweatshirt** das Sweatshirt
**sweet** *(not savoury)* süß
**sweetener** der Süßstoff
**sweets** die Süßigkeiten
**to swell** anschwellen
**to swim** schwimmen

**swimming costume** der Badeanzug

**swimming pool** das Schwimmbad

**swimsuit** der Badeanzug

**swing** *(for children)* die Schaukel

**Swiss** *adj* schweizerisch *m/f* der Schweizer/die Schweizerin

**switch** der Schalter

**to switch off** *(light)* ausschalten *(machine)* abschalten *(gas, water)* abstellen

**to switch on** *(light, machine)* einschalten *(gas, water)* anstellen

**Switzerland** die Schweiz

**swollen** geschwollen

**synagogue** die Synagoge

**syringe** die Spritze

# T

**table** der Tisch

**tablecloth** die Tischdecke

**tablet** *(pill)* die Tablette

**table tennis** das Tischtennis

**table wine** der Tafelwein

**to take** nehmen; *(medicine)* einnehmen *how long does it take?* wie lange dauert es?

**take-away food** das Essen zum Mitnehmen

**to take off** abfliegen

**talc** der Körperpuder

**to talk to** sprechen mit

**tall** groß

**tampons** die Tampons

**tangerine** die Mandarine

**tank** *(petrol)* der Tank *(fish)* das Aquarium

**tap** der Wasserhahn

**tap water** das Leitungswasser

**tape** die Kassette

**tape measure** das Maßband

**tape recorder** der Kassettenrekorder

**target** das Ziel

**taste** der Geschmack

**to taste** probieren *can I taste it?* darf ich es probieren?

**tax** die Steuer

**taxi** das Taxi

**taxi driver** der Taxifahrer/die Taxifahrerin

**taxi rank** der Taxistand

**tea** der Tee *herbal tea* Kräutertee *tea with milk* Tee mit Milch

**tea bag** der Teebeutel

**teapot** die Teekanne

**teaspoon** der Teelöffel

**tea towel** das Geschirrtuch

**to teach** unterrichten

**teacher** der Lehrer/die Lehrerin

**T**

**team** das Team
**tear** *(in material)* der Riss
**teat** *(on bottle)* der Sauger
**teenager** der Teenager
**teeth** die Zähne
**telegram** das Telegramm
**telephone** das Telefon
**to telephone** telefonieren
**telephone box** die Telefonzelle
**telephone call** der Anruf
**telephone card** die Telefonkarte
**telephone directory** das Telefonbuch
**telephone number** die Telefonnummer
**television** das Fernsehen
**to tell** erzählen
**temperature** die Temperatur
  *to have a temperature* Fieber haben
**temporary** provisorisch
**tenant** der Mieter
**tendon** die Sehne
**tennis** das Tennis
**tennis ball** der Tennisball
**tennis court** der Tennisplatz
**tennis racket** der Tennisschläger
**tent** das Zelt
**tent peg** der Hering
**terminal** das Terminal
**terrace** die Terrasse

**to test** testen
**testicles** die Hoden
**tetanus injection** die Tetanusimpfung
**than** als
**to thank** danken
  *thank you* danke
  *thanks very much* vielen Dank
**that** das
  *that one* das dort
**the** der, die, das
**theatre** das Theater
**theft** der Diebstahl
**their** *(with der words)* ihr
  *(with das words)* ihr
  *(with die words)* ihre
**them** ihnen
**there** *(over there)* dort
**there is/there are** es gibt
**these** diese
  *these ones* diese hier
**they** sie
**thick** *(not thin)* dick
**thief** der Dieb
**thigh** der Oberschenkel
**thin** dünn
**thing** das Ding
  *my things* meine Sachen
**to think** denken
**thirsty** durstig
  *to be thirsty* Durst haben
**this** dies
  *this one* das hier
**thorn** der Dorn

**those** jene
　*those ones* jene dort
**thread** der Faden
**throat** die Kehle
**throat lozenges** die Halspastillen
**through** durch
**to throw away** wegwerfen
**thumb** der Daumen
**thunder** der Donner
**thunderstorm** das Gewitter
**Thursday** der Donnerstag
**ticket** die Karte
　*(train, bus, etc)* die Fahrkarte
　*(entrance fee)* die Eintrittskarte
　*a single ticket* eine einfache Fahrkarte
　*a return ticket* eine Rückfahrkarte
**ticket inspector** der Schaffner/die Schaffnerin
**ticket office** der Fahrkartenschalter
**tide** die Gezeiten
　*high tide* die Flut
　*low tide* die Ebbe
**tidy** ordentlich
**to tidy up** aufräumen
**tie** die Krawatte
**tight** eng
**tights** die Strumpfhose
**tile** die Fliese
**till** *(cash desk)* die Kasse
**till** *(until)* bis
　*till 2 o'clock* bis zwei Uhr

**time** *(of day)* die Zeit
　*what time is it?* wie spät ist es?
**timer** die Schaltuhr
**timetable** der Fahrplan
**tin** *(can)* die Dose
**tinfoil** die Alufolie
**tin-opener** der Dosenöffner
**to tip** Trinkgeld geben
**tip** *(to waiter, etc)* das Trinkgeld
**tipped** *(cigarettes)* Filter-
**tired** müde
**tissues** die Papiertaschentücher
**to** zu (zum/zur)
　*(with names of places)* nach
　*to London* nach London
　*to the airport* zum Flughafen
**toadstool** der Giftpilz
**toast** der Toast
**tobacco** der Tabak
**tobacconist's** die Tabakwarenhandlung
**today** heute
**toddler** das Kleinkind
**toe** die Zehe
**together** zusammen
**toilet** die Toilette
　*disabled toilet* die Behindertentoilette
**toilet brush** die Toilettenbürste
**toilet paper** das Toilettenpapier

**T**

**toiletries** die Toilettenartikel

**toll** *(motorway)* die Maut

**tomato** die Tomate
 *tinned tomatoes* die Dosentomaten

**tomato juice** der Tomatensaft

**tongue** die Zunge

**tonic water** das Tonic

**tonight** heute Abend

**tonsillitis** die Mandelentzündung

**too** *(also)* auch
 *too big* zu groß
 *too small* zu klein
 *too noisy* zu laut

**tools** das Werkzeug

**toolkit** der Werkzeugkasten

**tooth** der Zahn

**toothache** die Zahnschmerzen
 *I have toothache* ich habe Zahnschmerzen

**toothbrush** die Zahnbürste

**toothpaste** die Zahnpasta

**toothpick** der Zahnstocher

**top:** *the top floor* das oberste Stockwerk

**top** *(of mountain)* der Gipfel
 *(lid)* der Deckel
 *(clothing)* das Oberteil
 *on top of...* oben auf...

**topless** oben ohne

**torch** *(flashlight)* die Taschenlampe

**torn** zerrissen

**total** *(amount)* die Endsumme

**to touch** anfassen

**tough** *(meat)* zäh

**tour** die Fahrt
 *guided tour* die Besichtigungstour

**tour guide** der Reiseführer/ die Reiseführerin

**tour operator** der Reiseveranstalter

**tourist** der Tourist/die Touristin

**tourist information** die Touristeninformation

**tourist office** das Fremdenverkehrsbüro

**tourist route** die Touristenroute

**tourist ticket** die Touristenkarte

**to tow** *(car)* abschleppen

**towbar** *(car)* die Abschleppstange

**tow rope** das Abschleppseil

**towel** das Handtuch

**tower** der Turm

**town** die Stadt
**town centre** das Stadtzentrum
**town hall** das Rathaus
**town plan** der Stadtplan
**toxic** giftig
**toy** das Spielzeug
**toy shop** der Spielzeugladen
**tracksuit** der Jogginganzug
**traditional** traditionell
**traffic** der Verkehr
**traffic jam** der Stau
**traffic lights** die Ampel
**traffic warden** die Politesse
**trailer** der Anhänger
**train** der Zug
  *by train* mit dem Zug
**trainers** die Trainingsschuhe
**tram** die Straßenbahn
**tranquilliser** das Beruhigungsmittel
**to translate** übersetzen
**to travel** reisen
**travel agent's** das Reisebüro
**travel documents** die Reisepapiere
**travel guide** der Reiseführer
**travel insurance** die Reiseversicherung
**travel sickness** die Reisekrankheit
**traveller's cheques** die Reiseschecks

**tray** das Tablett
**tree** der Baum
**trip** der Ausflug
**trolley** *(luggage)* der Gepäckwagen
  *(shopping)* der Einkaufswagen
**trousers** die Hose
**truck** der Laster
**true** wahr
**trunk** der Koffer
**trunks** die Badehose
**to try** versuchen
**to try on** anprobieren
**T-shirt** das T-Shirt
**Tuesday** der Dienstag
**tumble dryer** der Wäschetrockner
**tunnel** der Tunnel
**to turn** *(right/left)* abbiegen
**to turn around** umdrehen
**to turn off** *(light)* ausmachen
  *(TV, radio, etc)* ausschalten
  *(tap)* zudrehen
**to turn on** *(light)* anmachen
  *(TV, radio, etc)* anschalten
  *(tap)* aufdrehen
**turquoise** *(colour)* türkis
**tweezers** die Pinzette
**twice** zweimal
**twin-bedded room** das Zweibettzimmer
**twins** die Zwillinge
**to type** Maschine schreiben
**typical** typisch

**T**

**tyre** der Reifen
**tyre pressure** der Reifendruck
**Tyrol** das Tirol

## U

**ugly** hässlich
**ulcer** das Geschwür
**umbrella** der Regenschirm (sun) der Sonnenschirm
**uncle** der Onkel
**uncomfortable** unbequem
**unconscious** bewusstlos
**under** unter
**undercooked** nicht gar
**underground** die U-Bahn
**underpants** die Unterhose
**underpass** die Unterführung
**understand** verstehen
 *I don't understand* ich verstehe nicht
**underwear** die Unterwäsche
**unemployed** arbeitslos
**to unfasten** aufmachen
**United Kingdom** das Vereinigte Königreich
**United States** die Vereinigten Staaten
**university** die Universität
**unleaded petrol** das bleifreie Benzin
**unlikely** unwahrscheinlich
**to unlock** aufschließen
**to unpack** auspacken
**unpleasant** unangenehm

**to unplug** herausziehen
**to unscrew** aufschrauben
**until** bis
**unusual** ungewöhnlich
**up:** *to get up* aufstehen
**upside down** verkehrt herum
**upstairs** oben
**urgent** dringend
**urine** der Urin
**us** uns
**to use** benutzen
**useful** nützlich
**usual(ly)** gewöhnlich
**U-turn** die Wende

## V

**vacancy** *(in hotel)* Zimmer frei
**vacant** frei
**vacation** der Urlaub
**vaccination** die Impfung
**vacuum cleaner** der Staubsauger
**vagina** die Vagina
**valid** gültig
**valuable** wertvoll
**valuables** die Wertsachen
**value** der Wert
**valve** das Ventil
**van** der Lieferwagen
**vase** die Vase
**VAT** die Mehrwertsteuer (MWST)

**vegan:** *I'm vegan* ich bin Veganer

**vegetables** das Gemüse

**vegetarian** vegetarisch

**vehicle** das Fahrzeug

**vein** die Ader

**Velcro®** das Klettband

**vending machine** der Automat

**venereal disease** die Geschlechtskrankheit

**ventilator** der Ventilator

**very** sehr

**vest** das Unterhemd

**vet** der Tierarzt

**via** über

**to video** *(from TV)* auf Video aufnehmen
*(to film)* filmen

**video** das Video

**video camera** die Videokamera

**video cassette/tape** die Videokassette

**video game** das Videospiel

**video recorder** der Videorekorder

**Vienna** Wien

**view** die Aussicht

**villa** die Villa

**village** das Dorf

**vinegar** der Essig

**vineyard** der Weinberg

**virus** der Virus

**visa** das Visum

**visit** der Besuch

**to visit** *(person)* besuchen
*(place)* besichtigen

**visiting hours** *(hospital)* die Besuchszeit

**visitor** der Besucher

**vitamin** das Vitamin

**voice** die Stimme

**volcano** der Vulkan

**volleyball** der Volleyball

**voltage** die Spannung

**to vomit** erbrechen

**voucher** der Gutschein

# W

**wage** der Lohn

**waist** die Taille

**waistcoat** die Weste

**to wait for** warten auf

**waiter/waitress** der Kellner/die Kellnerin

**waiting room** der Warteraum

**to wake up** aufwachen

**Wales** Wales

**walk** der Spaziergang
*to go for a walk* einen Spaziergang machen

**to walk** spazieren gehen
*(go on foot)* zu Fuß gehen

**walking boots** die Wanderschuhe

**walking stick** der Wanderstock

**Walkman®** der Walkman®

171

**W**

wall die Mauer

wallet die Brieftasche

to want wollen
 *I want...* ich möchte...
 *we want...* wir möchten...

war der Krieg

ward *(hospital)* die Station

wardrobe der Kleiderschrank

warehouse die Lagerhalle

warm warm
 *it's warm* es ist warm

to warm up *(milk, etc)* aufwärmen

warning triangle das Warndreieck

to wash waschen
 *(to wash oneself)* sich waschen

wash and blow dry Waschen und Föhnen

washing machine die Waschmaschine

washing powder das Waschpulver

washing-up bowl die Abwaschschüssel

washing-up liquid das Spülmittel

wasp die Wespe

wasp sting der Wespenstich

waste bin der Abfalleimer

to watch zuschauen

watch die Armbanduhr

water das Wasser

hot water warmes Wasser

cold water kaltes Wasser

drinking water Trinkwasser

mineral water Mineralwasser

sparkling water Sprudelwasser

still water stilles Wasser

water heater das Heißwassergerät

waterproof wasserdicht

water sports der Wassersport

to water ski Wasserski fahren

water wings die Schwimmflügel

waves *(on sea)* die Wellen

way der Weg

way in *(entrance)* der Eingang

way out *(exit)* der Ausgang

we wir

weak schwach
 *(tea, coffee)* dünn

to wear tragen

weather das Wetter

weather forecast die Wettervorhersage

website die Webseite

wedding die Hochzeit

wedding anniversary der Hochzeitstag

wedding present das Hochzeitsgeschenk

Wednesday der Mittwoch

**week** die Woche
   *last week* letzte Woche
   *next week* nächste Woche
   *this week* diese Woche

**weekday** der Werktag

**weekend** das Wochenende

**weekly** wöchentlich

**weekly ticket** das Wochenticket

**to weigh** wiegen

**weight** das Gewicht

**welcome** willkommen

**well** gut
   *he's not well* ihm geht es nicht gut

**well** *(for water)* der Brunnen

**well-done** *(steak)* durch

**wellington boots** die Gummistiefel

**Welsh** *adj* walisisch
   *m/f* der Waliser/die Waliserin

**west** der Westen

**wet** nass

**wetsuit** der Taucheranzug

**what** was

**wheat** der Weizen

**wheel** das Rad

**wheelchair** der Rollstuhl

**wheel clamp** die Parkkralle

**when** wann

**where** wo

**which:** *which man?* welcher Mann?
   *which woman?* welche Frau?

**which book?** welches Buch?

**while** während
   *in a while* bald

**white** weiß

**who** wer

**whole** vollständig

**wholemeal bread** das Vollkornbrot

**whose** wessen

**why** warum

**wide** breit

**widow** die Witwe

**widower** der Witwer

**wife** die Frau

**wig** die Perücke

**to win** gewinnen

**wind** der Wind

**windmill** die Windmühle

**window** das Fenster
   *(of shop)* das Schaufenster

**windscreen** die Windschutzscheibe

**windscreen wipers** die Scheibenwischer

**to windsurf** surfen

**windy:** *it's windy* es ist windig

**wine** der Wein
   *dry wine* trockener Wein
   *house wine* Hauswein
   *red wine* Rotwein
   *rosé wine* Roséwein
   *sparkling wine* Schaumwein
   *sweet wine* süßer Wein
   *white wine* Weißwein

**W**

wine list die Weinkarte
wing der Flügel
wing mirror der Seitenspiegel
winter der Winter
wire der Draht
with mit
without ohne
witness der Zeuge
woman die Frau
wonderful wunderbar
wood (material) das Holz
wooden hölzern
woods (forest) der Wald
wool die Wolle
word das Wort
work die Arbeit
work permit die Arbeitsgenehmigung
to work (person) arbeiten (machine) funktionieren
world die Welt
worried besorgt
worse schlechter
worth: it's worth £50 es ist fünfzig Pfund wert
to wrap up einwickeln
wrapping paper das Geschenkpapier
wrist das Handgelenk
to write schreiben
please write it down bitte schreiben Sie das auf
writing paper das Briefpapier

wrong falsch
what's wrong? was stimmt nicht?

**X**

X-ray die Röntgenaufnahme
to x-ray röntgen

**Y**

yacht die Jacht
year das Jahr
this year dieses Jahr
next year nächstes Jahr
last year letztes Jahr
yearly jährlich
yellow gelb
Yellow Pages die Gelben Seiten
yes ja
yesterday gestern
yet: not yet noch nicht
yoghurt der Jogurt
plain yoghurt Naturjogurt
yolk das Eigelb
you (polite sing. and pl.) Sie (familiar sing.) du ; ihr (pl.)
young jung
your dein/Ihr
(with der words) dein/Ihr
(with das words) dein/Ihr
(with die words) deine /Ihre
youth hostel die Jugendherberge

# Z

**zebra crossing** der
  Zebrastreifen
**zero** null
**zip** der Reißverschluss
**zone** die Zone
**zoo** der Zoo
**zoom lens** der Zoom

# A

**Aal** m eel

**ab** off ; from
  *ab 8 Uhr* from 8 o'clock
  *ab Mai* from May onward

**abbestellen** to cancel

**abbiegen** to turn *(right/left)*

**Abbildung** f illustration

**abblenden** to dip *(lights)*

**Abblendlicht** nt dipped headlights

**Abend** m evening

**Abendessen** nt evening meal

**abends** in the evening(s)

**aber** but

**abfahren** to depart ; to leave

**Abfahrt** f departures

**Abfahrtszeit** f departure time

**Abfall** m rubbish

**Abfertigungsschalter** m check-in desk

**abfliegen** to take off

**Abflug** m flight departures
  *Abflug Inland* domestic departures
  *Abflug Ausland* international departures

**Abflughalle** f departure lounge

**Abflugzeit** f departure time

**Abfluss** m drain

**Abführmittel** nt laxative

**abholen** to fetch ; to claim *(baggage, etc)*
  *abholen lassen* to send for

**Abkürzung** f short cut

**abladen** to dump ; to offload

**ablaufen** to expire

**ablehnen** to refuse

**Abonnement** nt subscription

**Abreise** f departure

**absagen** to cancel

**Absatz** m heel

**abschalten** to switch off *(machine)*

**abschicken** to dispatch

**Abschleppdienst** m breakdown service

**abschleppen** to tow *(car)*

**Abschleppseil** nt towrope

**Abschleppstange** f towbar

**Abschleppwagen** m breakdown van

**Absender** m sender

**abstellen** to turn off ; to park car

**Abszess** m abscess

**Abtei** f abbey

**Abteil** nt compartment

**Abteilung** f department

**Abtreibung** f abortion

**Abtreibungspille** f abortion pill

**Abzug** m print *(photo)*

**Achse** f axle

**achten auf** to pay attention to

**Achtung** f caution ; danger

**Ader** f vein

**Adler** m eagle

**Adressbuch** nt address book

**Adresse** f address

**adressieren** to address

**Affe** m monkey

**ähnlich** similar

**Aktentasche** f briefcase

**Akzent** m accent (pronunciation)

**akzeptieren** to accept

**Alarmanlage** f alarm

**Alge** f seaweed

**Alkohol** m alcohol

**alkoholfrei** non-alcoholic

**alkoholisch** alcoholic (drink)

**alle** all ; everybody ; everyone
*alle zwei Tage* every other day

**Allee** f avenue

**allein** alone

**Allergie** f allergy

**allergisch gegen** allergic to

**Allerheiligen** nt All Saints' Day

**alles** everything ; all

**allgemein** general ; universal

**Alpen** pl Alps

**alt** old

**Altar** m altar

**Altbier** nt top-fermented dark beer

**Alter** nt age (of person)

**ältere(r/s)** older ; elder

**Altglascontainer** m bottle bank

**Alufolie** f aluminium foil

**am** at ; in ; on
*am Bahnhof* at the station
*am Abend* in the evening
*am Freitag* on Friday

**Ameise** f ant

**Amerika** nt America

**Amerikaner(in)** m/f American

**amerikanisch** adj American

**Ampel** f traffic light

**Amtszeichen** nt dialling tone

**Amüsierviertel** nt nightclub district

**an** at ; on (light, radio, etc) ; near
*Frankfurt an 1300* arriving Frankfurt at 1300

**an/aus** on/off

**Ananas** f pineapple

**anbauen** to grow (cultivate)

**anbieten** to offer

**andere(r/s)** other

**ändern** to change (to alter)

**Änderung** f change

**Anfall** m fit (seizure)

**Anfang** m start (beginning)

**anfangen** to begin ; to start

**Anfänger(in)** m/f beginner

**Anfängerhügel** m nursery slope

**Anfrage** f enquiry

**Angaben** pl details ; directions (to a place)

**angeben** to give

**Angebot** nt offer
im Angebot on offer

**Angehörige(r)** m/f relative

**angeln** to fish

**Angeln** nt fishing ; angling
Angeln verboten no fishing

**Angelrute** f fishing rod

**Angelschein** m fishing permit

**angenehm** pleasant

**Angestellte(r)** m/f employee

**Angina** f angina

**angreifen** to attack

**Angst haben vor** to be afraid of

**Anhänger** m trailer ; fan (supporter)

**Anker** m anchor

**ankommen** to arrive

**ankündigen** to announce

**Ankunft** f arrivals

**Anlage** f park ; grounds ; facilities

**öffentliche Anlage** public park

**Anlasser** m starter (in car)

**Anlegeplatz** m mooring

**Anlegestelle** f landing stage ; jetty

**anmachen** to turn on

**Anmeldeformular** nt registration form

**Anmeldung** f registration ; reception (place)

**Annahme** f acceptance ; reception

**annehmen** to assume ; to accept

**anprobieren** to try on

**Anruf** m phone call

**Anrufbeantworter** m answerphone

**anrufen** to phone

**anschalten** to turn on

**anschauen** to look at

**Anschlagbrett** nt notice board

**Anschluss** m connection (train, etc)

**Anschlussflug** m connecting flight

**anschnallen** to fasten

**Anschrift** f address

**anschwellen** to swell

**Ansicht** f view

**Ansichtskarte** f picture postcard

**anstatt** instead of

**ansteckend** infectious

**anstehen** to queue

**anstellen** to switch on *(gas, water)*

**Anteil** *m* share *(part)*

**Antenne** *f* aerial

**Antibiotikum** *nt* antibiotic

**antik** ancient

**Antiquitäten** *pl* antiques

**Antiquitätenladen** *m* antique shop

**Antiseptikum** *nt* antiseptic

**Antwort** *f* answer ; reply

**antworten** to answer ; to reply

**Anweisungen** *pl* instructions

**Anzahl** *f* number

**Anzahlung** *f* deposit

**Anzeige** *f* advertisement ; report *(to police)*

**Anzug(-züge)** *m* suit(s) *(man's)*

**anzünden** to light ; to set fire to

**Apfel (Äpfel)** *m* apple(s)

**Apfelsaft** *m* apple juice

**Apfelsine(n)** *f* orange(s)

**Apfelwein** *m* cider

**Apotheke** *f* pharmacy

**Apparat** *m* appliance ; camera ; extension

**Aprikose(n)** *f* apricot(s)

**April** *m* April

**Aquarium** *nt* fish tank

**Arbeit** *f* employment ; work

**arbeiten** to work *(person)*

**arbeitslos** unemployed

**Architekt(in)** *m/f* architect

**Architektur** *f* architecture

**arm** poor

**Arm** *m* arm

**Armband** *nt* bracelet

**Armbanduhr** *f* watch

**Ärmelkanal** *m* English Channel

**Art** *f* type ; sort ; manner

**Arthritis** *f* arthritis

**Artikel** *m* article ; item

**Arznei** *f* medicine

**Arzt (Ärztin)** *m/f* doctor

**Aschenbecher** *m* ashtray

**Aspirin** *nt* aspirin

**Ast** *m* branch *(of tree)*

**Asthma** *nt* asthma

**Atlantik** *m* Atlantic Ocean

**atmen** to breathe

**attraktiv** attractive

**auch** also ; too ; as well

**auf** onto ; on ; upon ; on top of
*auf Deutsch* in German
*auf Wiedersehen* goodbye

**aufdrehen** to turn on *(tap)*

**Aufenthalt** *m* stay ; visit

**Aufenthaltsraum** *m* lounge

**Auffahrt** *f* slip-road

**Aufführung** *f* performance ; show

**aufgeben** to quit ; to post ; to check in *(baggage)*

**A**

aufhalten to delay ; to hold up
*sich aufhalten* to stay

auflegen to hang up

aufmachen to open (shop, bank etc) ; to unfasten
*sich aufmachen* to set off

aufregend exciting

aufschließen to unlock

aufschrauben to unscrew

aufschreiben to write down

aufstehen to get up

Aufstieg m ascent

aufwachen to wake up

aufwärmen to heat up (food, milk)

Aufzug m lift/elevator

Auge(n) nt eye(s)

Augenblick m moment ; instant

Augentropfen pl eye drops

August m August

Auktion f auction

Au-pair-Mädchen nt au pair

aus off (light, radio, etc) ; made of... ; from ; out of

Ausdruck m expression ; print-out ; term (word)

Ausfahrt f exit (motorway)

Ausfall m failure (mechanical)

Ausflug(-flüge) m trip(s) ; excursion(s)

Ausfuhr f export(s)

ausführen to export ; to carry out (job)

ausfüllen to fill in (form)
*bitte nicht ausfüllen* please leave blank (on form)

Ausgabe f issue (of magazine) ; issuing counter

Ausgaben pl expenses

Ausgang m exit ; gate (at airport)

ausgeben to spend (money)

ausgehen to go out (for amusement)

ausgeschaltet off (radio)

ausgestellt issued at (passport)

ausgezeichnet excellent

auskugeln to dislocate (joint)

Auskunft information

Ausland nt foreign countries ; abroad ; international
*aus dem Ausland* from overseas

Ausländer(in) m/f foreigner

ausländisch foreign

Auslandsgespräch nt international call

auslassen to leave out ; to omit

auslaufen to sail (ship)

ausmachen to turn off (light) ; to put out (fire, etc)

**Ausnahme** f exception

**auspacken** to unpack

**Auspuffrohr** nt exhaust pipe

**Ausrüstung** f kit ; equipment

**ausschalten** to switch off (light, TV, radio)

**Ausschank** m bar ; drinks

**Ausschlag** m cold sore ; skin rash

**ausschließlich** excluding ; exclusive(ly)

**Außenseite** f outside

**Außenspiegel** m outside mirror

**außer Betrieb** out of order

**äußerlich** exterior

**Aussicht** f view ; prospect

**aussprechen** to pronounce

**Ausstattung** f equipment (of car)

**aussteigen** to get out of (vehicle)

**Ausstellung** f show ; exhibition

**Ausstellungsdatum** nt date of issue

**Austausch** m exchange

**Australien** nt Australia

**Australier(in)** m/f Australian

**australisch** adj Australian

**Ausverkauf** m sale

**ausverkauft** sold out

**Auswahl** f choice

**auswählen** to choose

**auswärts essen** to eat out

**ausweichen** to avoid

**Ausweis** m identity card ; pass (permit)

**auszahlen** to pay

**Auto(s)** nt car(s)

**Autobahn** f motorway

**Autobahngebühr** f toll

**Autofähre** f car-ferry

**Autokarte** f road map

**Automat** m vending machine
  *Automat wechselt* change given

**Automatikauto** nt automatic car

**automatisch** automatic

**Automobilklub** m automobile association

**Autor(in)** m/f author

**Autoreisezug** m motorail service

**Autoschlüssel** pl car keys

**Autovermietung** f car hire

# B

**Baby** nt baby

**Babyflasche** f baby's bottle

**Babymilch** f baby milk

**Babynahrung** f baby food

**Babyraum** m mother and baby room

**B**

Babysitter(in) *m/f* baby-sitter

Babytücher *pl* baby wipes

Bach *m* stream

Bäckerei *f* baker's

Backofen *m* oven

Bad *nt* bath ; spa

Badeanzug *m* swimsuit

Badehose *f* swimming trunks

Badekappe *f* bathing cap

Badelatschen *pl* flip flops

baden to bathe ; to swim
*Baden verboten* no swimming

Badezimmer *nt* bathroom

Baguette *nt* French bread

Bahn *f* railway ; rink
*per Bahn* by rail

Bahnhof *m* station ; depot

Bahnlinie *f* line *(railway)*

Bahnsteig *m* platform

Bahnübergang *m* level crossing

bald soon

Balkon *m* balcony

Ball *m* ball

Ballett *nt* ballet

Ballon *m* balloon

Banane(n) *f* banana(s)

Band (Bänder) *nt* ribbon(s) ; tape(s)

Band *f* band *(musical)*

Bank *f* bank ; bench

Bankkonto *nt* bank account

Bar *f* nightclub ; bar

Bär *m* bear *(animal)*

Bargeld *nt* cash

Bart *m* beard

Basel Basle

Batterie *f* battery

Bauarbeiten *pl* roadworks ; construction work

bauen to build

Bauer (Bäuerin) *m/f* farmer

Bauernhaus *nt* farmhouse

Bauernhof *m* farm(yard)

Baum *m* tree

Baumarkt *m* DIY shop

Baumwolle *f* cotton *(fabric)*

Baustelle *f* roadworks ; construction site

Bayern *nt* Bavaria

beachten to observe ; to obey

beantworten to answer

Bedarfshaltestelle *f* request stop

bedeckt cloudy *(weather)*

Bedeutung *f* meaning

bedienen to serve ; to operate
*sich bedienen* to help oneself

Bedienung *f* service charge

Bedingung *f* condition

Beefsteak *nt* steak
*deutsches Beefsteak* hamburger; beefburger

beenden to end ; to finish

**Beerdigung** f funeral

**Beere** f berry

**beginnen** to begin

**begrüßen** to greet ; to welcome

**behalten** to keep (retain)

**Behandlung** f treatment

**beheizt** heated

**behindert** disabled (person)

**Behindertentoilette** f toilet for disabled

**Behinderung** f obstruction ; handicap

**bei** near ; by (beside) ; at ; on ; during

**beide** both

**Beilage** f side-dish ; vegetables ; side-salad

**Bein** nt leg

**Beisel** nt pub (Austria)

**Beispiel(e)** nt example(s) **zum Beispiel** for example

**beißen** to bite

**Beitrag** m contribution ; subscription (to club)

**beitreten** to join (club)

**Bekleidungsgeschäft** nt clothes shop

**bekommen** to get (receive, obtain)

**beladen** to load (truck, ship)

**Belastung** f load

**belegt** no vacancies

**Beleuchtung** f lighting

**Belgien** nt Belgium

**beliebt** popular

**Belohnung** f reward

**benachrichtigen** to inform

**Benachrichtigung** f advice note

**benötigen** to require

**benutzen** to use

**Benzin** nt petrol

**bequem** comfortable

**Beratungsstelle** f advice centre

**berechtigt zu** entitled to

**Berechtigte(r)** m/f authorized person

**bereit** ready

**Bereitschaftsdienst** m emergency service

**Berg(e)** m mountain(s)

**bergab** downhill

**bergauf** uphill

**Bergführer(in)** m/f mountain guide

**Bergschuhe** pl climbing boots

**Bergtour** f hillwalk ; climb

**Bergwacht** f mountain rescue

**Bergwanderung** f hill-walking

**Bericht(e)** m report(s) ; bulletin(s)

**berichten** to report

**Berliner** m doughnut

**Beruf** m profession ; occupation

**beruflich** professional

Beruhigungsmittel nt tranquilliser

berühmt famous

berühren to handle ; to touch

beschädigen to damage

beschäftigt busy

Beschäftigung f employment ; occupation

Bescheinigung f certificate

beschreiben to describe

Beschreibung f description

Besen m brush (for sweeping floor)

besetzt engaged ; occupied

besichtigen to visit (place)

Besichtigungen pl sightseeing

Besichtigungstour f guided tour

Besitzer(in) m/f owner

besondere(r/s) particular ; special

besorgt worried

besser better

Besserung(en) f improvement(s)
  gute Besserung get well soon

bestätigen to confirm

Bestätigung f confirmation (flight, etc)

beste(r/s) best

Besteck nt cutlery

bestellen to book ; to order

Bestellung f order

Bestimmungen pl regulations

Bestimmungsort m destination

besuchen to visit (person)

Besucher(in) m/f visitor

Besuchszeit f visiting hours

beten to pray

Betrag m amount
  Betrag erhalten payment received

betreten to enter

Betrieb m business

betrunken drunk

Bett(en) nt bed(s)

Bettbezug m duvet cover

Bettdecke f duvet ; quilt

Betttuch nt sheet (on bed)

Bettzeug nt bedclothes

Beule f lump (swelling)

bewacht guarded

bewegen to move

Bewohner(in) m/f resident

bewölkt cloudy

bewusstlos unconscious

bezahlen to pay ; to settle bill

bezahlt paid

Bezahlung f payment

Bezirk m district

bezüglich concerning

BH m bra

**Bibliothek** f library

**Biene** f bee

**Bienenstich** m bee sting ; type of cream cake

**Bier** nt beer
*Bier vom Fass* draught beer

**Biergarten** m beer garden

**Bierkeller** m beer cellar

**Bierstube** f pub that specializes in beer

**bieten** to offer

**Bikini** m bikini

**Bild(er)** nt picture(s)

**Bilderrahmen** m picture frame

**Bildschirm** m screen *(TV, computer)*

**billig** cheap ; inexpensive

**billiger** cheaper

**Billigtarif** m cheap rate

**Birne(n)** f pear(s) ; lightbulb(s)

**bis** until ; till
*bis jetzt* up till now
*bis zu 6* up to 6
*bis bald* see you soon

**bisschen:** *ein bisschen* a little ; a bit of

**bitte** please

**bitte?** pardon?

**bitten um** to ask for

**bitter** bitter *(taste)*

**blass** pale

**Blase** f blister

**Blasenentzündung** f cystitis

**Blatt (Blätter)** nt sheet(s) *(of paper)* ; leaf (leaves)

**blau** blue

**Blaue Zone** f limited parking zone *(parking disk required)*

**Blei** nt lead *(metal)*

**bleiben** to stay *(to remain)*

**Bleichmittel** nt bleach

**Bleiersatz-Zusatz** nt lead additive

**bleifreies Benzin** nt unleaded petrol

**Bleistift** m pencil

**blind** blind *(person)*

**Blinddarmentzündung** f appendicitis

**Blinker** m indicator *(in car)*

**Blitz** m lightning

**Blitzlicht** nt flash *(for camera)*

**blockiert** jammed *(camera, lock)*

**Blockschrift** f block letters

**blond** fair *(hair)* ; blond

**Blumen** pl flowers

**Blumenladen** m florist's shop

**Bluse** f blouse

**Blut** nt blood

**Blutdruck** m blood pressure

**bluten** to bleed

**Bluterguss** m bruise

**Blutgruppe** f blood group

**blutig** rare *(steak)*

**Bluttest** m blood test

**Blutvergiftung** f blood poisoning

**Bockbier** nt strong beer

**Boden** m floor (of room) ; ground

**Bodensee** m Lake Constance

**Bohnen** pl beans
*grüne Bohnen* french beans

**Bohrer** m drill (tool)

**Boiler** m immersion heater

**Bombe** f bomb

**Bonbon** nt sweet

**Boot** nt boat (small)

**Bootsfahrt** f cruise

**Bootsrundfahrt** f round boat trip

**Bootsverleih** m boat hire

**Bordkarte** f boarding pass

**borgen** to borrow

**Böschung** f embankment

**botanischer Garten** m botanical gardens

**Botschaft** f embassy

**Bowle** f punch (drink)

**Brandwunde** f burn (on skin)

**Brat-** fried ; roast

**braten** to fry ; to roast

**Bratkartoffeln** pl fried potatoes

**Bratpfanne** f frying pan

**Bratwurst** f sausage

**Brauch** m custom (tradition)

**brauchen** to need

**Brauerei** f brewery

**braun** brown

**Bräune** f suntan

**Braut** f bride

**Bräutigam** m bridegroom

**Brechreiz** m nausea

**breit** wide

**Bremse(n)** f brake(s)

**bremsen** to brake

**Bremsflüssigkeit** f brake fluid

**Bremslicht** nt brake light

**brennen** to burn

**Brief** m letter (message)

**Briefkasten** m letterbox ; postbox

**Briefmarke(n)** f stamp(s)

**Briefpapier** nt writing paper

**Brieftasche** f wallet

**Briefträger(in)** m/f postman/woman

**Brille** f glasses (spectacles)

**Brillenetui** nt glasses case

**bringen** to bring

**britisch** British

**Brombeeren** pl blackberries

**Bronchitis** f bronchitis

**Bronze** f bronze

**Brosche** f brooch

**Broschüre** f brochure

**Brot** nt bread ; loaf

**Brötchen** nt bread roll

**Bruch** m fracture

Brücke f bridge

Bruder(Brüder) m brother(s)

Brühe f stock (for soup, etc)

Brühwürfel pl stock cubes

Brunnen m well (for water) ; fountain

Brust f breast ; chest

Buch nt book

buchen to book

Buchhandlung f bookshop

Büchsen- canned

Büchsenöffner m can-opener

Buchstabe m letter (of alphabet)

Bucht f bay (along coast)

Buchung f booking

Bügel m coat hanger
*Bügel drücken!* press down!

Bügelbrett nt ironing board

Bügeleisen nt iron (for clothes)

bügeln to iron

Bundes- federal

Bundesrepublik Deutschland f Federal Republic of Germany

Bungee-Springen nt bungee jumping

bunt coloured

Burg f castle ; fortress (medieval)

Bürger(in) m/f citizen

bürgerlich middle-class

Bürgermeister(in) m/f mayor(-ess)

Bürgersteig m pavement ; sidewalk

Büro nt agency ; office

Bürogebäude nt office block

Bürste f brush

Bus(se) m bus(es) ; coach(es)

Busbahnhof m bus/coach station

Busfahrschein m bus ticket

Busfahrt f bus tour

Bushaltestelle f bus stop

Buslinie f bus route

Busreise f coach trip

Busverbindung f bus service

Büstenhalter m bra

Butangas nt Calor gas®

Butter f butter

# C

campen to camp

Campingführer m camping guide(book)

Campingkocher m camping stove

Campingplatz m campsite

Campingtisch m picnic table

CD-Spieler m CD player

Champignon(s) m mushroom(s)

Charterflug m charter flight

Check-in m check-in

Chef(in) m/f boss

chemische Toilette f chemical loo

Chinarestaurant nt Chinese restaurant

Chips pl crisps ; chips (gambling)

Chor m choir

Cola f Coke®

Computer m computer

Computerprogramm nt computer program

Computerspiel nt computer game

Conditioner m conditioner (hair)

Cousin(e) m/f cousin

Creme f cream (lotion)

Creme(speise) f mousse

# D

da there
nicht da out (not at home)

Dach nt roof

Dachboden m attic

Dachgepäckträger m roof-rack

daheim at home

Damen pl ladies

Damenbinde(n) f sanitary towel(s)

Dampfer m steamer (boat)

danach after (afterwards)

Dänemark nt Denmark

danke thank you

danken to thank

Darmgrippe f gastric flu

das the ; that ; this ; which

Datei f file (computer)

Datum nt date (day)

Dauer f length ; duration

Dauerwelle f perm

Daumen m thumb

Decke f blanket ; ceiling

Deckel m top ; lid

dein your (singular familiar)

denken to think

Denkmal(-mäler) nt monument(s)

Deo nt deodorant

der the ; who(m) ; that ; this ; which

Desinfektionsmittel nt disinfectant

desinfizieren to disinfect

destilliertes Wasser nt distilled water

Details pl details

deutsch adj German

Deutsch nt German (language)

Deutsche(r) m/f German

Deutschland nt Germany

Devisen pl foreign currency

Dezember m December

**Dia(s)** nt slide(s)

**Diabetes** m diabetes

**Diabetiker(in)** m/f diabetic person

**Diamant** m diamond

**Diät** f diet (special)

**dick** fat

**die** the ; who(m) ; that ; this ; which

**Dieb(in)** m/f thief

**Diebstahl** m theft

**Dienst** m service
im Dienst on duty

**Dienstag** m Tuesday

**dienstbereit** open (pharmacy) ; on duty (doctor)

**Dienstreise** f business trip

**Dienstzeit** f office hours

**dies** this

**diese** these

**diese(r/s)** this (one)

**Diesel** m diesel

**Dieselöl** nt diesel oil

**Ding(e)** nt thing(s)

**Diplomat(in)** m/f diplomat

**direkt** direct (route, train)

**Direktflug** m direct flight

**Direktor(in)** m/f managing director

**Diskette** f computer disk (floppy)

**Disko** f disco

**Dokumente** pl documents

**Dollar** m dollar

**Dolmetscher(in)** m/f interpreter

**Dom** m cathedral

**Donner** m thunder

**Donnerstag** m Thursday

**Doppel-** double

**Doppelbett** nt double bed

**doppelt** double

**Doppelzimmer** nt double room

**Dorf(Dörfer)** nt village(s)

**Dorn** m thorn

**dort** there (over there) ; that one

**Dose** f box ; tin ; can

**Dosenöffner** m tin-opener

**Dozent(in)** m/f teacher (university)

**Drachenfliegen** nt hang gliding

**Draht** m wire

**Drahtseilbahn** f cable railway

**draußen** outdoors ; outside

**drehen** to turn ; to twist

**Dreibettabteil** nt three-berth compartment

**Dreieck** nt triangle

**Dreikönigstag** m Epiphany

**dringend** urgent

**drinnen** indoors

**Droge** f drug

**Drogerie** f chemist's (not for prescriptions)

**D**

drücken push
Druckschrift f block letters
du you (familiar form)
dumm stupid
dunkel dark
dunkelblau dark blue
dünn thin ; weak (tea)
dunstig misty
durch through ; well-done (steak)
Durchfahrt verboten no through traffic
Durchfall m diarrhoea
Durchgang m way ; passage
Durchgangsverkehr m through traffic
durchgehend direct (train, bus) ; 24 hour
Durchsage f announcement
durchwählen to dial direct
Durchzug m draught (of air)
dürfen to be allowed
Dürre f drought
Durst haben to be thirsty
durstig thirsty
Dusche f shower
Duschhaube f shower cap
Duschvorhang m shower curtain
Dutzend nt dozen

190

**E**

Ebbe f low tide
echt real ; genuine
Ecke f corner
Edelstein m jewel ; gem
ehemalig ex-
ehrlich honest
Ei(er) nt egg(s)
Eiche f oak
eifersüchtig jealous
Eigelb nt egg yolk
Eigentum nt property
Eigentümer(in) m/f owner
Eil- urgent
Eilbrief m express letter
Eilzustellung f special delivery
Eimer m bucket
ein (with 'das'/'der' words) a ; one
ein(geschaltet) on (machine)
Einbahnstraße f one-way street
Einbrecher(in) m/f burglar
einchecken to check in
eine (with 'die' words) a ; one
einfach simple ; single ticket ; plain (unflavoured)
Einfuhr f import
einführen to insert ; to import
Eingang m entrance
Eingangstür f front door
eingeschlossen included (in price)

**eingeschneit** snowed up

**Eingeweidebruch** m hernia

**eingießen** to pour

**einige(r/s)** some ; a few

**einkaufen** to shop

**Einkaufswagen** m shopping trolley

**Einkaufszentrum** nt shopping centre

**einladen** to invite

**Einladung** f invitation

**Einlass ab 18** no entry for under 18s

**einlaufen** to shrink

**einlösen** to cash (cheque)

**einmal** once

**einnehmen** to take (medicine)

**einordnen** to get in lane

**Einrichtungen** pl facilities

**eins** one

**einschalten** to switch on (light, TV)

**einschieben** to insert

**einschließlich** including

**Einschreiben** nt registered letter
per Einschreiben by recorded delivery

**einsteigen** to get in(to) (bus, etc)

**einstellen** to adjust ; to appoint ; to stop

**Eintopfgericht** nt stew

**eintreten** to enter

**Eintritt** m entry ; admission (fee)

**Eintritt frei** free entry

**Eintrittskarte(n)** f ticket(s)

**Eintrittspreis** m admission charge/fee

**einwerfen** to post ; to insert

**einwickeln** to wrap up (parcel)

**Einwurf** m slot ; slit
Einwurf 2 Mark insert 2 marks

**Einzahlung** f deposit

**Einzel-** (not double)

**Einzelbett** nt single bed

**Einzelfahrschein** m single ticket

**einzeln** single ; individual

**Einzelzimmer** nt single room

**Eis** nt ice cream ; ice

**Eisbahn** f skating rink

**Eisbecher** m knickerbocker glory

**Eisdiele** f ice-cream parlour

**Eisen** nt iron (metal)

**Eisenbahn** f railway

**Eisenwarenhandlung** f hardware shop

**Eiskaffee** m iced coffee

**Eistee** m iced tea

**Eiswürfel** pl ice cubes

**Eiweiß** nt egg white

**E**

**Elastikbinde** f elastic bandage
**elastisch** elastic
**Elektriker(in)** m/f electrician
**elektrisch** electric(al)
**elektrischer Schlag** m electric shock
**Elektrizität** f electricity
**Elektrorasierer** m electric razor
**Ellbogen** m elbow
**Eltern** pl parents
**E-Mail** f e-mail
**E-Mail-Adresse** f e-mail address
**Empfang** m reception
**empfangen** to receive (guest) ; to greet
**Empfangschef** m receptionist
**Empfangsdame** f receptionist
**Empfangsschein** m receipt
**empfehlen** to recommend
**Ende** nt end ; bottom (of page, etc)
**Endstand** m final score (of match)
**Endstation** f terminal
**Endsumme** f total (amount)
**eng** narrow ; tight (clothes)
**England** nt England
**Engländer(in)** m/f Englishman/woman
**Englisch** nt English (language)

**Enkel** m grandson
**Enkelin** f granddaughter
**entdecken** to discover
**Ente** f duck
**enteisen** to de-ice
**entfernt** distant
    *2 Kilometer entfernt* 2 km away
**Entfernung** f distance
**entfrosten** to defrost
**Enthaarungscreme** f depilatory cream
**enthalten** to hold (to contain)
**entkoffeinierter Kaffee** m decaffeinated coffee
**entkommen** to escape
**entrahmte Milch** f skimmed milk
**entschädigen** to reimburse
**Entschuldigung** f pardon ; excuse me
**entweder ... oder** either ... or
**entwickeln** to develop (photos)
**Entzündung** f inflammation
**Epileptiker(in)** m/f epileptic
**epileptischer Anfall** m epileptic fit
**er** he ; it
**erbrechen** to vomit
**Erbsen** pl peas
**Erdbeben** nt earthquake
**Erdbeeren** pl strawberries
**Erde** f earth

**Erdgeschoss** nt ground floor

**Erdnuss(-nüsse)** f peanut(s)

**Erdrutsch** m landslide

**erfreut** pleased

**Erfrischungen** pl refreshments

**erhalten** to obtain ; to receive

**erhältlich** available

**Erkältung** f cold (illness)

**erkennen** to realize ; to recognize

**erklären** to explain

**Erklärung** f explanation

**erlauben** to permit (something) ; to allow

**Ermäßigung** f reduction

**Ernte** f harvest

**Ersatz** m substitute ; replacement

**Ersatzrad** nt spare wheel

**Ersatzteile** pl car parts

**erste(r/s)** first
*erste Hilfe* first aid
*erste Klasse* first class

**ertrinken** to drown

**Erwachsene(r)** m/f adult

**erzählen** to tell

**es** it

**essbar** edible

**essen** to eat

**Essen** nt food ; meal

**Essen zum Mitnehmen** take-away food

**Essig** m vinegar

**Esslöffel** m tablespoon

**Esszimmer** nt dining room

**Etage** f floor ; storey

**Etagenbetten** pl bunk beds

**etwas** something

**Eule** f owl

**Euro** m Euro (currency)

**Europa** nt Europe

**europäisch** European

**Europäische Union (EU)** f European Union (EU)

**Euroscheck** m Eurocheque

**Exemplar** nt copy

**Experte (Expertin)** m/f expert

**exportieren** to export

# F

**Fabrik** f works ; factory

**Facharzt (Fachärztin)** m/f specialist (medical)

**Fächer** m fan (hand-held)

**Faden** m thread

**Fahne** f flag

**Fahrbahn** f carriageway

**Fähre** f ferry

**fahren** to drive ; to go

**Fahrer(in)** m/f driver (of car)

**Fahrgast** m passenger

**Fahrkarte** f ticket (train, bus, etc)

**Fahrkartenschalter** m ticket office

**Fahrplan** m timetable (trains, etc)

**Fahrplanhinweise** pl travel information

**Fahrpreis(e)** m fare(s)

**Fahrrad(-räder)** nt bicycle(s)

**Fahrradflickzeug** nt bicycle repair kit

**Fahrradschloss** nt bicycle lock

**Fahrradvermietung** f bike hire

**Fahrschein(e)** m ticket(s)

**Fahrscheinentwerter** m ticket stamping machine

**Fahrscheinheft** nt book of tickets

**Fahrspur(en)** f lane(s)

**Fahrstuhl** m lift ; elevator

**Fahrt** f journey ; drive ; ride (in vehicle)
*gute Fahrt!* safe journey!

**Fahrzeug** nt vehicle

**Fall** m instance
*im Falle von* in case of

**fallen** to fall

**fällig** due (owing)

**falsch** false (name, etc) ; wrong

**Falten** pl wrinkles

**Familie** f family

**Familienname** m surname

**Familienstand** m marital status

**Familienzimmer** nt family room

**Fan** m fan (football)

**Farbe** f colour ; paint ; suit (cards)

**färben** dye

**farbenblind** colour-blind

**Farbfilm** m colour film

**farbig** coloured

**Farbstoff** m dye

**Fasching** m carnival

**Fass** nt barrel
*vom Fass* on tap ; on draught

**Fassbier** nt draught beer

**Fastnachtsdienstag** m Shrove Tuesday

**faul** lazy

**Fax** nt fax

**faxen** to fax

**Faxnummer** f fax number

**Februar** m February

**Feder** f spring (coil) ; feather

**Federball** m badminton

**Federung** f suspension (in car)

**fehlen** to be missing

**Fehler** m fault ; mistake

**Fehlgeburt** f miscarriage

**feiern** to celebrate

**Feiertag** m holiday

**Feile** f file (nail)

**Feinkostgeschäft** nt delicatessen

**Feld** nt field

**Felsen** m cliff (in mountains)

**Fenster** nt window

**Fensterladen** m shutter (on window)

**Fensterplatz** m window seat

**Ferien** pl holiday(s)

**Ferienhaus** nt chalet (holiday)

**Ferienwohnung** f holiday flat

**Fern-** long-distance

**Fernbedienung** f remote control

**Ferngespräch** nt long-distance call

**Fernglas** nt binoculars

**Fernlicht** nt full beam (headlights)

**Fernsehen** nt television

**Fernseher** m TV set

**Fernsprecher** m public phone

**fertig** ready ; finished

**Fest** nt celebration ; party ; festival

**Festplatte** f hard disk

**Fett** nt fat ; grease

**fettarm** low-fat

**fettarme Milch** f low-fat milk

**fettig** greasy

**feucht** damp

**Feuchtigkeitscreme** f moisturizer

**Feuer** nt fire

**feuerfeste Form** f ovenproof dish

**feuergefährlich** inflammable

**Feuerlöscher** m fire extinguisher

**Feuermelder** m fire/smoke alarm

**Feuertreppe** f fire escape

**Feuerwehr** f fire brigade

**Feuerwehrauto** nt fire engine

**Feuerwerk** nt fireworks

**Feuerzeug** nt cigarette lighter

**Fieber** nt fever
*Fieber haben* to have temperature

**Filet** nt sirloin ; fillet (of meat, fish)

**Filiale** f branch (of store, bank, etc)

**Film** m film (at cinema, for camera)

**filmen** to film

**Filter** m filter

**Filzstift** m felt-tip pen

**finden** to find

**Finger** m finger

**Fingernagel** m fingernail

**Firma** f company (firm)

**Fisch** m fish

**Fischladen** m fishmonger's

**FKK-Strand** m nudist beach

**flach** flat (level)

**Flamme** f flame

**Flasche** f bottle

**F**

**Flaschenbier** nt bottled beer
**Flaschenöffner** m bottle opener
**Fleck** m mark (stain)
**Fleckenmittel** nt stain-remover
**Fleisch** nt meat ; flesh
**Fleischerei** f butcher's
**Flickzeug** nt puncture repair kit
**Fliege** f bow tie ; fly
**fliegen** to fly
**Flitterwochen** honeymoon
**Flöhe** pl fleas
**Flohmarkt** m flea market
**Flug(Flüge)** m flight(s)
**Fluggast** m passenger
**Fluggesellschaft** f airline
**Flughafen** m airport
**Flughafenbus** m airport bus
**Flugplan** m flight schedule
**Flugauskunft** f flight information
**Flugschein(e)** m plane ticket(s)
**Flugsteig** m gate
**Flugstrecke** f route ; flying distance
**Flugticket(s)** nt plane ticket(s)
**Flugzeug** nt plane, aircraft
**Flur** m corridor
**Fluss(Flüsse)** m river(s)

**Flussfahrt** f river trip
**Flüssigkeit** f liquid
**Flut** f flood ; high tide
**Föhn** m hairdryer
**föhnen** to blow-dry
**folgen** to follow
**Forelle** f trout
**Form** f shape ; form
**Formular** nt form (document)
**Fortsetzung** f sequel (book, film)
**Foto** nt photo
**Fotoapparat** m camera
**Fotogeschäft** nt photo shop
**Fotografie** f photography
**fotografieren** to take a photo
**Fotokopie** f photocopy
**fotokopieren** to photocopy
**Fracht** f cargo ; freight
**Frage** f question
**fragen** to ask
**frankieren** to stamp (letter)
**Frankreich** nt France
**Franzose (Französin)** m/f Frenchman/woman
**französisch** adj French
**Frau** f wife ; Mrs ; Ms ; woman
**Fräulein** nt Miss
**frei** free / vacant
**im Freien** outdoor

**Freibad** nt open-air pool

**freiberuflich** freelance ; self-employed

**Freigepäck** nt baggage allowance

**freimachen** to stamp

**Freitag** m Friday

**Freizeichen** nt ringing tone

**Freizeit** f spare time ; leisure

**Freizeitzentrum** nt leisure centre

**fremd** foreign ; strange (unknown)

**Fremde(r)** m/f stranger

**Fremdenführer(in)** m/f tourist guide

**Fremdenverkehrsbüro** nt tourist office

**Freude** f joy

**Freund** m friend ; boyfriend

**Freundin** f friend ; girlfriend

**freundlich** friendly

**Frieden** m peace

**Friedhof** m cemetery

**frisch** fresh ; wet (paint)

**Frischhaltefolie** f cling film

**Frischkäse** m cream cheese

**Friseur (Friseuse)** m/f hairdresser

**Frosch** m frog

**Frost** m frost

**Frostschutzmittel** nt antifreeze

**Früchte** pl fruit

**Früchtetee** m fruit tea

**Fruchtsaft** m fruit juice

**früh** early

**früher** earlier .

**Frühling** m spring (season)

**Frühstück** nt breakfast

**Fuchs** m fox

**fühlen** to feel

**führen** to lead

**Führer(in)** m/f guide

**Führerschein** m driving licence

**Führung(en)** f guided tour(s)

**füllen** to fill

**Füller** m pen

**Fundbüro** nt lost property office

**Fundsachen** pl lost property

**funktionieren** to work (machine)

**für** for
*Benzin für DM 50* DM 50 worth of petrol
*für immer* forever

**Fuß(Füße)** m foot(feet)
*zu Fuß gehen* to walk

**Fußball** m football ; soccer

**Fußballer(in)** m/f football player

**F**

**Fußballplatz** m football pitch

**Fußballspiel** nt football match

**Fußgänger(in)** m/f pedestrian

**Fußgängerüberweg** m pedestrian crossing

**Fußgängerzone** f pedestrian precinct

**Fußweg** m footpath

**füttern** to feed

# G

**Gabel** f fork (for eating)

**Gabelung** f fork (in road)

**Galerie** f gallery

**Gang** m course (of meal) ; aisle (theatre, plane)

**Gangschaltung** f gears

**Gans** f goose

**ganz** whole ; quite

**ganztägig** full-time

**Garage** f garage (private)

**Garantie** f guarantee ; warrant(y)

**Garderobe** f cloakroom

**Garten** m garden

**Gartenlokal** nt garden café

**Gärtner(in)** m/f gardener

**Gas** nt gas

**Gasflasche** f gas cylinder

**Gasherd** m gas cooker

**Gaspedal** nt accelerator

**Gasse** f alley ; lane (in town)

**Gast** m guest
nur für Gäste patrons only

**Gästezimmer** nt guestroom

**Gasthaus** nt inn

**Gasthof** m inn ; guesthouse

**Gastritis** f gastritis

**Gaststätte** f restaurant

**Gaststube** f lounge

**Gate** nt gate (airport)

**Gebäck** nt pastry (cake)

**gebacken** baked

**Gebäude** nt building

**gebeizt** cured ; marinated

**geben** to give

**Gebiet** nt region ; area

**Gebiss** nt dentures

**geboren** born
geborene Schnorr née Schnorr

**gebraten** fried

**gebrauchen** to use

**Gebraucht-** used (car, etc)

**gebrochen** broken

**Gebühr** f fee

**gebührenpflichtig** subject to fee

**Geburt** f birth

**Geburtsdatum** nt date of birth

**Geburtsort** m place of birth

Geburtstag *m* birthday

Geburtstagsgeschenk *nt* birthday present

Geburtstagskarte *f* birthday card

Geburtsurkunde *f* birth certificate

Gedeckkosten *pl* cover charge *(in restaurant)*

gedünstet steamed

Gefahr *f* danger

gefährlich dangerous

Gefälle *nt* gradient

Gefängnis *nt* prison

Geflügel *nt* poultry ; fowl

gefroren frozen *(food)*

gefüllt stuffed

gegen versus ; against ; toward(s)

Gegend *f* district ; region

gegenüber opposite ; facing

Gegenverkehr *m* two-way traffic

gegrillt grilled

gehen to go ; to walk
*wie geht es Ihnen?* how are you?

Gehirnerschütterung *f* concussion

gehören to belong to

gekocht boiled ; cooked

gelb yellow ; amber *(traffic lights)*

Gelbe Seiten *pl* Yellow Pages

Gelbsucht *f* jaundice

Geld *nt* money
*Geld einwerfen* insert money

Geldautomat *m* cash dispenser

Geldbeutel *m* purse

Geldrückgabe *f* coin return

Geldschein *m* banknote

Geldstrafe *f* fine *(to be paid)*

Geldstück *nt* coin

gelegentlich occasionally

Gelenk *nt* joint *(of body)*

Geltungsdauer *f* period of validity

gemischt mixed ; assorted

Gemüse *nt* vegetables

Gemüseladen *m* greengrocer's

genau accurate ; precise ; exact

Genehmigung *f* approval ; permit

genug enough

Genuss *m* enjoyment

geöffnet open

Gepäck *nt* luggage

Gepäckablage *f* luggage rack

Gepäckaufbewahrung *f* left-luggage office

Gepäckausgabe *f* baggage reclaim

Gepäckermittlung *f* luggage desk *(for queries)*

**Gepäcknetz** nt luggage rack (in train)

**Gepäckschließfach** nt left-luggage locker

**Gepäckträger** m luggage rack (on car) ; porter

**Gepäckversicherung** f luggage insurance

**Gepäckwagen** m luggage trolley

**gerade** even (number)

**geradeaus** straight ahead

**Gerät** nt appliance ; gadget

**geräuchert** smoked (food)

**Gericht** nt court (law) ; dish (food)

**gerieben** grated (cheese)

**geröstet** sauté ; fried ; toasted

**Geruch** m smell

**Gesamtsumme** f total amount

**Geschäft(e)** nt business ; shop(s)

**Geschäftsadresse** f business address

**Geschäftsführer(in)** m/f manager

**Geschäftspartner(in)** m/f partner (business)

**Geschäftsstunden** pl business hours

**geschehen** to happen

**Geschenk(e)** nt gift(s)

**Geschenkeladen** m gift shop

**Geschenkpapier** nt wrapping paper

**Geschichte** f history

**geschieden** divorced

**Geschirrspülmaschine** f dishwasher

**Geschirrspülmittel** nt washing-up liquid

**Geschirrtuch** nt tea/dish towel

**Geschlecht** nt gender ; sex

**Geschlechtskrankheit** f venereal disease

**geschlossen** closed/shut

**Geschmack** m taste ; flavour

**geschmort** braised

**geschnittenes Brot** nt sliced bread

**Geschoss** nt storey

**geschützt** sheltered

**Geschwindigkeit** f speed

**geschwollen** swollen

**Geschwür** nt ulcer

**Gesellschaft** f company

**Gesetz** nt law

**gesetzlicher Feiertag** m public holiday

**Gesicht** nt face

**Gesichtswasser** f cleanser (for face)

**Gesichtspflege** f facial (beauty treatment)

**gesperrt** closed

**Gespräch** nt talk ; phone call

**Gestank** m smell (unpleasant)

**gestattet** permitted

**gestern** yesterday

**gestochen** stung ; bitten (by insect)

**gestreift** striped

**gesund** healthy

**Gesundheit** f health ; bless you!

**Getränk(e)** nt drink(s)

**Getränkekarte** f list of beverages

**getrennt** separated (couple)
**getrennt bezahlen** to pay separately

**Getriebe** nt gearbox ; gears

**Gewehr** nt gun

**Gewicht** nt weight

**gewinnen** to win

**Gewitter** nt thunderstorm

**gewöhnlich** usual(ly)

**Gewürz** nt spice ; seasoning

**Gezeiten** pl tide

**gibt es...?** is/are there...?

**Gift** nt poison

**giftig** poisonous

**Gipfel** m summit ; mountain top

**Gips** m plaster (for broken limb)

**Gitarre** f guitar

**Glas** nt glass ; jar

**Glatteis** nt black ice

**Glatteisgefahr** f danger – black ice

**glatzköpfig** bald (person)

**glauben** to believe ; to think (be of opinion)

**gleich** same

**Gleise** pl platforms ; tracks

**Gletscher** m glacier

**Glocke** f bell

**Glück** nt happiness ; luck

**glücklich** happy ; lucky

**Glühbirne** f light bulb

**Gold** nt gold

**Golf** nt golf

**Golfplatz** m golf course

**Golfschläger** m golf club

**gotisch** Gothic

**Gott** m God

**Gottesdienst** m church service

**Grad** m degree (of heat, cold)

**Gramm** nt gram(me)

**Grapefruit** f grapefruit

**Gras** nt grass

**Gräte** f fish bone

**grau** grey

**Grenze** f frontier ; border (of country)

**Grenzpolizei** f border police

**Griff** m handle ; knob

**Grill** m barbecue ; grill

**grillen** to grill

## G

**Grillstube** f steak house ; grillroom

**Grillteller** m mixed grill

**Grippe** f flu

**groß** tall ; great ; big ; high (number, speed)

**Großbritannien** nt Great Britain

**Großbuchstabe** m capital letter

**Größe** f size (of clothes, shoes) ; height

**Großeltern** pl grandparents

**Großmutter** f grandmother

**Großvater** m grandfather

**großzügig** generous

**grün** green ; fresh (fish)

**Grünanlage** f park

**Grundstücksmakler** m estate agent's

**grüne Versicherungskarte** f green card (car insurance)

**grüner Salat** m green salad

**Gruppe** f group

**Gruß** m greeting

**Grußkarte** f greetings card

**Gulasch** nt goulash

**gültig** valid

**Gummi** m rubber ; elastic

**Gummiband** nt rubber band

**Gummihandschuhe** pl rubber gloves

**Gummistiefel** pl wellington boots

**günstig** convenient

**Gurke(n)** f cucumber(s) ; gherkin(s)

**Gürtel** m belt

**Gürtelrose** f shingles

**Gürteltasche** f bumbag ; moneybelt

**gut** good ; well ; all right (yes)

**alles Gute** all the best ; with best wishes

**guten Abend** good evening

**guten Appetit** enjoy your meal

**guten Morgen** good morning

**gute Nacht** good night

**guten Tag** hello ; good day/afternoon

**Güter** pl goods

**Gutschein** m voucher ; coupon

## H

**H-Milch** f long-life milk

**Haar** nt hair

**Haarbürste** f hairbrush

**Haare** pl hair

**Haargel** nt hair gel

**Haarklemme** f hairgrip

**Haarschnitt** m haircut

**Haarspray** nt hair spray

**haben** to have

**Hackfleisch** nt mince meat

**Hacksteak** nt hamburger

**Hafen** m harbour ; port

**Hafer** m oats

**Haftung** f liability

**Hagel** m hail

**Hahn** m tap *(for water)* ; cockerel

**Hähnchen** nt chicken

**halb** half
    zum halben Preis half-price

**halb durch** medium rare *(meat)*

**halber Fahrpreis** m half fare

**Halbfettmilch** f semi-skimmed milk

**Halbinsel** f peninsula

**Halbpension** f half board

**Hälfte** f half

**hallo** hello

**Hals** m neck ; throat

**Halskette** f necklace

**Halspastillen** pl throat lozenges

**Halsschmerzen** pl sore throat

**Halstuch** nt scarf *(round neck)*

**Halt** m stop

**Haltbarkeitsdatum** nt sell-by date

**Haltebucht** f layby

**halten** to hold ; to stop

**Halten verboten** no stopping

**Haltestelle** f bus stop

**Hammer** m hammer

**Hämorrhoiden** pl haemorrhoids

**Hand** f hand

**Handel** m trade ; commerce

**Handgelenk** nt wrist

**handgemacht** handmade

**Handgepäck** nt hand-luggage

**Handschuhe** pl gloves

**Handtasche** f handbag

**Handtuch** nt towel

**Handwerker(in)** m/f craftsperson

**Harke** f rake

**hart** hard *(not soft)*

**hart gekochtes Ei** nt hard-boiled egg

**Hase** m hare

**Haselnuss(-nüsse)** f hazelnut(s)

**hässlich** ugly

**häufig** frequent ; common

**Haupt-** major ; main

**Hauptbahnhof** m main station

**Hauptgericht** nt main course

**Hauptstadt** f capital *(city)*

**Hauptstraße** f major road

**Hauptverkehrszeit** f peak hours

**Haus** nt house ; home
    zu Hause at home

Hausarbeit f housework

Hausfrau (Hausmann) f/m housewife/ househusband

Haushaltswaren pl household goods

Hausschuhe pl slippers

Haustier nt pet

Hauswein m house wine

Haut f hide (leather) ; skin

Hecht m pike

Hefe f yeast

Heft nt exercise book

Hefter m stapler

Heftklammern pl staples

Heftpflaster nt sticking plaster

Heidelbeeren pl blueberries

heilig holy

Heiligabend m Christmas Eve

Heim nt home (institution) ; hostel

Heimweh haben to be homesick

heiraten to marry

heiß hot
heiße Schokolade f hot chocolate

heißen to be called
wie heißen Sie? what's your name?

Heißwassergerät nt water heater

Heizgerät nt heater

Heizkörper m radiator

Heizung f heating

helfen to help

Helikopter m helicopter

hell light (pale) ; bright

hellblau light blue

helles Bier nt lager

helles Fleisch nt white meat

Helm m helmet

Hemd(en) nt shirt(s)

Hepatitis f hepatitis

Herbst m autumn

Herd m cooker ; oven

herein in ; come in

hereinkommen to come in

Hering m herring ; tent peg

Herr m gentleman ; Mr

Herren gents (toilet)

heruntergehen to go down

Herz nt heart

Herzanfall m heart attack

herzliche Glückwünsche! congratulations!

Herzschrittmacher m pacemaker

Heuschnupfen m hay fever

heute today

heute Abend tonight

hier here

hiesig local (wine, speciality)

Hilfe f help

**Himbeeren** *pl* raspberries

**Himmel** *m* heaven ; sky

**hin** there

**Hin- und Rückfahrt** *f* round trip

**hineingehen** to go in

**hinten** behind

**hinten einsteigen** enter at rear

**hinter** behind

**Hinweis** *m* notice ; information

**Hirnhautentzündung** *f* meningitis

**historisch** historic

**hoch** high

**Hochsaison** *f* high season

**Höchstgeschwindigkeit** *f* maximum speed

**Höchsttarif** *m* peak rate

**Hochzeit** *f* wedding

**Hochzeitsgeschenk** *nt* wedding present

**Hochzeitskleid** *nt* wedding dress

**Hochzeitstag** *m* wedding anniversary

**Hochzeitstorte** *f* wedding cake

**Hoden** *pl* testicles

**Hof** *m* court

**hoffen** to hope

**höflich** polite

**Höhe** *f* altitude ; height

**hoher Blutdruck** *m* high blood pressure

**höher** higher
*höher stellen* to turn up *(heat, volume)*

**Höhle** *f* cave

**holen** to fetch

**holländisch** Dutch

**Holz** *nt* wood *(material)*

**Holzkohle** *f* charcoal

**Homöopathie** *f* homeopathy

**homosexuell** homosexual

**Honig** *m* honey

**hören** to hear

**Hörer** *m* receiver *(phone)*

**Hörgerät** *nt* hearing aid

**Hörnchen** *nt* croissant

**Hose** *f* trousers

**Hotel** *nt* hotel

**Hotel garni** *nt* bed and breakfast hotel

**hübsch** pretty

**Hubschrauber** *m* helicopter

**Hüfte** *f* hip

**Hügel** *m* hill

**Huhn** *nt* hen

**Hühnchen** *nt* chicken

**Hummer** *m* lobster

**Hund** *m* dog

**Hundeleine** *f* dog lead

**hundert** hundred

**Hunger haben** to be hungry

**Hupe** *f* horn *(of car)*

**husten** to cough

**H**

Husten *m* cough
Hustenbonbons *pl* cough sweets
Hustensaft *m* cough mixture
Hut *m* hat
Hütte *f* mountain hut

**I**

ich I
Idiotenhügel *m* nursery slope
ihm him
ihnen them
ihr(e) her ; their
Imbiss *m* snack
Imbissstube *f* snack bar
immer always
Immunisierung *f* immunisation
Impfung *f* vaccination
in in (place, position) ; inside ; into
in Ordnung all right (agreed)
Infektion *f* infection
Informationsbüro *nt* information office
Ingenieur(in) *m/f* engineer
Inhalationsapparat *m* inhaler (medication)
Inhalt *m* contents
inklusive inclusive
Inland *nt* domestic (flight, etc)

Inlandsgespräch(e) *nt* national call(s)
innen inside
Innenstadt *f* city centre
innerlich for internal use (medicine)
Insekt *nt* insect
Insektenschutzmittel *nt* insect repellent
Insel *f* island
Insulin *nt* insulin
intelligent intelligent
interessant interesting
Internet *nt* internet
Internet-Café *nt* internet café
Internet-Seite *f* website
Ire (Irin) *m/f* Irishman/woman
irgend jemand someone
irgendwo somewhere
irisch *adj* Irish
Irland *nt* Ireland
Irrtum *m* mistake
Italien *nt* Italy
Italiener(in) *m/f* Italian
italienisch *adj* Italian

**J**

ja yes
Jacht *f* yacht
Jachthafen *m* marina
Jacke *f* jacket ; cardigan
Jagderlaubnis *f* hunting permit

jagen to hunt

Jahr nt year

Jahrestag m anniversary

Jahreszeit f season

Jahrgang m vintage

Jahrhundert nt century

jährlich annual ; yearly

Jahrmarkt m fair

Januar m January

jeder everyone

Jeans pl jeans

jede(r/s) each

jemand somebody ;
someone

jene those

jetzt now

Jod nt iodine

joggen to jog

Jogginganzug m
tracksuit

Joghurt m yoghurt

Johannisbeere(n) f
currant(s)

Journalist(in) m/f
journalist

jucken to itch

Jude/Jüdin m/f Jew

Jugendherberge f youth
hostel

Jugendliche(r) m/f
teenager

Juli m July

jung young

Junge m boy

Junggeselle m bachelor

Juni m June

Juwelier m jeweller's

## K

Kabel nt cable ; lead
(electrical)

Kabelfernsehen nt cable
TV

Kabine f cabin ; berth
(train, ship)

Kaffee m coffee

Kaffeehaus nt café

Kaffeemaschine f
percolator

Kai m quayside

Kakao m cocoa

Kakerlake f cockroach

Kalb nt calf (young cow)

Kalbfleisch nt veal

kalt cold

Kamera f camera

Kameratasche f camera
case

Kamillentee m camomile
tea

Kamin m fireplace

Kamm m comb ; ridge

kämpfen to fight

Kanada nt Canada

Kanadier(in) m/f Canadian

kanadisch adj Canadian

Kanal m canal ; (English)
Channel

kandiert glacé

Kaninchen nt rabbit

**K**

Kanister m (petrol) can
Kanu nt canoe
Kapelle f chapel ; orchestra
kaputt broken ; out of order
kaputtmachen to break (object)
Kapuze f hood (of jacket)
Karaffe f decanter ; carafe
Karfreitag m Good Friday
Karotten pl carrots
Karte f card ; ticket ; map ; menu
Kartentelefon nt cardphone
Kartoffel(n) f potato(es)
Kartoffelpüree nt mashed potato
Kartoffelsalat m potato salad
Karton m box (cardboard) ; carton
Käse m cheese
Kasino nt casino
Kasse f cash desk
Kasserolle f casserole
Kassette f cassette ; cartridge ; tape
Kassettenrecorder m cassette player ; tape recorder
Kassierer(in) m/f cashier
Kastanie f chestnut
Katalog m catalogue
Kater m hangover

katholisch Catholic
Katze f cat
kaufen to buy
Kaufhaus nt department store
Kaugummi m chewing gum
Kaution f deposit
Kehle f throat
Keilriemen m fan belt
kein... no...
keine(r/s) no ; none
Keks(e) m biscuit(s) (sweet)
Keller m cellar
Kellner(in) m/f waiter/ waitress
kennen to be acquainted with
Keramik f pottery
Kern m pip
Kerze f candle
Kette f chain
Kfz-Versicherung f car insurance
Kiefer f pine
Kiefer m jaw
Kilo(gramm) nt kilo(gram)
Kilometer m kilometre
Kind(er) nt child(ren)
Kinderbett nt cot
Kindermädchen nt nanny
Kindersitz m child seat (car)
Kinderstuhl m high chair
Kinderteller m child's helping

**Kinderwagen** m pram

**Kinn** nt chin

**Kino** nt cinema

**Kiosk** m kiosk

**Kirche** f church

**Kirmes** f funfair

**Kirsche(n)** f cherry (cherries)

**Kissen** nt cushion ; pillow

**Kiste** f box (wooden)

**Klage** f complaint

**klar** clear

**Klarer** m schnapps

**Klärgrube** f septic tank

**Klasse** f class ; grade

**Klavier** nt piano

**Klebeband** f adhesive tape

**kleben** to stick (with glue)

**Klebstoff** m glue

**Kleid** nt dress

**Kleider** pl clothes

**Kleiderbügel** m coat hanger

**Kleiderschrank** m wardrobe

**klein** little (small) ; short

**Kleingeld** nt change (money)

**Klempner(in)** m/f plumber

**Klettband** nt Velcro®

**klettern** to climb (mountains)

**Klimaanlage** f air-conditioning

**klimatisiert** air-conditioned

**Klingel** f doorbell

**klingeln** to ring (bell, phone)

**Klinik** f clinic

**Klippe** f cliff (along coast)

**klopfen** to knock (on door)

**Kloß** m dumpling

**Kloster** nt monastery ; convent

**Kneipe** f pub

**Knie** nt knee

**Kniestrümpfe** pl pop socks

**Knoblauch** m garlic

**Knöchel** m ankle

**Knochen** m bone

**Knödel** m dumpling

**Knopf** m button ; knob (radio, etc)

**Knoten** m knot

**Koch** m chef

**kochen** to boil ; to cook

**Kocher** m cooker ; stove

**Köchin** f cook

**Kochschinken** m cooked ham

**Kochtopf** m saucepan

**Kode** m code

**Köder** m bait (for fishing)

**koffeinfreier Kaffee** m decaffeinated coffee

**Koffer** m suitcase ; trunk

**Kofferanhänger** m luggage tag

**Kofferraum** m carboot

**Kognak** m brandy

**Kohl** m cabbage

**Kohle** f coal

**Kohlrübe** f swede

**K**

Koje f berth (in ship) ; bunk

Kollege (Kollegin) m/f colleague

Köln Cologne

Kölnischwasser nt eau de cologne

komisch funny (amusing)

kommen to come

Kommode f chest of drawers

Komödie f comedy

Kompass m compass

Komponist(in) m/f composer

Kondensmilch f condensed milk

Konditorei f cake shop ; café

Kondom nt condom

Konferenz f conference

Konfitüre f jam

König m king

Königin f queen

königlich royal

können to be able to ; to know how to

Konsulat nt consulate

Kontaktlinsen pl contact lenses

Kontaktlinsenreiniger m contact lens cleaner

Konto nt bank account

Kontrolle f check ; control

kontrollieren to check (passports, tickets)

Konzert nt concert

Konzertsaal m concert hall

Kopf m head

Kopfhörer pl headphones

Kopfkissen nt pillow

Kopfsalat m lettuce

Kopfschmerzen pl headache

Kopftuch nt scarf (headscarf)

Kopie f copy (duplicate)

kopieren to copy

Korb m basket

Korinthe f currant

Korken m cork (of bottle)

Korkenzieher m corkscrew

Körper m body

Körperpuder m talc

Kortison nt cortisone

Kosmetiksalon m beauty salon

Kosmetiktücher pl paper tissues

kosten to cost

Kosten pl cost (price)

kostenlos free of charge

köstlich delicious

Kostüm nt suit (woman's)

Krabbe f crab

Kräcker m cracker

Kraftstoff m fuel

Kragen m collar

Krämpfe pl cramps

krank ill ; sick

Krankenhaus nt hospital

Krankenkasse f medical insurance

**Krankenwagen** m ambulance

**Krankheit** f disease

**Kräuter** pl herbs

**Kräutertee** m herbal tea

**Krawatte** f tie

**Krebs** m crab *(animal)* ; cancer *(illness)*

**Kreditkarte** f credit card

**Kreisverkehr** m roundabout

**Kreuz** nt cross *(also crucifix)*

**Kreuzfahrt** f cruise

**Kreuzschlitz-schraubenzieher** m Phillips screwdriver®

**Kreuzung** f junction ; crossroads

**Kreuzworträtsel** nt crossword

**Krieg** m war

**Kristall** nt crystal

**Krone** f crown

**Krücken** pl crutches

**Krug** m jug

**Küche** f kitchen ; cuisine

**Kuchen** m flan ; cake

**Küchenbrett** nt chopping board

**Küchenpapier** nt kitchen paper

**Kugel** f ball ; scoop *(of ice cream)*

**Kugelschreiber** m pen ; biro

**Kuh** f cow

**kühl** cool

**Kühlbox** f cool-box *(for picnic)*

**kühlen** to chill *(wine, food)*

**Kühler** m radiator *(of car)*

**Kühlschrank** m fridge

**Kümmel** m caraway seed ; cumin ; schnapps

**Kunde (Kundin)** m/f client ; customer

**Kunst** f art

**Kunstfaser** f man-made fibre

**Kunstgewerbearbeiten** pl crafts

**Kunsthalle** f art gallery

**Künstler(in)** m/f artist

**künstlich** artificial ; man-made

**künstliche Hüfte** f hip replacement

**Kupfer** nt copper

**Kupplung** f clutch *(of car)*

**Kurierdienst** m courier service

**Kurort** m spa

**Kurs** m course ; exchange rate

**Kurve** f curve ; corner ; bend

**kurz** short ; brief

**Kurz(zeit)parkplatz** m short-stay car park

**kurzsichtig** short-sighted

**Kurzwarengeschäft** nt haberdasher's

## K

**Kuss** m kiss
**küssen** to kiss
**Küste** f coast ; seaside
**Küstenwache** f coastguard

## L

**lächeln** to smile
**Lächeln** nt smile
**lachen** to laugh
**Lachs** m salmon
**Lack** m varnish
**Laden** m shop ; store
**Lagerhalle** f warehouse
**Lakritze** f liquorice
**Lamm** nt lamb
**Lampe** f lamp
**Land** nt country (Italy, France, etc) ; land
**landen** to land
**Landkarte** f map (of country)
**Landschaft** f countryside
**Landung** f landing (of plane)
**Landwein** m table wine
**lang** long
**Länge** f length
**Langlauf** m cross-country skiing
**langsam** slow(ly)
**langsamer werden** to slow down
**langweilig** boring
**Langzeitparkplatz** m long-stay car park

**Lappen** m cloth (rag)
**Laptop** m laptop
**Lärm** m noise
**lassen** to let (allow)
**Last** f load
**Laster** m truck
**Lastwagen** m truck ; lorry
**Lätzchen** nt bib (baby's)
**Lauch** m leek
**laufen** to run
**Laugenbrezel** f soft pretzel
**laut** noisy ; loud(ly) ; aloud
**läuten** to ring (doorbell)
**Lautsprecher** m loudspeaker
**Lautstärke** f volume (of sound)
**Lawine** f avalanche
**Lawinengefahr** f danger of avalanches
**leben** to live (exist)
**Lebensgefahr** f danger to life
**Lebensmittel** pl groceries
**Lebensmittelvergiftung** f food poisoning
**Lebensversicherung** f life insurance
**Leber** f liver
**Lebkuchen** m gingerbread
**Leck** nt leak (of gas, liquid)
**Lederwaren** pl leather goods
**ledig** single (not married)
**leer** empty ; flat (battery) ; blank

**Leerlauf** m neutral (gear)
**legen** to lay
**Lehrer(in)** m/f teacher (school) ; instructor
**leicht** light (not heavy) ; easy
**Leid** nt grief
  *es tut mir Leid* (I'm) sorry
**leider** unfortunately
**leihen** to rent (car) ; to lend
**Leihgebühr** f rental
**Leinen** nt linen (cloth)
**leise** quietly ; soft ; faint
  *leiser stellen* to turn down (volume)
**Leiter** f ladder
**Leitung** f telephone line
**Lenker** m handlebars
**Lenkrad** nt steering wheel
**lernen** to learn
**lesbisch** lesbian
**lesen** to read
**letzte(r/s)** last ; final
**Leuchtturm** m lighthouse
**Leute** pl people
**Licht** nt light
  *das Licht anschalten* to switch on lights
**Lichtmaschine** f alternator
**Lichtschalter** m light switch
**Lidschatten** m eye shadow
**liebe(r)** dear (in letter)
**Liebe** f love
**lieben** to love
**liebenswürdig** kind
**lieber** rather

**Lieblings-** favourite
**Lied** nt song
**Lieferwagen** m van
**Liegestuhl** m deckchair
**Liegewagen** m couchette
**Lift** m elevator ; lift
**Liftpass** m lift pass (on ski slopes)
**Likör** m liqueur
**Limonade** f lemonade
**Limone** f lime (fruit)
**Lineal** nt ruler
**Linie** f line (row, of railway)
**Linienflug** m scheduled flight
**linke(r/s)** left(-hand)
**links** to the left ; on the left
**Linkshänder(in)** m/f left-handed person
**Linse** f lens
**Linsen** pl lentils
**Lippen** pl lips
**Lippenpflegestift** m lip salve
**Lippenstift** m lipstick
**Liste** f list
**Liter** m litre
**Loch** nt hole
**lochen** to punch (ticket, etc)
**locker** loose (screw, tooth)
**Löffel** m spoon
**Loge** f box (in theatre)
**Lohn** m wage
**Loipe** f cross-country ski run

**L**

**Lokal** nt pub
**Lorbeerblatt** nt bayleaf
**los** loose
  **was ist los?** what's wrong?
**Los** nt lot (at auction) ; ticket (lottery)
**lösen** to buy (ticket)
**löslich** soluble
**Lounge** f lounge
**Löwe** m lion
**Luft** f air
**Luftfilter** m air filter
**Luftfracht** f air freight
**Luftkissenboot** nt hovercraft
**Luftmatratze** f air bed/mattress
**Luftpost** f air mail
**Luftpumpe** f pump (bike/air-mattress)
**Lüge** f lie (untruth)
**Lunge** f lung
**Lupe** f magnifying glass
**Lutscher** m lollipop
**Luxus** m luxury

**M**

**machen** to make ; to do
**Mädchen** nt girl
**Mädchenname** m maiden name
**Made** f maggot
**Magen** m stomach
**Magenschmerzen** pl stomachache

**Magentabletten** pl indigestion tablets
**Magenverstimmung** f indigestion
**Magermilch** f skimmed milk
**Magnet** m magnet
**Mai** m May
**Mais** m sweetcorn
**Make-up** nt make-up
**malen** to paint
**Malzbier** nt malt beer
**man** one
**managen** to manage (be in charge)
**manchmal** sometimes
**Mandarine** f tangerine
**Mandel** f almond ; tonsil
**Mandelentzündung** f tonsillitis
**Mangel** m flaw
**Mann** m man ; husband
**Männer** pl men
**männlich** masculine ; male
**Manschettenknöpfe** pl cufflinks
**Mantel** m coat
**Margarine** f margarine
**marineblau** navy blue
**mariniert** marinated
**Marke** f brand (of product) ; token (for phone)
**Markt** m market
**Marktplatz** m market place
**Marmelade** f jam

Marmor *m* marble

März *m* March

Maschine *f* machine

Maschine schreiben to type

Masern *pl* measles

Maßband *nt* tape measure

Maße *pl* measurements

Mast *m* mast

Material *nt* material

Matratze *f* mattress

Mauer *f* wall

Maus *f* mouse (animal/computer)

Maut *f* toll (motorway)

Mayonnaise *f* mayonnaise

Mechaniker(in) *m/f* mechanic

Medikament *nt* drug ; medicine

Medizin *f* medicine

Meer *nt* sea

Meeresfrüchte *pl* seafood

Mehl *nt* flour

mehr more

Mehrwertsteuer (MWST) *f* value-added tax (VAT)

meiden to avoid (person)

Meile *f* mile

mein my

meiste(n) most

Meisterwerk *nt* masterpiece

melden to report (tell about)

Melone *f* melon ; bowler hat

Menge *f* crowd

Messe *f* fair (commercial) ; mass (church)

Messegelände *nt* exhibition centre

messen to measure

Messer *nt* knife

Messing *nt* brass

Metall *nt* metal

Meter *m* metre

Metro *f* metro (underground)

Metzgerei *f* butcher's

mich me (direct object)

Mietauto *nt* hire car

Miete *f* rent

mieten to hire ; to rent (house, etc)

Mietgebühr *f* rental charge

Mietvertrag *m* lease (rental)

Migräne *f* migraine

Mikrowelle *f* microwave oven

Milch *f* milk

Milchprodukte *pl* dairy produce

Milchpulver *nt* powdered milk

Millimeter *m* millimetre

Million *f* million

minderwertig low-quality

Mindest- minimum

Mineralwasser *nt* mineral water

Minimum *nt* minimum

**Minister(in)** *m/f* minister
*(politics)*

**Minute(n)** f minute(s)

**Minze** f mint *(herb)*

**mir** me *(indirect object)*

**mischen** to mix

**Missverständnis** nt misunderstanding

**mit** with

**Mitfahrgelegenheit** f lift
*(in car)*

**Mitglied** nt member *(of
club, etc)*

**mitnehmen** to give a lift to
**zum Mitnehmen** take-
away *(food)*

**Mittag** m midday

**Mittagessen** nt lunch

**Mitte** f middle

**Mitteilung** f message

**Mittel** nt means
**ein Mittel gegen** a
remedy for

**mittelalterlich** medieval

**Mittelmeer-**
Mediterranean

**Mitternacht** f midnight

**Mittwoch** m Wednesday

**Mixer** m blender ; mixer

**Möbel** pl furniture

**Möbelpolitur** f furniture
polish

**Mobiltelefon** nt mobile
phone

**möbliert** furnished

**Modem** nt modem

**modern** fashionable ;
modern

**mögen** to enjoy *(to like)*

**möglich** possible

**Mohn** m poppy

**Möhre(n)** f carrot(s)

**Mole** f jetty

**Monat** m month

**monatlich** monthly

**Mond** m moon

**Montag** m Monday

**Moped** nt moped

**Morgen** m morning ;
tomorrow

**morgen** tomorrow

**Morgendämmerung** f
dawn

**Morgenmantel** m
dressing gown

**Moschee** f mosque

**Moskitonetz** nt mosquito
net

**Motor** m motor ; engine

**Motorboot** nt motor boat

**Motorhaube** f bonnet *(car)*

**Motorrad** nt motorbike

**Motte** f moth *(clothes)*

**Mountainbike** nt
mountain bike

**Mücke** f midge

**müde** tired

**Müll** m rubbish

**Müllbeutel** m bin liner

**Mülleimer** m bin *(dustbin)*

**Mumps** m mumps

München Munich
Mund *m* mouth
Mundwasser *nt* mouthwash
Münster *nt* cathedral
Münze(n) *f* coin(s)
Münzfernsprecher *m* payphone
Münztelefon *nt* payphone
Muscheln *pl* mussels
Museum *nt* museum
Musik *f* music
Muskat *m* nutmeg
Muskel *m* muscle
müssen to have to ; to must
mutig brave
Mutter *f* mother
Mütze *f* cap *(hat)*
MWST *f* VAT

# N

nach after ; according to ; to *(with names of places)*
Nachbar(in) *m/f* neighbour
Nachmittag *m* afternoon
nachmittags pm ; in the afternoon
Nachname *m* surname
Nachricht *f* note *(letter)* ; message
Nachrichten *pl* news
Nachspeise *f* dessert ; pudding
nächste(r/s) next

Nacht *f* night
 über Nacht overnight
Nachtdienst *m* night duty *(chemist)*
Nachthemd *nt* nightdress
Nachtisch *m* dessert
Nachtklub *m* night club
nachzahlen to pay extra
nackt nude ; naked ; bare
Nadel *f* needle
Nagel *m* nail *(metal)*
Nagelbürste *f* nailbrush
Nagelfeile *f* nail file
Nagellack *m* nail polish/varnish
Nagellackentferner *m* nail polish remover
Nagelschere *f* nail scissors
Nähe *f* proximity
 in der Nähe nearby
nähen to sew
Name *m* name ; surname
Narkose *f* anaesthetic
Nase *f* nose
nass wet
national national
Nationalität *f* nationality
Natur- natural
Naturlehrpfad *m* nature trail
Naturschutzgebiet *nt* nature reserve
Nebel *m* mist ; fog
neben by *(next to)* ; beside
Nebenstraße *f* minor road

neblig foggy

Neffe *m* nephew

Negativ *nt* negative *(photo)*

nehmen to catch *(bus, train)* ; to take *(remove)*

nein no

Nektarine *f* nectarine

Nelke *f* carnation

nennen to quote *(price)*

Nervenzusammenbruch *m* nervous breakdown

Nest *nt* nest

nett nice *(person)* ; kind

Netto- net *(income, price)*

Netz *nt* net ; network

neu new

neueste(r/s) newest ; latest

Neujahr(stag) *m* New Year's Day

Neuseeland *nt* New Zealand

nicht not ; non-

Nichte *f* niece

Nichtraucher *m* non-smoker

nichts nothing

nie never

Niederlande *pl* Netherlands

Niedersachsen *nt* Lower Saxony

niedrig low

Niedrigwasser *nt* low tide

niemand no one ; nobody

Niere(n) *f* kidney(s)

niesen to sneeze

nirgends nowhere

noch still *(up to this time)* ; yet

noch ein(e) extra *(more)* ; another

Norden *m* north

Nordirland *nt* Northern Ireland

nördlich north ; northern

Nordsee *f* North Sea

Normal(benzin) *nt* regular *(petrol)*

Normal- standard *(size)*

Notarzt *m* emergency doctor

Notaufnahme *f* accident & emergency

Notausgang *m* emergency exit

Notdienstapotheke *f* on-duty chemist

Notfall *m* emergency

nötig necessary

Notizblock *m* note pad

Notruf *m* emergency number

Notrufsäule *f* emergency phone *(on motorway)*

Notsignal *nt* distress signal

notwendig essential ; necessary

November *m* November

nüchtern sober

Nudeln *pl* pasta ; noodles

Null *f* nil ; zero ; nought

numerieren to number

Nummer *f* number ; act

Nummernschild *nt* numberplate

nur only

Nürnberg Nuremberg

Nuss (Nüsse) *f* nut(s)

nützlich useful

# O

oben upstairs ; above ; this side up

oben auf on top of...

Oberschenkel *m* thigh

obligatorisch compulsory

Obst *nt* fruit

Obstkuchen *m* fruit tart

oder or

offen open
*offene Weine pl* wine served by the glass

öffentlich public

öffnen to open ; to undo

Öffnungszeiten *pl* business hours

oft often

ohne without

ohnmächtig fainted

ohnmächtig werden to faint

Ohr(en) *nt* ear(s)

Ohrenschmerzen *pl* earache

Ohrringe *pl* earrings

okay OK

ökonomisch economic

Oktober *m* October

Öl *nt* oil

Ölfilter *m* oil filter

Olive *f* olive

Olivenöl *nt* olive oil

Ölstandsanzeiger *m* oil gauge

Ölwechsel *m* oil change

Omelett *nt* omelette

Onkel *m* uncle

Oper *f* opera

Operation *f* operation *(surgical)*

Optiker *m* optician's

orange orange *(colour)*

Orange *f* orange *(fruit)*

Orangensaft *m* orange juice

Orchester *nt* orchestra

Ordner *m* file *(for papers)*

Oregano *m* oregano

organisch organic

organisieren to organize

Organspenderausweis *m* donor card

Ort *m* place
*an Ort und Stelle* on the spot

örtlich local

örtliche Betäubung *f* local anaesthetic

Ortschaft *f* village ; town

**O** Ortsgespräch nt local call

Ortszeit f local time

Osten m east

Osterei nt Easter egg

Ostermontag m Easter Monday

Ostern nt Easter

Österreich nt Austria

Österreicher(in) m/f Austrian

österreichisch adj Austrian

Ostersonntag m Easter Sunday

östlich eastern

Ozean m ocean

# P

Paar nt pair ; couple
ein paar a couple of

packen to pack (luggage)

Paket nt parcel ; packet

Palast m palace

Pampelmuse(n) f grapefruit(s)

Panne f breakdown (of car)

Papier(e) nt paper(s)

Papiertaschentücher pl tissues

Pappe f cardboard

Paprikaschote f pepper (vegetable)

Parfüm nt perfume

Parfümerie f perfumery

Park m park

parken to park

Parken verboten no parking

Parkett nt stalls (in theatre)

Parkhaus nt multi-storey car park

Parkkralle f wheel clamp

Parkplatz m car park

Parkscheibe f parking disk

Parkschein m parking ticket (to display)

Parkuhr f parking meter

Parkverbot nt no parking zone

Partei f political party

Partner(in) m/f partner (boy/girlfriend)

Party f party (celebration)

Pass m passport ; pass (in mountains)
Pass geschlossen pass closed

Passagier m passenger

passen to fit

passieren to happen

Passkontrolle f passport control

Passnummer f passport number

Patient(in) m/f patient (in hospital)

Pauschalreise f package tour

Pauschaltarif m flat-rate tariff

Pause f pause ; interval
keine Pausen no intervals

Pelz m fur

Pelzmantel m fur coat

Pendelverkehr m shuttle (service)

Penis m penis

Penizillin nt penicillin

Pension f boarding house

pensioniert retired

per via ; by
  per Express by express mail
  per Post by post

perfekt perfect

Periode f period (menstruation)

Perlen pl pearls

perlend sparkling

Person f person

Personal nt staff

Personalausweis m identity card

Personalien pl particulars

persönlich personal(ly)

Perücke f wig

Pessar nt cap (diaphragm)

Petersilie f parsley

Pfalz f Palatinate

Pfannkuchen m pancake

Pfarrer(in) m/f church minister

Pfeffer m pepper (spice)

Pfefferkuchen m gingerbread

Pfefferminzbonbon nt mint (sweet)

Pfefferminztee m mint tea

Pfeife f pipe (smoker's)

Pferd nt horse

Pferderennen nt horse-racing

Pfirsich(e) m peach(es)

Pflanze f plant (green)

Pflaster nt plaster (for cut)

Pflaume(n) f plum(s)

Pforte f gate

Pfund nt pound

Pfund Sterling nt sterling (pound)

Picknick nt picnic

Picknickdecke f picnic rug

Pier m jetty ; pier

pikant savoury

Pille f pill

Pilot(in) m/f pilot

Pils/Pilsner nt lager

Pilz(e) m mushroom(s)

Pilzkrankheit f thrush (candida)

Pinzette f tweezers

Pistazie f pistachio

Piste f runway ; ski run

Pizza f pizza

planmäßig scheduled

Planschbecken nt paddling pool

Plastik- plastic (made of)

Plastikbeutel m plastic bag

Platte f plate ; dish ; record

**P**

**Platz** m seat ; space ; square (in town) ; court

**Plätzchen** nt biscuit(s)

**Platzkarte** f seat reservation (ticket)

**Plombe** f filling (in tooth)

**plötzlich** suddenly

**pochiert** poached (egg, fish)

**Polen** nt Poland

**Polizei** f police

**Polizeirevier** nt police station

**Polizeiwache** f police station

**Polizist(in)** m/f policeman/woman

**Pommes frites** pl chips (french fries)

**Pony** nt pony

**Ponyreiten** nt pony trekking

**Porree** m leek

**Portier** m porter (for door)

**Portion** f portion

**Portrait** nt portrait

**Portugal** nt Portugal

**Portugiese/Portugiesin** m/f Portuguese

**portugiesisch** adj Portuguese

**Post** f post ; post office

**Post-** postal

**Postamt** nt post office

**Postanweisung** f money order

**Poster** nt poster

**Postkarte** f postcard

**postlagernd** poste restante

**Postleitzahl** f postcode

**praktisch** handy ; practical

**Pralinen** pl chocolates

**Präservativ** nt condom

**Praxis** f doctor's surgery

**Preis** m prize ; price

**Preisliste** f price list

**Priester** m priest

**Prinz** m prince

**Prinzessin** f princess

**privat** private

**Privatstrand** m private beach

**Privatweg** m private road

**pro** per
   *pro Stunde* per hour
   *pro Kopf* per person
   *pro Jahr* per annum

**probieren** to taste ; to sample

**Problem** nt problem

**Programm** nt programme

**Programmierer(in)** m/f computer programmer

**prost!** cheers!

**protestantisch** Protestant

**provisorisch** temporary

**Prozent** nt per cent

**prüfen** to check (oil, water, etc)

Prüfung f exam *(school, university)*

Publikum nt audience

Puderzucker m icing sugar

Pullover m sweater ; jumper

Pulver nt powder

pulverförmig in powder form

Pulverkaffee m instant coffee

pünktlich on schedule ; punctual

Puppe f doll ; puppet

Puppenspiel nt puppet show

pur straight *(drink)*

Pute f turkey

Pyjama m pyjamas

## Q

Qualität f quality

Qualitätswein m good quality wine

Qualle f jellyfish

Quantität f quantity

Quarantäne f quarantine

Quelle f spring *(of water)* ; source

quetschen to squeeze

Quetschung f bruise

Quittung f receipt

Quiz nt quiz show

## R

Rabatt m discount

Rad nt wheel ; bicycle

Rad fahren to cycle

Radfahrer(in) m/f cyclist

Radiergummi m rubber *(eraser)*

Radieschen pl radishes

Radio nt radio

Radweg m cycle track

Rahmen m frame *(picture)*

Rand m verge ; border ; edge

Randstein m kerb

Rang m circle *(in theatre)* ; rank

Rasen m lawn

Rasierapparat m shaver ; razor

Rasiercreme f shaving cream

rasieren to shave

Rasierklinge f razor blade

Rasierschaum m shaving foam

Rasierwasser nt aftershave lotion

Rasthof m service area; travel inn

Rastplatz m picnic area

Raststätte f service area

raten to advise

Rathaus nt town hall

rau rough

**Rauch** m smoke
**rauchen** to smoke
  *Rauchen verboten* no smoking
**Raucher(in)** m/f smoker
**Raum** m space (room)
**rechnen** to calculate
**Rechnung** f bill (account) ; invoice
**rechte(r/s)** right (not left)
**rechts** to the right ; on the right
**Rechtsanwalt** m lawyer ; solicitor
**Rechtsanwältin** f lawyer ; solicitor
**reden** to speak
**reduzieren** to reduce
**Reformhaus** nt health food shop
**Regal** nt shelf
**Regen** m rain
**Regenmantel** m raincoat
**Regenschirm** m umbrella
**regnen** to rain
**Reibe** f grater
**reich** rich (person)
**Reich** nt empire
**reichhaltig** rich (food)
**reif** ripe ; mature (cheese)
**Reifen** m tyre
**Reifendruck** m tyre pressure
**Reifenpanne** f flat tyre
**Reihe** f row (line) ; tier

**rein** pure
**reinigen** to clean
**Reinigung** f dry-cleaner's
**Reis** m rice
**Reise** f trip (journey)
  *gute Reise!* have a good trip!
**Reisebüro** nt travel agency
**Reiseführer** m guidebook
**Reiseführer(in)** m/f tour guide
**Reisegruppe** f party (of tourists)
**Reisekrankheit** f travel sickness
**reisen** to travel
**Reisepapiere** pl travel documents
**Reisepass** m passport
**Reisescheck** m traveller's cheque
**Reiseveranstalter** m tour operator
**Reiseziel** nt destination
**Reißverschluss** m zip
**reiten** to ride (horse)
**Reiten** nt riding
**Rennbahn** f racecourse
**rennen** to run
**Rennen** nt race (sport)
**Rentner(in)** m/f pensioner ; senior citizen
**Reparatur** f repair
**Reparaturwerkstatt** f car repairs

**reparieren** to repair ;
to mend

**reservieren** to book ;
to reserve

**reserviert** reserved

**Reservierung** f booking
*(in hotel)*

**Reservierungen** pl
reservations

**Restaurant** nt restaurant

**Restgeld** nt change *(money)*

**retten** to rescue ; to save
*(person)*

**Rettungsboot** nt lifeboat

**Rettungsinsel** f life raft

**Rettungsring** m lifebelt

**Rettungsschwimmer(in)**
m/f lifeguard

**Rezept** nt prescription ;
recipe

**R-Gespräch** nt reverse
charge call

**Rhein** m Rhine

**Rheinfahrten** pl Rhine
cruises

**Rheumatismus** m
rheumatism

**Richter(in)** m/f judge

**richtig** correct ; right ;
proper

**Richtung** f direction

**riechen** to smell

**Rinderbraten** m roast beef

**Rindfleisch** nt beef

**Ring** m ring

**Ringstraße** f ring road

**Riss** m tear *(in material)*

**Rock** m skirt

**Roggenbrot** nt rye bread

**roh** raw

**Rohr** nt pipe *(drain, etc)*

**Rollo** nt blind *(for window)*

**Rollschuhe** pl roller skates

**Rollstuhl** m wheelchair

**Rolltreppe** f escalator

**Roman** m novel

**romanisch** Romanesque

**Röntgenaufnahme** f X-ray

**rosa** pink

**Rose** f rose *(flower)*

**Rosenkohl** m Brussels
sprouts

**Rosenmontag** m carnival
*(Monday before Shrove
Tuesday)*

**Roséwein** m rosé wine

**Rosine(n)** f raisin(s)

**Rost** m rust ; grill

**Rost-** roast

**Rostbraten** m roast

**rosten** to rust

**rostfreier Stahl** m stain-
less steel

**rostig** rusty

**Röstkartoffeln** pl sautéed
potatoes

**rot** red

**Rote Bete** f beetroot

**Röteln** pl German measles ;
rubella

rote Johannisbeeren *pl* redcurrants

Rotwein *m* red wine

Rücken *m* back

Rückerstattung *f* refund

Rückfahrkarte *f* return ticket

Rückfahrt *f* return journey

Rückflugticket *nt* return airticket

Rückgrat *nt* spine

Rücklicht *nt* rear light

Rucksack *m* rucksack

Rückspiegel *m* rearview mirror

rückwärts backwards

rückwärts fahren to reverse *(car)*

Rückwärtsgang *m* reverse gear

Ruder *nt* rudder ; oar

Ruderboot *nt* rowing boat

rudern to row *(boat)*

rufen to shout

Rufnummer *f* telephone number

Ruhe *f* rest *(repose)* ; peace *(calm)*
*Ruhe!* be quiet!

ruhen to rest

ruhig calm ; quiet(ly) ; peaceful

Rührei *nt* scrambled egg

Ruine *f* ruin *(castle, etc)*

rund round

Rundfahrt *f* tour ; round trip

Rundreise *f* round trip

Rundwanderweg *m* circular trail for ramblers

Rutschbahn *f* slide *(chute)*

rutschen to slip

rutschig slippery

# S

Saal *m* hall (room)

Sache *f* thing

Sachen *pl* stuff *(things)* ; belongings

Sachsen *nt* Saxony

Sackgasse *f* cul-de-sac

Safe *m* safe *(for valuables)*

Saft *m* juice

sagen to say ; to tell *(fact, news)*

Sahne *f* cream *(dairy)*
*mit Sahne* with whipped cream

Saison *f* season

Salat *m* salad

Salatsoße *f* salad dressing

Salbe *f* ointment

Salz *nt* salt

Salzkartoffeln *pl* boiled potatoes

Salzwasser *nt* salt water

Samstag *m* Saturday

Sand *m* sand

**Sandalen** pl sandals

**Sandstrand** m sandy beach

**Satellitenfernsehen** nt satellite TV

**satt** full

**Sattel** m saddle

**Satteltaschen** pl panniers (for bike)

**Satz** m set (collection) ; sentence

**sauber** clean

**säubern** to clean

**sauer** sour

**Sauerkraut** nt sauerkraut

**Sauerstoff** m oxygen

**Sauger** m teat (on bottle)

**Säule** f petrol pump

**Saum** m hem

**Sauna** f sauna

**Säure** f acid

**saure Sahne** f soured cream

**S-Bahn** f suburban railway

**Schach** nt chess

**Schaden** m damage

**schädlich** harmful

**Schaf** nt sheep

**Schaffner(in)** m/f conductor (bus, train) ; guard

**Schale** f shell (egg, nut) ; dish

**schälen** to peel (fruit)

**Schallplatte** f record (music)

**Schalter** m switch

**Schaltgetriebe** nt manual (gear change)

**Schaltknüppel** m gear lever ; gearshift

**Schaltuhr** f timer

**scharf** hot (spicy) ; sharp

**Schatten** m shade

**schätzen** to value ; to estimate

**Schauer** m rain shower

**Schaufel und Handfeger** dustpan and brush

**Schaufenster** nt shop window

**Schaukel** f swing (for children)

**Schaum** m foam

**Schaumbad** nt bubble bath

**Schaumfestiger** m hair mousse

**Schaumwein** m sparkling wine

**Schauspiel** nt play

**Schauspieler(in)** m/f actor/actress

**Scheck** m cheque

**Scheckbuch** nt cheque book

**Scheckkarte** f cheque card

**Scheibe** f slice

**Scheibenputzmittel** nt screenwash

**Scheibenwischer** pl windscreen wipers

**S**

Schein(e) m banknote(s) ; certificate(s)

scheinen to shine (sun, etc) ; to seem

Scheinwerfer m headlight ; floodlight ; spotlight
*Scheinwerfer anschalten* switch on headlights

Schere f scissors (pair of)

scherzen to joke

Scheuerlappen m floorcloth

Scheune f barn

Schi- see Ski-

schicken to send

schießen to shoot

Schiff nt ship

Schild nt sign ; label

Schinken m ham

Schirm m umbrella ; screen

Schlachterei f butcher's

schlafen to sleep

Schlafsack m sleeping bag

Schlaftablette f sleeping pill

Schlafwagen m sleeping car (on train)

Schlafzimmer nt bedroom

Schlag m shock (electric)

Schlaganfall m stroke (medical)

schlagen to hit

Schläger m racket (tennis, etc)

Schlagloch nt pothole

Schlagsahne f whipped cream

Schlange f queue ; snake

Schlangenbiss m snake bite

Schlauch m hosepipe ; inner tube

Schlauchboot nt dinghy (rubber)

schlecht bad ; badly

Schlepplift m ski tow

schließen to shut ; to close

Schließfach nt locker

schlimm serious

Schlitten m sleigh ; sledge

Schlittschuh laufen to ice skate

Schlittschuh(e) m ice skate(s)

Schlittschuhbahn f ice rink

Schloss nt castle ; lock (on door, etc)

Schluss m end

Schlüssel m key

Schlüsselbein nt collar bone

Schlüsselkarte f cardkey (for hotel)

Schlüsselring m keyring

Schlusslichter pl rear lights

Schlussverkauf m sale

schmecken to taste

schmelzen to melt

Schmerz m pain ; ache

**schmerzhaft** painful

**Schmerzmittel** *nt* painkiller

**Schmerztablette** *f* painkiller

**Schmuck** *m* jewellery ; decorations

**schmutzig** dirty

**Schnaps** *m* schnapps ; spirit

**schnarchen** to snore

**Schnee** *m* snow

**Schneebrille** *f* snow goggles

**Schneeketten** *pl* snow chains

**Schneepflug** *m* snowplough

**schneiden** to cut

**schnell** fast ; quick

**Schnellboot** *nt* speedboat

**Schnellimbiss** *m* snack bar

**Schnellzug** *m* express train

**Schnittbohnen** *pl* green beans

**Schnittlauch** *m* chives

**Schnittwunde** *f* cut

**Schnorchel** *m* snorkel

**Schnuller** *m* dummy *(for baby)*

**Schnur** *f* string

**Schnurrbart** *m* moustache

**Schnürschuhe** *pl* boots *(ankle)*

**Schnürsenkel** *pl* shoelaces

**Schokolade** *f* chocolate

**schön** lovely ; fine ; beautiful ; good *(pleasant)*

**Schornstein** *m* chimney

**Schotte (Schottin)** *m/f* Scot

**schottisch** Scottish

**Schottland** *nt* Scotland

**Schrank** *m* cupboard

**Schraube** *f* screw

**Schraubenmutter** *f* nut *(for bolt)*

**Schraubenschlüssel** *m* spanner

**Schraubenzieher** *m* screwdriver

**schrecklich** awful

**schreiben** to write

**Schreibmaschine** *f* typewriter

**Schreibtisch** *m* desk

**Schreibwarenhandlung** *f* stationer's

**schriftlich** in writing

**Schritt** *m* pace ; step *Schritt fahren!* dead slow

**Schublade** *f* drawer

**Schuh(e)** *m* shoe(s)

**Schuhcreme** *f* shoe polish

**Schuhgeschäft** *nt* shoe shop

**Schuhputzmittel** *nt* shoe polish

**schulden** to owe

**Schulden** pl debts

**Schule** f school

**Schulter** f shoulder

**Schuppen** pl scales (of fish) ; dandruff

**Schürze** f apron

**Schüssel** f bowl (for soup, etc)

**Schuster** m shoe mender's

**Schutzhelm** m helmet (for bike)

**Schutzimpfung** f vaccination

**schwach** weak

**Schwager** m brother-in-law

**Schwägerin** f sister-in-law

**Schwamm** m sponge

**schwanger** pregnant

**schwarz** black

**Schwarzbrot** nt brown bread

**schwarze Johannisbeeren** pl black-currants

**Schwarzweißfilm** m black and white film

**Schwein** nt pig

**Schweinefleisch** nt pork

**Schweiß** m sweat

**Schweiz** f Switzerland

**Schweizer(in)** m/f Swiss

**schweizerisch** adj Swiss

**Schwellung** f swelling

**schwer** heavy

**Schwester** f sister ; nurse ; nun

**Schwiegermutter** f mother-in-law

**Schwiegersohn** m son-in-law

**Schwiegertochter** f daughter-in-law

**Schwiegervater** m father-in-law

**schwierig** hard (difficult)

**Schwimmbad** nt swimming pool

**schwimmen** to swim

**Schwimmflossen** pl flippers

**Schwimmweste** f life jacket

**schwindelig** dizzy

**schwitzen** to sweat

**See** f sea

**See** m lake

**seekrank** seasick

**Segel** nt sail

**Segelboot** nt sailing boat

**segeln** to sail

**sehen** to see

**Sehenswürdigkeit** f sight

**Sehne** f tendon

**sehr** very

**seicht** shallow (water)

**Seide** f silk

**Seife** f soap

**Seil** nt rope

**Seilbahn** f cable railway ; funicular

**sein(e)** his

**sein** to be

**seit** since

**Seite** f page ; side

**Seitenspiegel** m wing mirror

**Seitenstraße** f side street

**Seitenstreifen** m hard shoulder

**Sekretär(in)** m/f secretary

**Sekt** m sparkling wine

**Sekunde** f second (time)

**Selbstbedienung** f self-service

**selten** rare (unique)

**seltsam** strange (odd)

**Senf** m mustard

**September** m September

**servieren** to serve (food)

**Serviette** f napkin

**Servolenkung** f power steering

**Sessel** m armchair

**Sessellift** m chairlift

**setzen** to place ; to put
*sich setzen* to sit down
*setzen Sie sich bitte*
please take a seat

**Sex** m sex (intercourse)

**Shampoo** nt shampoo

**Shorts** pl shorts

**sicher** sure ; safe ; definite

**Sicherheit** f safety

**Sicherheitsgurt** m seatbelt ; safety belt

**Sicherheitsnadel** f safety pin

**Sicherung** f fuse

**Sicherungskasten** m fuse box

**sie** she ; they

**Sie** you (polite singular and plural)

**Sieb** nt sieve ; colander

**Silber** nt silver

**Silvester** m New Year's Eve

**singen** to sing

**Sitz** m seat

**sitzen** to sit

**Ski(er)** m ski(s)
*Ski fahren* to ski

**Skianzug** m ski suit

**Skihose** f ski pants

**Skijacke** f ski jacket

**Skilanglauf** m cross-country skiing

**Skilaufen** nt skiing

**Skilehrer(in)** m/f ski instructor

**Skilift** m ski lift

**Skipass** m ski pass

**Skipiste** f ski run

**Skistiefel** pl ski boots

**Skistock** m ski stick/pole

**Skiverleih** m ski hire

**Slip** m knickers ; underpants

**Slipeinlage** f panty liner

**Snack** m snack

**Snowboard** nt snow board

**Socken** pl socks

**Soda** nt soda water

**Sodbrennen** nt heartburn

**Sofa** nt sofa

**Sofabett** nt sofa bed

**sofort** at once ; immediately

**Software** f computer software

**Sohle** f sole (of shoe)

**Sohn** m son

**Sojabohnen** pl soya beans

**Sojamilch** f soya milk

**Sommer** m summer

**Sommerfahrplan** m summer railway timetable

**Sommerferien** pl summer holidays

**Sonder-** special

**sonn- und feiertags** Sundays and public holidays

**Sonnabend** m Saturday

**Sonne** f sun

**Sonnenaufgang** m sunrise

**sonnenbaden** to sunbathe

**Sonnenbrand** m sunburn

**Sonnenbräune** f suntan

**Sonnenbrille** f sunglasses

**Sonnencreme** f sunblock

**Sonnendach** nt sunroof

**Sonnenöl** nt suntan oil

**Sonnenschirm** m sun umbrella ; sunshade

**Sonnenstich** m sunstroke

**Sonnenuntergang** m sunset

**sonnig** sunny

**Sonntag** m Sunday

**Sonntagsdienst** m Sunday duty (chemist, doctor, etc)

**sorgen für** to look after ; to take care of

**Soße** f dressing ; sauce

**Souterrain** nt basement

**Souvenir** nt souvenir

**Spanien** nt Spain

**Spanier(in)** m/f Spaniard

**spanisch** adj Spanish

**Spannung** f voltage

**sparen** to save (money)

**Spargel** m asparagus

**Sparpreis** m economy fare

**Spaß** m fun ; joke

**spät** late

**Spaten** m spade

**Spätvorstellung** f late show

**Spaziergang** m stroll ; walk

**Speck** m bacon

**Speise** f dish ; food

**Speiseeis** nt ice cream

**Speisekarte** f menu

**Speisewagen** m dining car

**Spesen** pl expenses

**Spezialität** f speciality

**Spiegel** m mirror

**Spiegelei** nt fried egg

**Spiel** nt game ; pack (of cards)

**Spielbank** f casino

**spielen** to gamble ; to play

**Spielkarte** f card (playing)

**Spielplatz** m playground

**Spielzeug** nt toy

**Spielzeugladen** m toy shop

**Spielzimmer** nt playroom

**Spinat** m spinach

**Spirale** f coil (IUD) ; spiral

**Spirituosen** pl spirits (alcohol)

**Spitze** f lace ; point (tip)

**Splitter** m splinter

**Sportartikel** pl sports equipment

**Sportgeschäft** nt sports shop

**Sporttauchen** nt scuba diving

**Sprache** f speech ; language

**Sprachführer** m phrase book

**Spraydose** f aerosol

**sprechen** to speak
**sprechen mit** to talk to

**springen** to jump

**Spritze** f injection ; hypodermic needle

**sprudelnd** fizzy

**Sprudelwasser** nt sparkling water

**Sprungschanze** f ski jump

**Spülbecken** nt sink (kitchen)

**spülen** to flush toilet ; to rinse

**Spülkasten** m cistern (of toilet)

**Spülmittel** nt washing-up liquid

**Spur** f lane (of motorway/main road)

**Staatsangehörigkeit** f nationality

**Stachel** m sting

**Stadion** nt stadium

**Stadt** f town ; city

**Stadtführung** f guided tour of the town

**Stadtmitte** f city centre

**Stadtplan** m map (of town)

**Stadtzentrum** nt town/city centre

**Stahl** m steel

**Stand** m stall ; taxi rank

**ständig** permanent(ly) ; continuous(ly)

**Standlicht** nt sidelight

**stark** strong

**Starthilfekabel** nt jump leads

**Station** f station ; stop ; hospital ward

**statt** instead of

**stattfinden** to take place

**Statue** f statue

**Stau** m traffic jam

**Staub** m dust

**Staubsauger** m vacuum cleaner

**Staubtuch** nt duster

**stechen** to bite (insect)

**Stechmücke** f mosquito ; gnat

**Steckdose** f socket (electrical)

**Stecker** m plug (electric)

**stehen** to stand

**stehlen** to steal

**steil** steep

**Stein** m stone

**Stelle** f job ; place; point (in space)

**stellen** to set (alarm) ; to put

**stempeln** to stamp (visa)

**Steppdecke** f quilt

**sterben** to die

**Stereoanlage** f stereo

**Stern** m star

**Steuer** f tax

**Steuerung** f controls

**Steward (Stewardess)** m/f steward/stewardess

**Stich** m bite (by insect) ; stitch (sewing) ; sting

**Stiefel** pl boots (long)

**Stiefmutter** f stepmother

**Stiefvater** m stepfather

**Stil** m style

**still** still (motionless)

**stilles Wasser** nt still water

**Stimme** f voice

**stimmt so!** keep the change!

**Stirn** f forehead

**Stock** m cane (walking stick) ; stick ; floor

**Stockwerk** nt storey

**Stoff** m cloth (fabric)

**Stoppschild** nt stop (sign)

**Stöpsel** m plug (in sink)

**stören** to disturb (interrupt) *bitte nicht stören* do not disturb

**stornieren** to cancel

**Stornierung** f cancellation

**Störung** f hold-up ; fault ; medical disorder

**Stoßdämpfer** m shock absorber

**stoßen** to knock ; to push

**Stoßstange** f bumper (car)

**Stoßzeit** f rush hour

**Strafe** f punishment ; fine

**Strafzettel** m parking ticket (fine)

**Strand** m beach

**Strandkorb** m wicker beach chair with a hood ; beach hut

**Straße** f road ; street *Straße gesperrt* road closed

**Straßenarbeiten** pl roadworks

**Straßenbahn** f tram

**Straßenkarte** f road map

**Streichhölzer** pl matches

**Streifenkarte** f multiple journey travelcard

**Streik** m strike (industrial)

**streiten** to quarrel

**Stress** m stress

**stricken** to knit

**Strickjacke** f cardigan

**Stricknadel** f knitting needle

**Strohhalm** m straw (for drinking)

**Strom** m current ; electricity

**Stromanschluss** m electric point

**Strömung** f current (water)

**Stromzähler** m electricity meter

**Strümpfe** pl stockings

**Strumpfhose** f tights

**Stück** nt bit ; piece ; cut of meat ; play (theatre)

**Student(in)** m/f student m/f

**Studentenermäßigung** f student discount

**Stufe** f step (stair)

**Stuhl** m chair

**stumpf** blunt (knife, blade)

**Stunde** f hour ; lesson

**Sturm** m storm

**Sturzhelm** m crash helmet

**suchen** to look for

**Süden** m south

**südlich** southern

**Summe** f sum (total amount)

**Sumpf** m marsh

**Super(benzin)** nt four-star petrol

**Supermarkt** m supermarket

**Suppe** f soup

**Surfbrett** nt surfboard

**surfen** to surf

**süß** sweet

**Süßigkeiten** pl sweets

**Süßstoff** m sweetener ; saccharin

**Süßwaren** pl confectionery

**Synagoge** f synagogue

**Szene** f scene

# T

**Tabak** m tobacco

**Tabakwarenhandlung** f tobacconist's

**Tablett** nt tray

**Tablette(n)** f tablet(s) ; pill(s)

**Tachometer** nt speedometer

**Tafel** f table ; board ; bar of chocolate

**Tafelwein** m table wine

**Tag** m day
    *jeden Tag* every day

**Tageskarte** f day ticket ; menu of the day

Tagespauschale f daily unlimited rate

Tagessuppe f soup of the day

täglich daily

Taille f waist

Tal nt valley

Tampons pl tampons

Tank m fuel/petrol tank

Tankanzeige f fuel gauge

Tankdeckel m petrol cap

Tanksäule f petrol pump

Tankstelle f petrol station

Tanne f fir

Tante f aunt

Tanz m dance

tanzen to dance

Tarif m rate ; tariff

Tasche f pocket ; bag

Taschenbuch nt paperback

Taschendieb m pickpocket

Taschenlampe f torch ; flashlight

Taschenmesser nt penknife

Taschenrechner m calculator

Taschentuch nt handkerchief

Tasse f cup

Taste f button ; key (on keyboard)
*Taste drücken* push button

taub deaf

Taube f pigeon

tauchen to dive

Tauchen nt diving

Taucheranzug m wetsuit

Taucherbrille f goggles (swimming)

tauschen to exchange

tausend thousand

Taxi nt taxi ; cab

Taxifahrer(in) m/f taxi driver

Taxistand m taxi rank

Tee m tea

Teebeutel m tea bag

Teekanne f teapot

Teelöffel m teaspoon

Teig m pastry

Teil nt part

teilen to divide ; to share

Teilkaskoversicherung f third party, fire and theft insurance

Telefon nt telephone

Telefonauskunft f directory enquiries

Telefonbuch nt phone directory

telefonieren to telephone

Telefonkarte f phonecard

Telefonnummer f phone number

Telefonzelle f phonebox

Telegramm nt telegram

Teller m plate

**Tempel** m temple

**Temperatur** f temperature

**Tennis** nt tennis

**Tennisplatz** m tennis court

**Tennisschläger** m tennis racket

**Teppich** m rug

**Teppichboden** m fitted carpet

**Termin** m date ; deadline ; appointment

**Terminal** m terminal *(airport)*

**Terminkalender** m diary ; Filofax®

**Terminplaner** m personal organizer

**Terrasse** f patio ; terrace *(of café)*

**Terrorist(in)** m/f terrorist

**Tesafilm®** m Sellotape®

**teuer** dear *(expensive)*

**Theater** nt theatre

**Theke** f counter *(in shop, bar, etc)*

**Thermometer** nt thermometer

**Thermosflasche** f flask *(thermos)*

**Thunfisch** m tuna

**Thüringen** nt Thuringia

**Thymian** m thyme

**tief** deep ; low *(in pitch)*

**Tiefkühltruhe** f deep freeze ; freezer

**Tier** nt animal

**Tierarzt (Tierärztin)** m/f vet

**Tinte** f ink

**Tintenfisch** m octopus ; squid

**Tisch** m table

**Tischdecke** f tablecloth

**Tischler(in)** m/f carpenter

**Tischtennis** nt table tennis

**Tischwein** m table wine

**Toastbrot** nt sliced white bread for toasting

**Tochter** f daughter

**Toilette** f toilet ; lavatory

**Toilettenartikel** pl toiletries

**Toilettenbürste** f toilet brush

**Toilettenpapier** nt toilet paper

**Tollwut** f rabies

**Tomate** f tomato

**Tomatenpüree** nt tomato purée

**Tomatensaft** m tomato juice

**Tomatensoße** f tomato sauce

**Ton** m sound ; tone ; clay

**Tönung** f hair dye

**Töpferwaren** pl pottery

**Tor** nt gate ; goal *(sport)*

**Törtchen** nt cake *(small)*

**Torte** f gâteau ; tart

**tot** dead

**töten** to kill

**Tourist(in)** m/f tourist
**Touristeninformation** f tourist information
**Touristenkarte** f tourist ticket
**Touristenklasse** f economy class
**Touristenroute** f tourist route
**Touristenticket** nt tourist ticket
**tragbar** portable
**tragen** to carry ; to wear
**Tragflügelboot** nt hydrofoil
**Trainingsschuhe** pl trainers
**trampen** to hitchhike
**Trauben** pl grapes
**traurig** sad
**Treffen** nt meeting
**treffen** to meet (by chance)
**Treppe** f stairs
**Tresor** m safe
**Tretboot** nt pedalo
**trinken** to drink
**Trinkgeld** nt tip (for waiter, etc)
**Trinkwasser** nt drinking water
**trocken** dry ; stale (bread)
**Trockenmilch** f powdered milk
**Trockenobst** nt dried fruit
**trocknen** to dry
**Truthahn** m turkey
**Tschechien** nt Czech Republic

**tschüs** cheerio ; bye
**T-shirt** nt T-shirt
**Tuch** nt cloth ; scarf ; towel ; shawl
**tun** to do ; to put
  *das macht nichts* that doesn't matter
**Tunnel** m tunnel
**Tür** f door
**türkis** turquoise (colour)
**Turm** m tower
**Turnschuhe** pl gym shoes
**typisch** typical

# U

**u.A.w.g.** RSVP
**U-Bahn** f metro ; underground
**übel** sick (nauseous) ; bad
**über** over ; above ; about ; via
**überall** everywhere
**überbuchen** to overbook
**Überfahrt** f crossing (sea)
**Überfall** m mugging
**überfällig** overdue
**überfüllt** crowded (train, shop, etc)
**übergeben** to hand over ; to present (give)
  *sich übergeben* to vomit
**Übergewicht** nt excess baggage ; overweight
**überhitzen** to overheat
**überholen** to overtake

**Überholverbot** nt no overtaking

**Übernachtung mit Frühstück** bed and breakfast

**überprüfen** to check (to examine)

**Überschwemmung** f flash flood

**übersetzen** to translate

**Übersetzung** f translation

**überweisen** to transfer (money)

**Überzelt** nt fly sheet

**Überzieher** m overcoat

**übrig** left over ; extra (spare)

**Ufer** nt bank (of river) ; shore

**Uhr** f clock ; watch

**Uhrarmband** nt watch strap

**Uhrmacher** m watchmaker's

**um** around
*um 4 Uhr* at 4 o'clock

**umdrehen** to turn around

**umgeben von** surrounded by

**Umgehungsstraße** f ring road ; bypass (road)

**Umkleidekabine** f changing room (at swimming pool, in shop)

**Umleitung** f diversion

**Umschlag** m envelope

**umsonst** free (costing nothing)

**umsteigen** to change

**umstoßen** to knock over (object)

**Umweg** m detour

**Umwelt** f environment

**unbefugt** unauthorized
*Unbefugten Zutritt verboten* no entry to unauthorized persons

**unbegrenzt** unlimited

**und** and

**Unfall** m accident

**Unfallstation** nt casualty department

**ungefähr** approximately

**ungefährlich** safe (not dangerous)

**ungerade** odd (number)

**ungewöhnlich** unusual

**Unglück** nt accident

**ungültig** invalid

**ungültig werden** to expire (ticket, passport)

**Universität** f university

**unmöglich** impossible ; unsafe

**uns** us

**unser(e)** our

**unsicher** uncertain (fact)

**unten** downstairs ; below
*nach unten* downward(s) ; downstairs

**unter** under(neath)

**unter Wasser** underwater

**unterbrechen** to interrupt

239

**Unterbrecher** m circuit breaker

**Unterbrecherkontakte** pl points (in car)

**untere(r/s)** lower ; bottom

**Unterführung** f subway ; underpass (for pedestrians)

**Unterhemd** nt vest

**Unterhose** f underpants

**Unterkunft** f accommodation

**unterrichten** to teach

**Unterrichtsstunde** f lesson

**unterschreiben** to sign

**Unterschrift** f signature

**Untersuchung** f test ; medical examination

**Untertasse** f saucer

**Untertitel** pl subtitles

**Unterwäsche** f underwear ; lingerie

**unwohl** unwell

**Urin** m urine

**Urlaub** m leave ; holiday
*auf Urlaub* on holiday ; on leave

**Urlaubsgebiet** nt resort (holiday)

**Ursprungsland** nt country of origin

**USA** pl USA

**V**

**Vagina** f vagina

**Vanille** f vanilla

**Vanilleeis** nt vanilla ice cream

**Vanillesoße** f custard

**Vase** f vase

**Vater** m father

**Vegetarier(in)** m/f vegetarian

**vegetarisch** vegetarian

**Veilchen** nt violet (flower)

**Ventil** nt valve

**Ventilator** m fan (electric) ; ventilator

**Verband** m bandage

**Verbandskasten** m first aid kit

**verbinden** to connect (join)

**Verbindung** f connection (train, etc) ; service (bus, etc) ; line (phone)

**verbleit** leaded

**verboten** forbidden

**Verbrechen** nt crime

**verbrennen** to burn

**Verbrennung** f burn

**verbringen** to spend (time)

**verderben** to go bad (food) ; to spoil

**verdienen** to deserve ; to earn

**verdorben** bad (fruit, vegetables)

**Verein** m society (club)

**vereinbaren** to agree upon ; to arrange

**Vereinbarung** f agreement

**Vereinigtes Königreich** nt United Kingdom

**Vereinigte Staaten (von Amerika)** pl United States (of America)

**Verfallsdatum** nt expiry date ; eat-by date

**verfault** rotten (fruit, etc)

**vergeben** to forgive

**vergessen** to forget

**vergewaltigen** to rape

**Vergewaltigung** f rape

**Vergnügen** nt enjoyment ; pleasure
viel Vergnügen! have a good time!

**Vergnügungspark** m amusement park

**vergoldet** gold-plated

**Vergrößerung** f enlargement

**verhaften** to arrest

**verheiratet** married

**verhindern** to prevent

**Verhütungsmittel** nt contraceptive

**Verkauf** m sale

**verkaufen** to sell

**Verkäufer(in)** m/f salesman/woman

**Verkehr** m traffic

**Verkehrspolizist(in)** m/f traffic warden

**Verkehrszeichen** nt road sign

**verkehrt** wrong

**verkehrt herum** upside down

**Verlängerungskabel** nt extension cable

**Verleih** m rental company ; hire company

**verletzen** to injure

**verletzt** injured (person)

**Verletzung** f injury

**verlieren** to lose

**verlobt** engaged (to be married)

**Verlobte(r)** m/f fiancé(e)

**verloren** lost (object)

**vermeiden** to avoid

**vermieten** to rent ; to let (room, house)

**Vermieter(in)** m/f landlord/lady

**Vermietung** f hire

**vermisst** missing (person)

**Vermittlung** f telephone exchange ; operator

**verpassen** to miss (plane, train, etc)

**Verrenkung** f sprain

**verschieben** to postpone

**verschieden** different

**verschiedene** several ; different

**verschlucken** to swallow

**verschmutzt** polluted

verschreiben to prescribe
verschwinden to disappear
verschwunden missing
versichern to insure
versichert sein to be insured
Versicherung f insurance
Versicherung-sbescheinigung f insurance certificate
versilbert silver-plated
verspätet delayed
Verspätung f delay
versprechen to promise
Verstauchung f sprain
verstecken to hide
verstehen to understand
verstopft blocked (pipe); blocked (road); constipated
versuchen to try
Vertrag m contract
Vertreter(in) m/f sales rep
Verwandte(r) m/f relative
verwenden to use
verwirrt confused
Verzeihung! sorry; excuse me
verzollen to declare goods (customs)
Video nt video
Videokamera f video camera
Videokassette f video cas-sette/tape
viel much

viele many
vielleicht perhaps
Viertel nt quarter
Viertelstunde f quarter of an hour
vierzehn Tage fortnight
Villa f villa
violett purple
Virus nt virus
Visitenkarte f business card
Visum nt visa
Vitamin nt vitamin
Vogel m bird
Volkslied nt folk song
Volkstanz m folk dance
voll full
Volleyball m volleyball
Vollkornbrot nt dark rye bread; wholemeal bread
Vollmilchschokolade f milk chocolate
Vollnarkose f general anaesthetic
Vollpension f full board
vollständig whole
voll tanken to fill tank (petrol)
von from; of
vor before; in front of
vor 4 Jahren 4 years ago
voraus ahead
im Voraus in advance
vorbei past
vorbereiten to prepare

**Vorbestellung** f reservation

**Vorder-** front

**Vorderradantrieb** m front-wheel drive

**Vorfahrt** f right of way (on road)
**Vorfahrt beachten** give way

**vorgekocht** ready-cooked

**Vorhang** m curtain

**Vorhängeschloss** nt padlock

**Vorname** m first name

**vorne einsteigen** enter by front door

**Vorschrift** f regulation (rule)

**Vorsicht** f caution

**Vorspeise** f starter (in meal) ; hors d'œuvre

**Vorstellung** f performance

**Vor- und Zuname** m first name and surname

**Vorverkauf** m advance booking

**Vorwahl(nummer)** f dialling code

**vorziehen** to prefer

**Vulkan** m volcano

# W

**Waage** f scales (weighing)

**wach** awake

**Wache** f security guard

**Wachsbehandlung** f waxing

**Waffe** f gun

**Wagen** m car ; carriage (railway)

**Wagenheber** m jack (for car)

**Wahl** f choice ; election

**wählen** to dial (number) ; to choose

**Wählton** m dialling tone

**während** while ; during

**Währung** f currency

**Wald** m wood ; forest

**Waldlehrpfad** m nature trail

**Wales** nt Wales

**Waliser(in)** m/f Welshman/woman

**walisisch** Welsh

**Walnuss(-nüsse)** f walnut(s)

**wandern** to hike

**Wanderschuhe** pl walking boots

**Wanderstock** m walking stick

**Wanderung** f hike

**Wanderweg** m trail for ramblers

**Wange** f cheek

**wann?** when?

**Waren** pl goods

**warm** warm

**Wärmflasche** f hot-water bottle

**Warmwasser** nt hot water

**Warnblinkanlage** f hazard warning lights

Warndreieck nt warning triangle

Warnung f warning

Wartehalle f lounge (at airport)

warten (auf) to wait (for)

Wartesaal m waiting room

warum? why?

was? what?

waschbar washable

Waschbecken nt washbasin

Wäsche f linen ; washing (clothes)

Wäscheklammer f clothes peg

Wäscheleine f clothes line

waschen to wash

Waschen und Föhnen wash and blow dry

Wäscheraum m laundry room

Wäscherei f laundry

Wäschereiservice m laundry service

Wäschetrockner m tumble dryer

Waschmaschine f washing machine

Waschmittel nt detergent

Waschpulver nt washing powder

Waschsalon m launderette

Wasser nt water

wasserdicht waterproof

Wasserfall m waterfall

Wasserhahn m tap

Wassermelone f water melon

Wassermotorrad nt jet ski

Wasserski fahren to water ski

Wassertreter m pedal boat/pedalo

Watte f cotton wool

Wattebausch m cotton bud

Wechsel m change

Wechselgeld nt change (small coins)

Wechselkurs m exchange rate

wechseln to change (money) ; to give change

Wechselstube f bureau de change

Weckdienst m early morning call

Wecker m alarm clock

Weckruf m alarm call

weder ... noch neither ... nor

Weg m path ; way ; country lane

wegfahren to leave in vehicle

weggehen to leave on foot

Wegweiser m signpost

Wegwerfwindeln pl disposable nappies

weh tun to ache ; to hurt (be painful)

weiblich female ; feminine

weich soft

weich gekochtes Ei nt soft-boiled egg

Weihnachten nt Christmas

Weihnachtsgeschenk nt Christmas present

Weihnachtskarte f Christmas card

weil because

Wein m wine

Weinberg m vineyard

Weinbrand m brandy

weinen to cry (weep)

Weinhandlung f wine shop

Weinkarte f wine list

Weinkeller m wine cellar

Weinprobe f wine-tasting

Weinstube f wine bar

Weintrauben pl grapes

weiß white

Weißbrot nt white bread

Weißwein m white wine

weit far ; loose (clothing)

weiter farther ; further on

weitermachen to continue

weitsichtig long sighted

Weizen m wheat

welche(r/s) which ; what ; which one

Wellen pl waves (on sea)

Welt f world

Wende f U-turn (in car)

wenden to turn

wenig little

weniger less

wenn if ; when (with present tense)

wer? who?

Werbespot m advert (on TV)

werden to become

Werk nt plant (factory) ; work (of art)

Werkstatt f garage (for repairs)

Werktag m weekday

Werkzeug nt tool

Werkzeugkasten m toolkit

Wert m value

Wertbrief m registered letter

Wertsachen pl valuables

wertvoll valuable

wesentlich essential

Wespe f wasp

wessen? whose?

Weste f waistcoat

Westen m west

westlich western

Wetter nt weather

Wetterbericht m weather forecast

Wettervorhersage f weather forecast

Wettkampf m match (sport)

Whirlpool m jacuzzi

wichtig important

wie like ; how
   wie viel? how much?
   wie viele? how many?

wieder again

**W**

wiederaufladen to recharge *(battery)*

wiederholen to repeat

wiegen to weigh

Wien Vienna

Wiese *f* lawn ; meadow

Wild *nt* game *(hunting, meat)*

Wildleder *nt* suede

Wildschwein *nt* boar

willkommen welcome

Wimpern *pl* eyelashes

Wimperntusche *f* mascara

Wind *m* wind

Windeln *pl* nappies ; diapers

windig windy

Windmühle *f* windmill

Windpocken *pl* chickenpox

Windschutz *m* windbreak *(camping)*

Windschutzscheibe *f* windscreen

windstill calm *(weather)*

Winter *m* winter

Winterreifen *pl* snow tyres

wir we

wirksam effective *(remedy, etc)*

Wirt(in) *m(f)* landlord (landlady)

Wirtschaft *f* pub ; inn ; economy

wissen to know *(facts)*

Witwe(r) *f(m)* widow(er)

Witz *m* joke

wo? where?

Woche *f* week

Wochenende *nt* weekend

Wochentag *m* weekday

wöchentlich weekly

woher? where from?

wohin? where to?

Wohnadresse *f* home address

wohnen to stay ; to live *(reside)*

Wohnheim *nt* hostel

Wohnmobil *nt* dormobile

Wohnort *m* home address

Wohnung *f* flat *(apartment)*

Wohnwagen *m* caravan

Wohnzimmer *nt* living room ; lounge *(in house)*

wolkig cloudy

Woll- woollen

Wolldecke *f* blanket

Wolle *f* wool

wollen to want *(wish for)*

Wort *nt* word
in Worten in words *(on cheques)*

Wörterbuch *nt* dictionary

Wunde *f* wound *(injury)*

Würfel *m* dice

Wurst *f* sausage

Würstchenbude *f* hot-dog stand

würzig spicy

Würzmischung *f* seasoning

Yachthafen m marina

zäh tough *(meat)*
Zahl f number *(figure)*
zahlen to pay
Zähler m meter
Zahn m tooth
Zahnarzt (Zahnärztin) m/f dentist
Zahnbürste f toothbrush
Zahncreme f toothpaste
Zähne pl teeth
Zahnpasta f toothpaste
Zahnschmerzen pl toothache
Zahnseide f dental floss
Zahnstocher m toothpick
Zange f pliers
Zäpfchen nt suppository
z.B. e.g.
Zebrastreifen m zebra crossing
Zehe f toe
Zeichentrickfilm m cartoon
Zeichnung f drawing
zeigen to show
Zeit f time *(of day)*
Zeitkarte f season ticket
Zeitschrift f magazine
Zeitung f newspaper

Zeitungskiosk m newsstand
Zelt nt tent
Zeltboden m groundsheet
zelten to camp
Zentimeter m centimetre
zentral central
Zentralheizung f central heating
Zentralverriegelung f central locking *(car)*
Zentrum nt centre
zerbrechlich fragile ; breakable
zerrissen torn
Ziege f goat
Ziegel m brick
ziehen pull
Ziel nt destination ; goal ; target
ziemlich quite *(rather)*
Zigarette(n) f cigarette(s)
Zigarettenpapier nt cigarette papers
Zigarre(n) f cigar(s)
Zimmer nt room *(in house, hotel)*
  Zimmer frei vacancies
Zimmermädchen nt chambermaid
Zimmernummer f room number
Zimmerservice m room service
Zirkus m circus

**Z**

Zitrone f lemon
Zitronentee m lemon tea
Zoll m customs/toll
zollfrei duty-free
Zone f zone
Zoo m zoo
Zopf m plait
zornig angry
zu to ; off ; too ; at
  zu Hause at home
  zu mieten for hire
  zu verkaufen for sale
  zu viel too much
  zu viel berechnen to
  overcharge
zubereiten to prepare
Zucchini pl courgettes
Zucker m sugar
zuckerfrei sugar-free
Zuckerkrankheit f diabetes
zudrehen to turn off (tap)
Zug m train
Zuhause nt home
zuhören to listen
Zukunft f future
Zulassung f log book (car)
zum Beispiel f for example
Zuname m surname
Zündkerzen pl spark plugs
Zündschlüssel m ignition
  key
Zündung f ignition
Zunge f tongue
zurück back

zurückfahren to go back
(by car)
zurückgeben to give back
zurückgehen to go back
(on foot)
zurückkommen to come
back
zurücklassen to leave
behind
zusammen together
Zusammenstoß m crash
(collision)
zusätzlich extra ; additional
zuschauen to watch
Zuschlag m surcharge ;
supplement
zuschließen to lock
Zustellung f delivery (of
mail)
Zutaten pl ingredients
Zutritt m entry ; admission
  Zutritt verboten no entry
zu viel too much
  zu viel berechnen to
  overcharge
zuzüglich extra
zwanglose Kleidung f
informal dress
zwei two
Zweigstelle f branch (office)
zweimal twice
zweite(r/s) second
zweite Klasse f second
class
Zwiebel f bulb ; onion

**Zwillinge** *pl* twins
**zwischen** between
**Zwischenstecker** *m* adaptor
**Zyste** *f* cyst

## NOUNS

In German all nouns begin with a capital letter. The plural forms vary from noun to noun – there is no universal plural as in English (cat – cats, dog – dogs):

| singular | plural |
|----------|--------|
| **Mann** | **Männer** |
| **Frau** | **Frauen** |
| **Tisch** | **Tische** |

(In the dictionary, plural forms appear where they may be useful.)

German nouns are *masculine (m)*, *feminine (f)* or *neuter (nt)*, and this is shown by the words for **the** and **a(n)** used before them:

| | masculine | feminine | neuter |
|---|-----------|----------|--------|
| **the** | **der Mann** | **die Frau** | **das Licht** |
| **a, an** | **ein Mann** | **eine Frau** | **ein Licht** |

The plural for **the** for all forms is **die**:

| | | |
|---|---|---|
| **die Männer** | **die Frauen** | **die Lichter** |

There is no plural for the **ein** form. The plural noun is used on its own.

From the phrases in this book you will see that the endings for the word for **the** vary according to what part the noun plays in the sentence:

If the noun is the subject of the sentence, i.e. carrying out the action, then it is in the *nominative* case (the one found in dictionaries), e.g. **der Mann steht auf (the man stands up)**. The subject **der Mann** comes before the verb.

If the noun is the direct object of the sentence, i.e. the action of the verb is being carried out on the noun, then the noun is in the *accusative* case, e.g. **ich sehe den Mann (I see the man)**. Note how the ending of **der** has changed to **den**. The same applies to **ein**, e.g. **ich sehe einen Mann (I see a man)**.

If you see in front of the English noun **of**, or after it, **'s** or **s'**, then the noun is in the *genitive* case (i.e. it belongs to someone or something), e.g. **das Haus der Frau (the woman's house)**. Note how the ending of **die** (Frau) has changed to **der**. The same applies to **ein**, e.g. **das Haus einer Frau (a woman's house)**.

If you see **to the** or **to a** in front of the English noun, then the noun is in the *dative* case, e.g. **ich gebe es der Frau (I give it to the woman)**. Note how the ending of **die** (Frau) has changed to **der**. The same applies to **ein**, e.g. **ich gebe es einer Frau (I give it to a woman)**.

Several other words used before nouns have similar endings to **der** and **ein**.
Those like **der** are:
**dieser this ; jener that ; jeder each ; welcher which**
Those like **ein** are:
**mein my ; dein your** (familiar sing.) **; Ihr your** (polite sing. and plural) **; sein his ; ihr her ; unser our ; euer your** (familiar plural)**; ihr their**

Here are the cases for **der**:

|  | masculine | feminine | neuter | plural |
|---|---|---|---|---|
| Nominative | der Mann | die Frau | das Licht | die Frauen |
| Accusative | den Mann | die Frau | das Licht | die Frauen |
| Genitive | des Mannes | der Frau | des Lichtes | der Frauen |
| Dative | dem Mann | der Frau | dem Licht | den Frauen |

Here are the cases for **ein**:

|  | masculine | feminine | neuter |
|---|---|---|---|
| Nominative | ein Mann | eine Frau | ein Licht |
| Accusative | einen Mann | eine Frau | ein Licht |
| Genitive | eines Mannes | einer Frau | eines Lichtes |
| Dative | einem Mann | einer Frau | einem Licht |

The word **kein** (**no, not any**) also has the same endings as for **ein**, except that it can be used in the plural:

| | |
|---|---|
| Nominative | keine Männer |
| Accusative | keine Männer |
| Genitive | keiner Männer |
| Dative | keinen Männern |

## ADJECTIVES

When adjectives are used before a noun, their endings vary like the words for **der** and **ein**, depending on the gender (*masculine, feminine* or *neuter*) and whether the noun is plural, and how the noun is used in the sentence (whether it is the subject, object, etc.). Here are examples using the adjective **klug – clever**

| | masculine | feminine |
|---|---|---|
| Nominative | der kluge Mann | die kluge Frau |
| | ein kluger Mann | eine kluge Frau |
| Accusative | den klugen Mann | die kluge Frau |
| | einen klugen Mann | eine kluge Frau |
| Genitive | des klugen Mannes | der klugen Frau |
| | eines klugen Mannes | einer klugen Frau |
| Dative | dem klugen Mann | der klugen Frau |
| | einem klugen Mann | einer klugen Frau |

| | neuter | plural |
|---|---|---|
| Nominative | das kluge Kind | die klugen Männer |
| | ein kluges Kind | kluge Frauen |
| Accusative | das kluge Kind | die klugen Männer |
| | ein kluges Kind | kluge Frauen |
| Genitive | des klugen Kindes | der klugen Männer |
| | eines klugen Kindes | kluger Frauen |
| Dative | dem klugen Kind | den klugen Männern |
| | einem klugen Kind | klugen Frauen |

When the adjective follows the verb, then there is no agreement:

**der Mann ist klug**
**die Frau ist klug**
**das Kind ist klug**

## MY, YOUR, HIS, HER

These words all take the same endings as for **ein** and they agree with the noun they accompany, i.e. whether *masculine, feminine, neuter, plural* and according to the function of the noun (*nominative, accusative,* etc.):

**mein Mann kommt** my husband is coming (nom.)
**ich liebe meinen Mann** I love my husband (acc.)
**das Auto meines Mannes** my husband's car (gen.)
**ich gebe es meinem Mann** I give it to my husband (dat.)
**meine Kinder kommen** my children are coming (nom. pl.)
**ich liebe meine Kinder** I love my children (acc. pl.)
**die Spielsachen meiner Kinder** my children's toys (gen. pl.)
**ich gebe es meinen Kindern** I give it to my children (dat. pl.)

Other words which take these endings are:
**dein** your (familiar sing.) ; **sein** his ; **ihr** her ; **unser** our ; **euer** your (familiar plural) ; **Ihr** your (polite sing. and plural) ; **ihr** their

## PRONOUNS

| *subject* | | *direct object* | |
|---|---|---|---|
| **I** | ich | **me** | mich |
| **you** (familiar sing.) | du | **you** (familiar sing.) | dich |
| **he/it** | er | **him/it** | ihn |
| **she/it** | sie | **her/it** | sie |
| **it** (neuter) | es | **it** (neuter) | es |
| **we** | wir | **us** | uns |
| **you** (familiar plural) | ihr | **you** (familiar plural) | euch |
| **you** (polite sing. & pl.) | Sie | **you** (polite sing. & pl.) | Sie |
| **they** (all genders) | sie | **them** (all genders) | sie |

Indirect object pronouns are:
**to me** mir ; **to you** (familiar sing.) dir ; **to him/it** ihm ; **to her/it** ihr ; **to it** (neuter) ihm ; **to us** uns ; **to you** (familiar plural) euch ; **to you** (polite sing. and plural) Ihnen ; **to them** ihnen

## YOU

There are two ways of addressing people in German: the familiar form – **du** (when talking to just one person you know well), **ihr** (when talking to more than one person you know well), and the polite form – **Sie** (always written with a capital letter), which can be used for one or more people.

## VERBS

There are two main types of verb in German – **weak** verbs (which are regular) and **strong** verbs (which are irregular).

|  | *weak* | *strong* |
|---|---|---|
|  | **SPIELEN** | **HELFEN** |
|  | **to play** | **to help** |
| ich | spiele | helfe |
| du | spielst | hilfst |
| er/sie/es | spielt | hilft |
| wir | spielen | helfen |
| ihr | spielt | helft |
| Sie | spielen | helfen |
| sie | spielen | helfen |

Other examples of **strong** verbs are:

|  | **SEIN** | **HABEN** |
|---|---|---|
|  | **to be** | **to have** |
| ich | bin | habe |
| du | bist | hast |
| er/sie/es | ist | hat |
| wir | sind | haben |
| ihr | seid | habt |
| Sie | sind | haben |
| sie | sind | haben |

To make a verb negative, add **nicht**:

| ich verstehe nicht | **I don't understand** |
|---|---|
| das funktioniert nicht | **it doesn't work** |

## PAST TENSE

Here are a number of useful past tenses:

| | |
|---|---|
| ich war | **I was** |
| wir waren | **we were** |
| Sie waren | **you were** *(polite)* |
| ich hatte | **I had** |
| wir hatten | **we had** |
| Sie hatten | **you had** *(polite)* |
| ich/er/sie/es spielte | **I/he/she/it played** |
| Sie/wir/sie spielten | **you/we/they played** |
| | |
| ich/er/sie/es half | **I/he/she/it helped** |
| Sie/wir/sie halfen | **you/we/they helped** |

Another past form corresponds to the English **have ...ed** and uses the verb **haben to have**:

| | |
|---|---|
| ich habe gespielt | **I have played** |
| wir haben geholfen | **we have helped** |

In German the present tense is very often used where we would use the future tense in English:

| | |
|---|---|
| ich schicke ein Fax | **I will send a fax** |
| ich schreibe einen Brief | **I will write a letter** |